# JIM CORBETT'S INDIA

Jim Corbett stands in the centre, behind his mother, Mary Jane, his sister Maggie and the seated figure of (it is thought) his eldest brother Tom. This scene is Naini Tal, c. 1899.

# Jim Corbett's India

Stories selected by

## R. E. HAWKINS

Oxford   New York

OXFORD UNIVERSITY PRESS

1986

Oxford University Press, Walton Street, Oxford OX2 6DP

Oxford  New York  Toronto
Delhi  Bombay  Calcutta  Madras  Karachi
Petaling Jaya  Singapore  Hong Kong  Tokyo
Nairobi  Dar es Salaam  Cape Town
Melbourne  Auckland

and associated companies in
Beirut  Berlin  Ibadan  Nicosia

Oxford is a trade mark of Oxford University Press

Selection and Introduction © Oxford University Press

First published 1978
First issued as an Oxford University Press paperback 1986

British Library Cataloguing in Publication Data
Corbett, Jim
Jim Corbett's India.
1. Tiger hunting—India—History—
20th century
I. Title   II. Hawkins, R. E.
799.2'774428   SK305.T5
ISBN 0-19-282042-7

Printed in Great Britain by
Richard Clay (The Chaucer Press) Ltd.
Bungay, Suffolk

# Contents

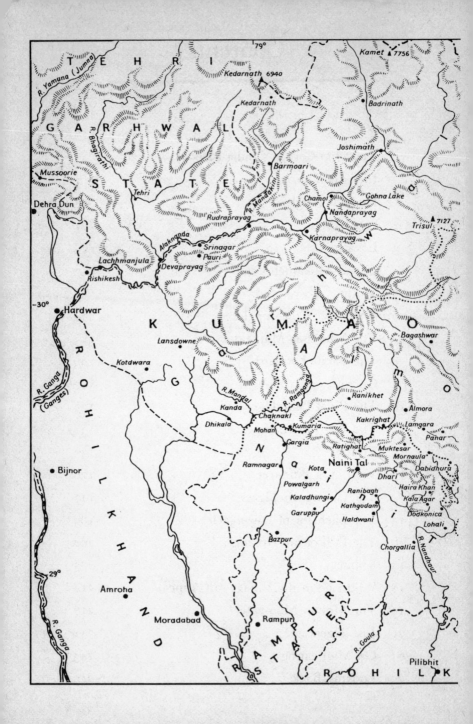

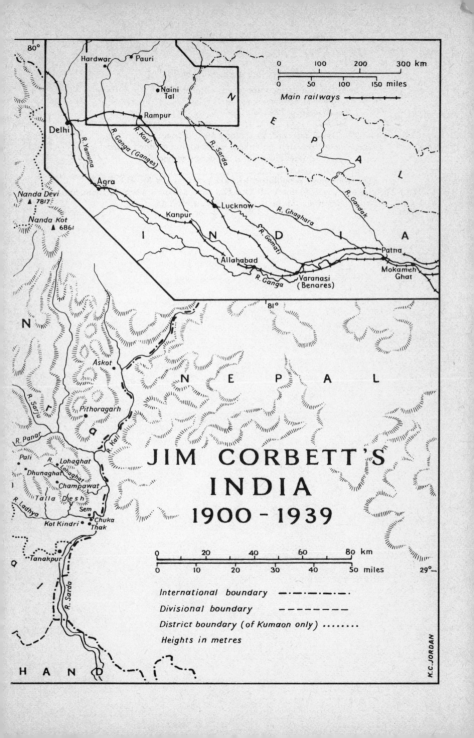

JIM CORBETT'S
INDIA
1900 - 1939

International boundary  —·—·—·—
Divisional boundary  — — — — —
District boundary (of Kumaon only)  ········
Heights in metres

Main railways  +—+—+—+

K.C. JORDAN

*Sources and acknowledgements*

The stories and extracts are taken (numbered as overleaf) from
*Man-eaters of Kumaon* (1944): 10, 14, 15, 16, 17, 19, 20, 21;
*The Man-eating Leopard of Rudraprayag* (1947): 11, 12, 13;
*My India* (1952): 1, 3, 4, 5, 6; *Jungle Lore* (1953): 2, 22;
*The Temple Tiger and More Man-eaters of Kumaon* (1954): 7, 8;
*Jungle Stories* (privately published, n.d.): 18; unpublished papers: 9.
The dates given are those of first publication.

The frontispiece is published with the permission of Mr D.C.Kala.
The publishers wish to thank Mr G.R.Kala and Mukul Prakashan, Delhi, for
permission to use the passages quoted on pages 3–4.

# Introduction

The frontispiece shows part of a large Victorian family. The mother has been twice widowed. She was married at 14 and had borne four children by the time her husband was killed in the Mutiny. A year or two later, at the age of 23, she married Christopher Corbett, a widower with two sons and a daughter, and this second marriage added six sons and three daughters. Maggie, the lady in the feathery hat, often kept house for Jim, who is standing at the back. I have not been able to identify the man sitting in front. Perhaps it is Tom, Jim's eldest brother and hero, a professional soldier.

Jim, or to give him his full name Edward James Corbett, was born on 25 July 1875, so this photograph was taken round about 1900. Christopher William Corbett, the father, had taken part in the First Afghan War (1839–42) and seems to have remained in the army till after 1857, when he had the rank of Apothecary, or Assistant Surgeon. By the time of his second marriage on 13 October 1859 he had joined the postal service and in 1862 he was appointed postmaster at Naini Tal, the hill station which later became the summer capital of the United Provinces. Soon after his arrival, Christopher Corbett was given a plot of land at the foot of the hills, at a place called Kaladhungi, and there he built a large house to which his family moved in the cold weather. The Naini Tal lake – *tal* means lake – lies at about 6,400 ft, the Corbett house (Gurney House, outside which I think the photograph was taken) is about a thousand feet higher, and pockets of snow are found on Cheena (or Naina, 8,568 ft), the peak which dominates the lake, as late as March. Very many people and birds move down from the hills to the plains in the winter months.

Gurney House still stands, and still contains some of the Corbett furniture, including their piano. There is a tall pile of sheet music, and among the books several prizes awarded to Maggie Corbett for her playing. The library was evidently a good one: besides theological and medical works, books on sport, natural history, travel and photography, the nineteenth-century poets and novelists are well represented, sometimes by first editions. The Corbett children had a cultured, comfortable home.

I have been asked to make this selection from Jim Corbett's writing because, as representative of the Oxford University Press in India, I received and published most of his books and, by correspondence, came to know him well, though I only met him briefly in Bombay and London, and his sister Maggie in London and Nyeri. Jim had taken Maggie to London for a cataract operation when she was nearing 80, and while she was out of action, with her eyes bandaged, a friend encouraged her to reminisce and made shorthand notes. When later I introduce a sentence with 'Maggie testifies' it means I rely on these notes. I am also indebted to Mr D.C.Kala, whose biography of Jim Corbett is soon to be published in Delhi, for much help.

Jim Corbett published only six books. The first, *Man-eaters of Kumaon* (1944), was followed ten years later by *The Temple Tiger and More Man-eaters of Kumaon* (1954), and about half of this selection comes from those two books. The other half comes from the autobiographical *My India* (1952) and *Jungle Lore* (1953). There are also three extracts from his longest story, *The Man-eating Leopard of Rudraprayag* (1948), which many people find the most enthralling of all. Written twenty years after the chase described, it provides ample evidence of Corbett's story-telling skill and exceptional power of recall. His last book, *Tree Tops*, which was published just after his death at the age of 80, in 1955, and which recounts the night he spent on guard over the Princess who became Queen Elizabeth, is not represented here. I have, however, included 'Goongi', originally intended for *My India*, as it is the only unpublished material I know of. It is a good example of Corbett's thorough investigation and independent, logical deduction.

Both Geoffrey Cumberlege, with whom Jim and Maggie stayed in England, and Lord Hailey, who was Governor of the United Provinces in 1928–30 and 1931–4 and often went into the jungles with Jim and Maggie, have in their Introductions to the World's Classics edition of *Man-eaters* and to *Tree Tops* given accounts of Jim Corbett's family and life. I have arranged the selections in this book as far as I am able in chronological order, so that anyone who reads straight through will get an idea of the course of Jim's life.

After leaving school at 17½ Jim went to work as a railway fuel inspector on a salary of Rs100 a month[1] – his father had died when he was 6 and his mother had been left with nine children to bring up – and

[1] £6 13s. The exchange rate in 1895 was 1s. 4d. to the rupee, almost the same as in January 1978.

when he was 20 Jim took on the contract from the railways for handling the transhipment of goods across the Ganges, described in 'Mokameh Ghat'. He was considered too old to join the army in 1914, but in 1917 was given the rank of Captain to take a labour force of 500 Kumaonis to France. He proudly brought back 499. Thereafter he saw fighting in the Third Afghan War and about 1920, at the age of 45, settled down at Naini Tal to look after his mother, his sister Maggie, and his step-sister Mary Doyle. His mother died in 1924 and Mary in 1940.

In 1922 he took a share with Percy Wyndham in a coffee estate on the slopes of Mount Kilimanjaro and used to go to it for about three months each year. Maggie testifies: 'As there was no proper living accommodation on the estate, nothing but huts, Jim set to work, and with his own hands laid every brick of a two-storeyed house, with a veranda upstairs. He was very pleased to find, on measuring the building when it was finished, that it was not out by an inch anywhere.'

During his time on the railway Jim had spent many holidays at Kaladhungi and in the early years of the century had bought a deserted village, Choti Haldwani. With a mile of wire he enclosed an area, divided it into plots, and built new houses. As he could afford it, he increased the circumference to three miles and built a 5-foot stone wall instead of the wire. The village was soon flourishing.

A Garhwali who was a Government servant in Kumaon at the time, Govind Ram Kala, refers to Wyndham and Corbett in his book *Memoirs of the Raj*. Of Wyndham he says:

Tiger hunting was Mr Wyndham's first love. He spent most of his career hunting either in Mirzapur district (the Wyndham Falls are named after him) or in the Naini Tal Tarai.[1] He was Jim Corbett's friend and a colourful person in his own right. He spent 12 years in Kumaon Division as its Commissioner. He was of medium build, of robust constitution and generally indifferent to his dress. His technique of administration was to strike terror in the hearts of his subordinates.

Kala gives the title 'Corbett's Kaladhungi' to one of his chapters, and writes:

Jim Corbett, now a famous man after his classic *Man-eaters of Kumaon*, was a resident of Kaladhungi, a small Bhabar town 15 miles away from Naini Tal, where he farmed and did small business in winter when not otherwise gainfully

---

[1] The author is referring to the tarai (or terai) in the Naini Tal District. The Himalayan foothills, well-drained and cultivable, are known as bhabar land, and farther south is a tract, formerly swampy and malarial, known as the terai.

occupied arranging their shoots for high-ups in the Government and their guests. Corbett was a constant companion of Mr Wyndham whenever he was out looking for tigers in the Bhabar and Tarai. A bachelor, he lived with his two sisters in a bungalow of his own. He had completely identified himself with the local population which affectionately called him 'Carpet Saab'. He always had a word of cheer for all those in trouble and was generous with his money. He was quite unlike the general run of the hoity-toity white man. I came in touch with Corbett at Kaladhungi where I was posted as a naib tahsildar in the year 1920–21. He was of middle size and rather dark. One could see him going about in shorts, shirt, a thick coat of coarse material and a hat. He went about without a tie.

The tahsildars and naib tahsildars of Bhabar and Tarai often came in contact with him for the arrangement of porters and bullock carts for the big shoots. Corbett, of course, was in overall charge of every important shoot. His kindly nature and sympathetic attitude encouraged us to visit him.

Corbett also owned a bungalow at Naini Tal where he lived with his sisters from April to October. Whenever I visited him at Naini Tal, I found his house crowded, so popular was he.

Jim was a member of the Naini Tal Municipal Board from 1920 to 1944. He was a pioneer conservationist and one of the editors of a short-lived journal called *Indian Wild Life*. A contribution which he made to the *Review of the Week* of 31 August 1932 appears as 'Wild Life in the Village' in this selection. At this period also he began to give lectures to local schools and societies to stimulate awareness of the natural beauty surrounding them and the need to conserve the forests and their wild life. A girl who was at Wellesley School, Naini Tal, in the early 1930s describes his annual visits as 'one of the highlights of my childhood'. There were no slides or films, but Jim would imitate the warning calls of monkeys, birds, and deer and end up, with the room in darkness, with terrifying tiger noises. His fluency in animal languages was demonstrated to more critical audiences when he used them to call up a man-eater or to drown the whirr of his camera when filming tigers.

In the Second World War Jim again raised a labour corps and recruited 1,400 Kumaonis. In 1942 an attack of typhus reduced his weight from 12½ to 7 stone and he was told he would have to spend the rest of his life in a wheel-chair. In February 1944, however, he was commissioned Lieutenant-Colonel in order that he could teach men to survive in the Burmese jungles. After a year of this strenuous life – the training camps were in Central India, but first he went to Burma – he had a bad attack of malaria.

In 1947 a major decision was taken. Maggie testifies:

It was hard for us to imagine ourselves living anywhere but in India. Our home and the home of our ancestors, which we so dearly loved, with its simple, kindly people, with its beautiful mountains, lakes and rivers, all seemed a part of our very selves; but the time came when we felt we should leave India, and find a new home for ourselves in some other part of the world. The reason being that neither of us could face the thought of living on in either our house in Naini Tal or the little house in Kaladhungi, when only one of us was left, for neither of us was young and the time could not be far distant when the parting would have to come.

So Jim and Maggie went to Kenya. Soon after his arrival in Nyeri Jim founded a Wild Life Preservation Society and became its Honorary Secretary. He was also made an honorary game warden. It was at Nyeri that he wrote most of his books. Maggie testifies:

He worked very hard; did his own typing, all with one finger, and made four copies of each book – three for the publishers, London, New York and Bombay, and the fourth copy for ourselves, known as 'The Home Copy'. He was very neat and if there was even one mistake on a page, he would scrap the page and type it all over again. He always wanted a sentence to read 'smoothly' and would take infinite pains in making it do so.

But Miss Marjorie Clough, an American Red Cross worker who spent a few days with Maggie and Jim at Kaladhungi in October 1945, when *The Man-eating Leopard of Rudraprayag* was being written, is probably nearer the truth. She reported:

In this most recent venture of story-writing Maggie has been of inestimable value to Jim with her keen memory of dates and events, and flair for writing. They sit together night after night before their wood fire, he at his typewriter and she brewing the after-dinner cup of tea. They ponder over words to properly describe to the outside world, you might say, something of the inmost secrets of the jungle they love and know so well.

Jim recognized two turning-points in his life. The first when, at the age of 8 or 9, he learnt to control his fear; the second when, at some undetermined date, he resolved never again to shoot an animal except for food or if it was a 'dangerous' beast. In *Jungle Lore* he recounts how Dansay, 'an Irishman steeped to the crown of his head in every form of superstition', used to tell ghost stories to the children who had come down to Kaladhungi for their winter holidays. One of his most terrifying stories was of a banshee living in the forest, to hear whose screams would bring calamity to the hearer and all his family. One evening Jim was in thick jungle, hurrying to get home before a thunderstorm broke, when he heard the banshee scream. 'A few weeks previously', he writes, 'I had run from a tiger as I thought I should never run again, but I did not know then that terror of the unknown could lend wings to one's feet.' He arrived home as windows and doors were being closed against the storm, so that his excited state was not noticed; and he did not say anything himself as he feared he would be blamed for the coming calamity. But, he continues, 'danger of any kind has an attraction for everyone, including small boys', so he haunted the area where he had heard the scream, and one windy day heard it again. This time, with beating heart, he crept towards the sound as slowly and noiselessly as a shadow, comforting himself with the thought that no calamity had yet overtaken him and that the banshee might have pity on so small a boy. The screaming sound, he discovered, was made by two branches which sawed against each other in strong wind. 'From that day', he writes, 'I date the desire I acquired of following up and getting to the bottom of every unusual thing I saw or heard in the jungles.'

The other turning-point was reached, he told the Reverend A.G.Atkins, pastor of the Union Church at Naini Tal in the early 1930s, when, having taken three officers out for a duck-shoot, he was sickened by the senseless slaughter of 300 birds.

The typescript of *Man-eaters of Kumaon* arrived with commendations from a viceroy, Lord Linlithgow, and the Governor of the United Provinces, Sir Maurice Hallett. It was dedicated to 'the gallant soldiers, sailors and airmen of the United Nations who during this war have lost their sight in the service of their country', and the author directed that all his royalties on the first edition should be sent to St Dunstan's Hostel for Indian soldiers blinded in the war that was still being fought. I never had any doubt that the book would be successful, but it was not until an American war correspondent who was then in Bombay, Preston Grover, returned the set of proofs I had lent him saying he had read the stories three times, that I realized I was on to something big. *Man-eaters of Kumaon* appeared in August 1944, when the end of the war was in sight. Years of massive, indiscriminate slaughter and regimentation had eroded faith in the significance of the individual. It was immensely refreshing to read of this contemporary dragon-killer, who in perfect freedom roamed the countryside, cheerfully facing danger and hardship to rid the world of tigers and leopards convicted of man-eating. Sir Galahad rode again. Truth and justice had returned.

I do not know how many copies of *Man-eaters of Kumaon* have been printed. It was an immediate success in India and was chosen by book clubs in England and America, the first printing of the American Book-of-the-Month Club being 250,000. It was not many years before it had been issued as a Talking Book for the Blind and translated into at least fourteen European languages,[1] eleven Indian languages,[2] Afrikaans and Japanese. The later books, too, were widely translated, though the only language into which all Corbett's books have been translated, including *Tree Tops*, seems to be Bengali. There is no doubt that his appeal is universal.

Jim Corbett was the most modest, companionable, and unassuming of men. When he was working on the railways it was said he was the only man who would be equally welcome if he visited the Agent or a ticket-collector. In later life he was equally at home with a viceroy or a poacher. He never sought the limelight, but it is satisfactory to be able to record that he was publicly honoured by the Government of India both before and after Independence. In British times he was awarded the Kaiser-i-Hind Gold Medal, made a Companion of the Order of the Star of India and an Officer of the Order of the British Empire, and given the Freedom of the Forests, a very rare distinction. In 1957, after Jim's death, the game sanctuary in Kumaon was renamed the Corbett National Park. The house at Kaladhungi is kept as a Corbett Museum, and besides many photographs, including the family group shown in the frontispiece, it contains a copy of Dr J.S.Phelan's short study entitled *The Sense of Imminent Danger*, a sixth sense which Corbett firmly believed he possessed. In January 1976 the Government of India issued a 25-paise stamp to commemorate Jim's birth in 1875. A new, Annamese, race of tigers was in 1968 named *Panthera tigris corbetti*. His literary distinction has been recognized by the inclusion of two of his books in the World's Classics series.

I have not found anyone who knew Corbett to cast doubt on the factual truth of his stories: as a man he inspired complete confidence

[1] Bulgarian, Czech, Danish, Dutch, Finnish, French, German, Italian, Norwegian, Portuguese, Serbo-Croat, Slovene, Spanish, Swedish.
[2] Bengali, Gujarati, Hindi, Kannada, Malayalam, Oriya, Sindhi, Sinhalese, Tamil, Telugu, Urdu.

and as a shikari he was unrivalled. It has, however, sometimes been hinted that Jim Corbett did not write his own stories; they must have been written by his friends, or his publishers. The only foundation for the first hypothesis seems to be natural scepticism: for an unknown author to produce at the age of 69 a first book which is a best-seller is too good to be true. For the second hypothesis there is the evidence that in his will Jim Corbett made bequests to his publishers – I myself received a carpet (a pun?) and his nine-volume, two-column Shakespeare. For authors to remember their publishers in their wills is regrettably rare – in my forty years indeed, unique – but Jim Corbett was a most unusual man.

The *Pioneer* of Lucknow of 26 December 1925 reports a statement made in the Legislative Council that the district authorities of Rudraprayag 'had been fortunate in securing the voluntary assistance of a European gentleman of considerable experience and proved courage', who did not wish his name to be disclosed, in the pursuit of a man-eating leopard which had killed 114 human beings. There follows, in the same issue, an anonymous letter which, from internal evidence, was written by Jim to A.W.Ibbotson, then Deputy Commissioner of Garhwal. It concludes:

I must give you my impressions of the leopard for I have told you I both saw and heard him. From the fact that he was visible on a dark night and overcast sky I conclude he is a very light coloured animal. He did not appear to be very long but looked thickset and powerfully built. Hearing him was the strangest experience I have ever had. I never heard any animal's body before and cannot in any way account for the sound. It was loud enough to be heard at 30 yards and was exactly like a woman walking in a stiff silk dress. The field had been lately planted with wheat and there was not a leaf or blade of grass in it. No, the sound did not come from his feet but from his body.

The *Pioneer* of 15 May 1926 carried on its front page the news that the Rudraprayag man-eater had at last been shot and killed by Captain Corbett of Naini Tal, and printed a three-column report of the affair from 'a Naini Tal correspondent'. In its issue of 21 May is reprinted a letter from G.B.Lambert, Chief Secretary to Government, United Provinces, to Captain Corbett of Gurney House, Naini Tal, conveying the Governor in Council's 'sincere thanks and his congratulations on a fine achievement'.

(Characteristically, Corbett does not mention this letter in his book, but instead recounts how, at a party for wounded Indian soldiers in

1942, one of them said: 'And now, sahib, I will go back to my home with great joy in my heart, for I shall be able to tell my father that with my own eyes I have seen you and, maybe, if I can get anyone to carry me to the fair that is held every year at Rudraprayag to commemorate the death of the man-eater, I shall tell all the people I meet there that I have seen and had speech with you.' And he goes on to comment: 'A typical son of Garhwal, of that simple and hardy hill-folk, and of that greater India, whose sons only those few who live among them are privileged to know. It is these big-hearted sons of the soil, no matter what their caste or creed, who will one day weld the contending factions into a composite whole, and make of India a great nation.')

*The Man-eating Leopard of Rudraprayag* was Corbett's second book, and the story told in it agrees closely with that outlined in the dispatch from their Naini Tal correspondent to the *Pioneer* so many years before. On pp.38–9 of the book (published, remember, in 1948) we read:

The rain was soon over – leaving me chilled to the bone – and the clouds were breaking up when the white stone was suddenly obscured, and a little later I heard the leopard eating. The night before, he had lain in the ravine and eaten from that side; so expecting him to do the same this night, I had placed the stone on the near side of the kill. Obviously, the rain had formed little pools in the ravine, and to avoid them the leopard had taken up a new position and in doing so had obscured my mark. This was something I had not foreseen; however, knowing the habits of leopards, I knew I should not have to wait long before the stone showed up again. Ten minutes later the stone was visible, and almost immediately thereafter I heard a sound below me and saw the leopard as a light yellowish object disappearing under the rick. His light colour could be accounted for by old age, but the sound he made when walking I could not then, nor can I now, account for; it was like the soft rustle of a woman's silk dress, and could not be explained by stubble in the field – for there was none – or by the loose straw lying about.

Who can doubt that this passage was written by the anonymous shikari quoted in the *Pioneer* of 1925?

There remains the suggestion that Corbett's books were rewritten by his publishers. As the person who received most of his typescripts I can assert without fear of contradiction that all I ever did before publishing them was to tidy up the punctuation and spelling, occasionally substituting a past tense for a present participle. A final example can be taken from the story 'The Pipal Pani Tiger' which seems to have been the first Corbett ever wrote. It appeared in 1931, in Vol.IV of the *Hoghunters' Annual* issued by the Times of India Press, Bombay. It was

included in the little book entitled *Jungle Stories* of which Jim had 100
copies printed for his friends. It was also included in *Man-eaters of
Kumaon*. Scarcely a word is different in the three versions. Jim was a
very careful writer, and a sentence he had once composed was seldom
modified.

A century ago the population of India comprised 200 million men,
women and children, and in the same area there are about 700 million
today. It is this pressure of population that has changed the face of Jim
Corbett's India. Motor roads with roaring buses have fragmented the
forested areas, crop-protection guns were easily available in the years
immediately after 1947, and the very existence of the tiger was
threatened. In 1972 the World Wildlife Fund donated a million U.S.
dollars to the Government of India to prevent the extinction of the
species and in its 5th Five-year Plan the Government of India spent
another six crores of rupees (7 million U.S. dollars) on Project Tiger
and has established seven sanctuaries, one of them in the Corbett
National Park. There is now a complete ban on the shooting of tigers
and leopards, except for the occasional man-eater.

If man saves the tiger presumably he will save himself, and by the year
2000 the continuing pressure of population will bring about prodigious
changes. Water will be so valuable that chains of lakes and canals will
radiate from the Himalayas and the Western Ghats, the headwaters and
catchment areas will be protected by forests, and maybe these forests will
be protected so strictly that they will teem with game as in Jim Corbett's
boyhood.

Life at Mokameh Ghat is also quite different. There is a railway
bridge across the Ganges. Income-tax is more than 4 pies in the rupee –
2 per cent – and there are trade unions. No employer could now be
found to distribute 80 per cent of his profits to his workmen as Jim did.
Pilgrims to Badrinath can now go by bus to within a few hundred yards
of the shrine. Though no railway has reached Naini Tal there is an
excellent motor road from Kathgodam, and a less good one from
Kaladhungi. When she first came from Agra to Naini Tal, Jim's
mother had made the first part of the journey, across the plains, by
doolie dak, a doolie being a box-like contrivance suspended from poles
and carried by four stalwart bearers, and the last steep ascent by
dandy, a hammock slung from a single pole which the occupant had to
clutch to avoid being tipped out. Jim used to walk up from

Kaladhungi, starting before dawn to attend the Municipal Council meetings in Naini Tal, and getting home after dark. Spatial communications have changed dramatically, and verbal too, for though there are, in all, many more people unable to read and write than there were a century ago – the percentage of literates having meanwhile risen from 3 to 30 per cent – transistor radios are in every village and television in the big cities. Times change, but human nature changes very much more slowly, and Jim Corbett will long be admired as hunter, story-teller, and Christian gentleman. If he were still alive, he would repeat the dedication which appeared in his third book, *My India*: 'To my friends, the poor of India.'

R. E. H.

# I

## Kunwar Singh

Kunwar Singh was by caste a Thakur, and the headman of Chandni Chauk village. Whether he was a good or a bad headman I do not know. What endeared him to me was the fact that he was the best and the most successful poacher in Kaladhungi, and a devoted admirer of my eldest brother Tom, my boyhood's hero.

Kunwar Singh had many tales to tell of Tom, for he had accompanied him on many of his shikar expeditions, and the tale I like best, and that never lost anything in repetition, concerned an impromptu competition between brother Tom and a man by the name of Ellis, whom Tom had beaten by one point the previous year to win the B.P.R.A. gold medal for the best rifle-shot in India.

Tom and Ellis, unknown to each other, were shooting in the same jungle near Garuppu, and early one morning, when the mist was just rising above the tree-tops, they met on the approach to some high ground overlooking a wide depression in which, at that hour of the morning, deer and pig were always to be found. Tom was accompanied by Kunwar Singh, while Ellis was accompanied by a shikari from Naini Tal named Budhoo, whom Kunwar Singh despised because of his low caste and his ignorance of all matters connected with the jungles. After the usual greetings, Ellis said that, though Tom had beaten him by one miserable point on the rifle range, he would show Tom that he was a better game shot; and he suggested that they should each fire two shots to prove the point. Lots were drawn and Ellis, winning, decided to fire first. A careful approach was then made to the low ground, Ellis carrying the ·450 Martini–Henry rifle with which he had competed at the B.P.R.A. meeting, while Tom carried a ·400 D.B. express by Westley Richards of which he was justly proud, for few of these weapons had up to that date arrived in India.

The wind may have been wrong, or the approach careless. Anyway, when the competitors topped the high ground, no animals were in sight on the low ground. On the near side of the low ground there was a strip of dry grass beyond which the grass had been burnt, and it was on this burnt ground, now turning green with sprouting new shoots, that animals were to be seen both morning and evening. Kunwar Singh was of the opinion that some animals might be lurking in the strip of dry grass, and at his suggestion he and Budhoo set fire to it.

When the grass was well alight and the drongos, rollers, and starlings were collecting from the four corners of the heavens to feed on the swarms of grasshoppers that were taking flight to escape from the flames, a movement was observed at the farther edge of the grass, and presently two big boar came out and went streaking across the burnt ground for the shelter of the tree jungle three hundred yards away. Very deliberately Ellis, who weighed fourteen stone, knelt down, raised his rifle and sent a bullet after the hindmost pig, kicking up the dust between its hind legs. Lowering his rifle, Ellis adjusted the back sight to two hundred yards, ejected the spent cartridge, and rammed a fresh one into the breach. His second bullet sent up a cloud of dust immediately in front of the leading pig.

This second bullet deflected the pigs to the right, bringing them broadside on to the guns, and making them increase their speed. It was now Tom's turn to shoot, and to shoot in a hurry, for the pigs were fast approaching the tree jungle, and getting out of range. Standing four-square, Tom raised his rifle and, as the two shots rang out the pigs, both shot through the head, went over like rabbits. Kunwar Singh's recital of this event invariably ended up with: 'And then I turned to Budhoo, that city-bred son of a low-caste man, the smell of whose oiled hair offended me, and said, "Did you see that, you, who boasted that your sahib would teach mine how to shoot? Had my sahib wanted to blacken the face of yours he would not have used two bullets, but would have killed both pigs with one".' Just how this feat could have been accomplished, Kunwar Singh never told me, and I never asked, for my faith in my hero was so great that I never for one moment doubted that, if he had wished, he could have killed both pigs with one bullet.

Kunwar Singh was the first to visit me that day of days when I was given my first gun. He came early, and as with great pride I put the old double-barrelled muzzle-loader into his hands he never, even by the flicker of an eyelid, showed that he had seen the gaping split in the right barrel, or the lappings of brass wire that held the stock and the barrels together. Only the good qualities of the left barrel were commented on, and extolled; its length, thickness, and the years of service it would give. And then, laying the gun aside, he turned to me and gladdened my eight-year-old heart and made me doubly proud of my possession by saying: 'You are now no longer a boy, but a man; and with this good gun you can go anywhere you like in our jungles and never be afraid, provided you learn how to climb trees; and I will now tell you a story to show how necessary it is for us men who shoot in the jungles to know how to do so.

'Har Singh and I went out to shoot one day last April, and all would have been well if a fox had not crossed our path as we were leaving the village. Har Singh, as you know, is a poor shikari with little knowledge of the jungle folk, and when, after seeing the fox, I suggested we should turn round and go home he laughed at me and said it was child's talk to say that a fox would bring us bad luck. So we continued on our way. We had started when the stars were paling, and near Garuppu I fired at a chital stag and unaccountably missed it. Later Har Singh broke the wing of a peafowl, but though we chased the wounded bird as hard as we could it got away in the long grass, where we lost it. Thereafter, though we combed the jungles we saw nothing to shoot, and towards the evening we turned our faces towards home.

'Having fired two shots, and being afraid that the forest guards would be looking for us, we avoided the road and took a sandy nullah that ran through dense scrub and thorn-bamboo jungle. As we went along talking of our bad luck, suddenly a tiger came out into the nullah and stood looking at us. For a long minute the tiger stared and then it turned and went back the way it had come.

'After waiting a suitable time we continued on our way, when the tiger again came out into the nullah; and this time, as it stood and looked at us, it was growling and twitching its tail. We again stood quite still, and after a time the tiger quietened down and left the nullah. A little later a number of junglefowl rose cackling out of the dense scrub, evidently disturbed by the tiger, and one of them came and sat on a haldu tree right in front of us. As the bird alighted on a branch in full view of us, Har Singh said he would shoot it and so avoid going home empty-handed. He added that the shot would frighten away the tiger, and before I could stop him he fired.

'Next second there was a terrifying roar as the tiger came crashing through the brushwood towards us. At this spot there were some runi trees growing on the edge of the nullah, and I dashed towards one while Har Singh dashed towards another. My tree was the nearer to the tiger, but before it arrived I had climbed out of reach. Har Singh had not learnt to climb trees when a boy, as I had, and he was still standing on the ground, reaching up and trying to grasp a branch, when the tiger, after leaving me, sprang at him. The tiger did not bite or scratch Har Singh, but standing on its hind legs it clasped the tree, pinning Har Singh against it, and then started to claw big bits of bark and wood off the far side of the tree. While it was so engaged, Har Singh was screaming and the tiger was roaring. I had taken my gun up into the tree with me, so now, holding on with my bare feet, I cocked the hammer and fired the gun off into the air. On hearing the shot so close to it the tiger bounded away, and Har Singh collapsed at the foot of the tree.

'When the tiger had been gone some time, I climbed down very silently, and went to Har Singh. I found that one of the tiger's claws had entered his stomach and torn the lining from near his navel to within a few fingers' breadth of the backbone, and that all his inside had fallen out. Here was great trouble for me. I could not run away and leave Har Singh, and not having any experience in these matters, I did not know whether it would be best to try and put all that mass of inside back into Har Singh's stomach, or cut it off. I talked in whispers on this matter with Har Singh, for we were afraid that if the tiger heard us it would return and kill us, and Har Singh was of the opinion that his inside should be put back into his stomach. So, while he lay on his back on the ground, I stuffed it all back, including the dry leaves and grass and bits of sticks that were sticking to it. I then wound my pugree round him, knotting it tight to keep everything from falling out again, and we set out on the seven-mile walk to our village, myself in front, carrying the two guns, while Har Singh walked behind.

'We had to go slowly, for Har Singh was holding the pugree in position, and on the way night came on and Har Singh said he thought it would be better to go to the hospital at Kaladhungi than to our village; so I hid the guns, and we went the extra three miles to the hospital. The hospital was closed when we arrived, but the doctor babu who lives nearby was awake, and when he heard our story he sent me to call Aladia the tobacco-seller, who is also postmaster at Kaladhungi and who receives five rupees pay per month from Government, while he lit a lantern and went to the hospital hut with Har Singh. When I returned with Aladia, the doctor had laid Har Singh on a string bed and, while Aladia held the lantern and I held the two pieces of flesh together, the doctor sewed up the hole in Har Singh's stomach. Thereafter the doctor, who is a very kind man of raw years and who refused to take the two rupees I offered him, gave Har Singh a drink of very good medicine to make him forget the pain in his stomach and we went home and found our womenfolk crying, for they thought we had been killed in the jungle by dacoits, or by wild animals. So you see, sahib, how necessary it is for us men who shoot in the jungles to know how to climb trees, for if Har Singh had had someone to advise him when he was a boy, he would not have brought all that trouble on us.'[1]

I learnt many things from Kunwar Singh during the first few years that I carried the old muzzle-loader, one of them being the making of mental maps. The jungles we hunted in, sometimes together, but more often alone – for Kunwar Singh had a horror of dacoits and there were times when for weeks on end he would not leave his village – were many hundreds of miles square with only one road running through them. Times without number when returning from a shoot I called in at Kunwar Singh's village, which was three miles nearer the forest than my house was, to tell him I had shot a chital or sambur stag, or maybe a big pig, and to ask him to retrieve the bag. He never once failed to do so, no matter in how great a wilderness of tree or scrub or grass jungle I had carefully hidden the animal I had shot, to protect it from vultures. We had a name for every outstanding tree, and for every water-hole, game track, and nullah. All our distances were measured by imaginary flight of a bullet fired from a muzzle-loader, and all our directions fixed by the four points of the compass. When I had hidden an animal, or Kunwar Singh had seen vultures collected on a tree and suspected that a leopard or a tiger had made a kill, either he or I would set out with absolute confidence that we would find the spot indicated, no matter what time of day or night it might be.

After I left school and started work in Bengal I was only able to visit Kaladhungi for about three weeks each year, and I was greatly distressed to find on one of these annual visits that my old friend Kunwar Singh had fallen a victim to the curse of our foothills, opium.

---

[1] The runi tree against which the tigress – who evidently had just given birth to cubs in that area, and who resented the presence of human beings – pinned Har Singh was about eighteen inches thick, and in her rage the tigress tore away a third of it. This tree became a landmark for all who shot or poached in the Garuppu jungles until, some twenty-five years later, it was destroyed by a forest fire.

Har Singh, in spite of the rough-and-ready treatment he received at the hands of his three friends, and in spite of the vegetation that went inside him, suffered no ill effects from his wound, and lived to die of old age.

With a constitution weakened by malaria the pernicious habit grew on him, and though he made me many promises he had not the moral strength to keep them. I was therefore not surprised, on my visit to Kaladhungi one February, to be told by the men in our village that Kunwar Singh was very seriously ill. News of my arrival spread through Kaladhungi that night, and next day Kunwar Singh's youngest son, a lad of eighteen, came hot-foot to tell me that his father was at death's door, and that he wished to see me before he died.

As headman of Chandni Chauk, paying Government land revenue of four thousand rupees, Kunwar Singh was an important person, and lived in a big stone-built house with a slate roof in which I had often enjoyed his hospitality. Now as I approached the village in company with his son, I heard the wailing of women coming, not from the house, but from a small one-roomed hut Kunwar Singh had built for one of his servants. As the son led me towards this hut, he said his father had been moved to it because the grandchildren disturbed his sleep. Seeing us coming, Kunwar Singh's eldest son stepped out of the hut and informed me that his father was unconscious, and that he only had a few minutes to live.

I stopped at the door of the hut, and when my eyes had got accustomed to the dim light, made dimmer by a thick pall of smoke which filled the room, I saw Kunwar Singh lying on the bare floor, naked, and partly covered with a sheet. His nerveless right arm was supported by an old man sitting on the floor near him, and his fingers were being held round the tail of a cow. (This custom of a dying man being made to hold the tail of a cow – preferably that of a black heifer – has its origin in the Hindu belief that when the spirit leaves its earthly body it is confronted with a river of blood, on the far side of which sits the Judge before whom the spirit must appear to answer for its sins. The heifer's tail is the only way by which the departing spirit can cross the river, and if the spirit is not provided with means of transit it is condemned to remain on earth, to be a torment to those who failed to enable it to appear before the judgement seat.) Near Kunwar Singh's head was a brazier with cowdung cakes burning on it, and by the brazier a priest was sitting intoning prayers and ringing a bell. Every available inch of floor space was packed with men, and with women who were wailing and repeating over and over again, 'He has gone! He has gone!'

I knew men died like this in India every day, but I was not going to let my friend be one of them. In fact, if I could help it he would not die at all, and anyway not at present. Striding into the room, I picked up the iron brazier, which was hotter than I expected it to be, and burnt my hands. This I carried to the door and flung outside. Returning, I cut the bark rope by which the cow was tethered to a peg driven into the mud floor, and led it outside. As these acts, which I had performed in silence, became evident to the people assembled in the room, the hubbub began to die down, and it ceased altogether when I took the priest's arm and conducted him from the room. When, standing at the door, I ordered everyone to go outside, the order was obeyed without a murmur or a single protest. The number of people, both old and young, who emerged from the hut was incredible. When the last of them had crossed the doorstep, I told Kunwar Singh's eldest son to warm two seers of fresh milk and to bring it to me with as little delay as possible. The man looked at me in blank surprise, but when I repeated the order he hurried off to execute it.

I now re-entered the hut, pulled forward a string bed which had been pushed against the wall, picked Kunwar Singh up and laid him on it. Fresh air, and plenty of it, was urgently needed, and as I looked round I saw a small window which had been boarded up. It did not take long to tear down the boards and let a stream of clean sweet air blow directly from the jungles into the overheated room which reeked with the smell of human beings, cowdung, burnt ghee, and acrid smoke.

When I picked up Kunwar Singh's wasted frame, I knew there was a little life in it, but only a very little. His eyes, which were sunk deep into his head, were closed, his lips were blue, and his breath was coming in short gasps. Soon, however, the fresh, clean air began to revive him and his breathing became less laboured and more regular, and presently, as I sat on his bed and watched through the door the commotion that was taking place among the mourners whom I had ejected from the death-chamber, I became aware that he had opened his eyes and was looking at me; and without turning my head, I began to speak.

'Times have changed, uncle, and you with them. There was a day when no man would have dared to remove you from your own house, and lay you on the ground in a servant's hut to die like an outcaste and a beggar. You would not listen to my words of warning and now the accursed drug has brought you to this. Had I delayed but a few minutes in answering your summons this day, you know you would by now have been on your way to the burning-ghat. As headman of Chandni Chauk and the best shikari in Kaladhungi, all men respected you. But now you have lost that respect, and you who were strong and who ate the best, are weak and empty of stomach, for as we came your son told me nothing has passed your lips for sixteen days. But you are not going to die, old friend, as they told you you were. You will live for many more years, and though we may never shoot together again in the Garuppu jungles, you will not want for game, for I will share all I shoot with you, as I have always done.

'And now, here in this hut, with the sacred thread round your fingers and a pipal leaf in your hands, you must swear an oath on your eldest son's head that never again will you touch the foul drug. And this time you will, and you *shall* keep your oath. And now, while we wait for the milk your son is bringing, we will smoke.'

Kunwar Singh had not taken his eyes off me while I was speaking, and now for the first time he opened his lips and said, 'How can a man who is dying smoke?'

'On the subject of dying', I said, 'we will say no more, for as I have just told you, you are not going to die. And as to how we will smoke, I will show you.'

Then, taking two cigarettes from my case, I lit one and placed it between his lips. Slowly he took a pull at it, coughed, and with a very feeble hand removed the cigarette. But when the fit of coughing was over, he replaced it between his lips and continued to draw on it. Before we had finished our smoke, Kunwar Singh's son returned carrying a big brass vessel, which he would have dropped at the door if I had not hurriedly relieved him of it. His surprise was understandable, for the father whom he had last seen lying on the ground dying, was now lying on the bed, his head resting on my hat, smoking. There was nothing in the hut to drink from, so I sent the son back to the house for a cup; and when he had brought it I gave Kunwar Singh a drink of warm milk.

I stayed in the hut till late into the night, and when I left Kunwar Singh had drunk a seer of milk and was sleeping peacefully on a warm and comfortable bed. Before I left I warned the son that he was on no account to allow anyone to come near the hut; that he was to sit by his father and give him a drink of milk every time he awoke; and that if on my return in the morning I found Kunwar Singh dead, I would burn down the village.

The sun was just rising next morning when I returned to Chandni Chauk to find both Kunwar Singh and his son fast asleep and the brass vessel empty.

Kunwar Singh kept his oath, and though he never regained sufficient strength to accompany me on my shikar expeditions, he visited me often and died peacefully four years later in his own house and on his own bed.

## 2

## *Schooldays*

When I was ten years of age I was considered old enough to join the school cadet company of the Naini Tal Volunteer Rifles. Volunteering was very popular and was taken very seriously in India in those days, and all able-bodied boys and men took pride and pleasure in joining the force. There were four cadet companies and one adult company in our battalion with a combined strength of 500 which, for a population of 6,000, meant that every one in twelve was a volunteer.

The Principal of our school of seventy boys was also captain of the school cadet company, which mustered fifty strong. The holder of these dual posts was an ex-army man and it was his burning, and very praiseworthy, ambition to have the best cadet company in the battalion and to satisfy this ambition we small boys suffered, and suffered greatly. Twice a week we drilled on the school playground, and once a week we drilled with the other four companies on the Flats, an open stretch of ground at the upper end of the Naini Tal lake.

Our captain never missed, nor did he ever overlook, a fault, and all mistakes made on the drill grounds were atoned for after evening school. Taking up a position four feet from his target and wielding a four-foot-long cane, the captain was a marksman of repute who had earned for himself the title of 'Dead-eye Dick'. I do not know if he made private bets with himself, but we small boys laid wagers of marbles, tops, pen-knives, and even on occasions the biscuit that formed our breakfast, that nine times out of ten our captain could lay his cane along the most painful weal left on the hand by the previous day's or previous week's caning, and the boy – usually a newcomer – who betted against the odds always lost. The cadets of the other three companies hotly disputed our reputation of being the best drilled company, but they did not dispute our claim of our being the best turned-out company. This claim was justified, for before being marched down to drill with the other companies we were subjected to an inspection that detected the minutest particle of dirt under a finger-nail, or speck of dust on the uniform.

Our uniforms – passed down when grown out of – were of dark blue serge of a quality guaranteed to stand hard wear and to chafe every tender part of the skin they came in contact with, and, further, to show every speck of dust. Hot and uncomfortable as the uniform was it was surpassed in discomfort by the helmet that was worn with it. Made of some heavy compressed material, this instrument of torture was armed with a four-inch-long fluted metal spike, the threaded butt end of which projected down inside the helmet for an inch or more. To keep the threaded end from boring into the brain the inner band had to be lined with paper, and when the helmet had been fixed to the head like a vice it was held in that position by a heavy metal chin-strap mounted on hard leather. After three hours in the hot sun few of us left the drill ground without a splitting headache which made repetition of lessons prepared the previous night difficult, with the result that the four-foot cane was used more freely on drill days than on any other.

On one of our drill days on the Flats the battalion was inspected by a visiting officer of senior rank. After an hour of musketry drill and marching and countermarching, the battalion was marched up to the Suka Tal (dry lake) rifle range. Here the cadet companies were made to sit down on the hillside while the adult company demonstrated to the visiting officer their prowess with the ·450 Martini rifle. The battalion prided itself on having some of the best rifle shots in India in its ranks, and this pride was reflected in every member of the force. The target, standing on a masonry platform, was made of heavy sheet-iron and the experts could tell from the ring of the bullet on the iron sheet whether it had struck the centre of the target or the edge of it.

Each cadet company had its hero in the adult company, and adverse comments against the marksmanship of a selected hero would that morning have resulted in many sanguinary fights, had fighting in uniform not been frowned on. After the scores of the best shots had been announced, the cadets were ordered to fall in and march down from the 500- to the 200-yard range. Here four senior cadets were selected from each company and we juniors were ordered to pile arms and sit down behind the firing point.

Inter-school competition in all forms of sport, and most of all on the rifle range, was very keen and every shot fired that morning by the four competing teams was eagerly watched and fiercely commented on by friend and foe alike. The scores ran close, for the best shots in each company had been selected by the respective company commanders, and there was great jubilation in our ranks when it was announced that

our team had come out second in the competition and that we had
been beaten by only one point by the school that had three times our
membership.

While we – the rank and file – were commenting on the achievements of the recent competitors, the Sergeant-Major was seen to detach
himself from the group of officers and instructors standing at the
firing point, and come towards us bellowing in a voice that it was
claimed could be heard a mile away, 'Corbett, Cadet Corbett!'
Heavens! What had I done now that merited punishment? True I had
said that the last shot that had put the rival company one point ahead
of us had been a fluke, and someone had offered to fight me, but there
had been no fight for I did not even know who the challenger was, and
here now was that awful Sergeant-Major again bellowing, 'Corbett,
Cadet Corbett!' 'Go on.' 'He's calling you.' 'Hurry up or you'll catch
it,' was being said on all sides of me; and at last, in a very weak voice, I
answered 'Yes, sir.' 'Why didn't you answer? Where is your carbine?
Fetch it at once,' were rapped out at me all in one breath. Dazed by
these commands I stood undecided until a push from behind by a
friendly hand and an urgent 'Go on, you fool' set me off at a run for my
carbine.

On our arrival at the 200-yard range those of us who were not
competing had been made to pile arms, and my carbine had been used
to lock one of the piles. In my effort now to release my carbine the
whole pile of arms clattered to the ground and while I was trying to set
the pile up again the Sergeant-Major yelled, 'Leave those carbines you
have mucked up alone, and bring yours here.' 'Shoulder arms, right
turn, quick march,' were the next orders I received. Feeling far worse
than any lamb could possibly ever have felt I was led off to the firing
point, the Sergeant-Major whispering over his shoulder as we started,
'Don't you dare disgrace me.'

At the firing point the visiting officer asked if I was the youngest cadet
in the battalion, and on being told that I was, he said he would like to
see me fire a few rounds. The way in which this was said – and the
kindly smile that went with it – gave me the feeling that of all the
officers and instructors who were standing round, the visiting officer
was the only one who realized how alone, and how nervous, a small
boy suddenly called upon to perform before a large and imposing
gathering can feel.

The ·450 Martini carbine the cadets were armed with had the most vicious kick of any small-arms weapon ever made, and the musketry course I had recently been put through had left my shoulder – which was not padded with overmuch flesh – very tender and very painful, and the knowledge that it would now be subjected to further kicks added to my nervousness. However, I would have to go through with it now, and suffer for being the youngest cadet. So on the command of the Sergeant-Major I lay down, picked up one of the five rounds that had been laid down for me, loaded the carbine and raising it very gently to my shoulder took what aim I could and pressed the trigger. No welcome ring came to my anxious ears from the iron target, only a dull thud, and then a quiet voice said, 'All right, Sergeant-Major, I will take over now,' and the visiting officer, in his spotless uniform, came and lay down beside me on the oily drugget. 'Let me have a look at your carbine,' he said, and when I passed it over to him a steady hand carefully adjusted the back-sight to 200 yards, a detail I had omitted to attend to. The carbine was then handed back to me with the injunction to take my time, and each of the following four shots brought a ring from the target. Patting me on the shoulder the visiting officer got to his feet and asked what score I had made and on being told that I had made ten, out of a possible twenty, with the first shot a miss, he said, 'Splendid. Very good shooting indeed,' and as he turned to speak to the officers and instructors I went back to my companions, walking on air. But my elation was short-lived, for I was greeted with: 'Rotten shot.' 'Disgraced the Company.' 'Could have done better with my eyes closed.' 'Crumbs, did you see that first shot, went and hit the 100-yard firing point.' Boys are like that. They just speak their minds without any thought or intention of being cruel or unkind.

The visiting officer who befriended me that day on the Suka Tal rifle range when I was feeling lonely and nervous, later became the nation's hero and ended his career as Field-Marshal Earl Roberts. When I have been tempted, as many times I have been, to hurry over a shot or over a decision, the memory of that quiet voice telling me to take my time has restrained me and I have never ceased being grateful to the great soldier who gave me that advice.

The Sergeant-Major, who for many years ruled the Naini Tal Volunteers with a rod of iron, was short and fat with a neck like a bull's and a heart of gold. After our last drill on the Flats that term he asked me if I would like to have a rifle. Surprise and delight rendered me speechless; however, no reply appeared to be expected, and he went on to say, 'Come and see me before you leave for the holidays and I will give you a service rifle and all the ammunition you want, provided you promise to keep the rifle clean, and to return me the empties.'

So that winter I went down to Kaladhungi armed with a rifle, and without any anxiety about ammunition. The rifle the good Sergeant-Major had selected for me was dead accurate, and though a ·450 rifle firing a heavy bullet may not have been the best type of weapon for a boy to train on, it served my purpose. The bow and arrow had enabled me to penetrate farther into the jungles than the catapult, and the muzzle-loader had enabled me to penetrate farther than the bow and arrow; and now, armed with a rifle, the jungles were open to me to wander in wherever I chose to go.

Fear stimulates the senses of animals, keeps them 'on their toes', and adds zest to the joy of life; fear can do the same for human beings. Fear had taught me to move noiselessly, to climb trees, to pin-point sound; and now, in order to penetrate into the deepest recesses of the jungle and enjoy the best in nature, it was essential to learn how to use my eyes, and how to use my rifle.

A human being has a field of vision of 180 degrees, and when in a jungle in which all forms of life are to be met with, including poisonous snakes and animals that have been wounded by others, it is necessary to train the eyes to cover the entire field of vision. Movements straight in front are easy to detect and easy to deal with, but movements at the edge of the field of vision are vague and indistinct and it is these vague and indistinct movements that can be most dangerous, and are most to be feared. Nothing in the jungle is deliberately aggressive, but circumstances may arise to make some creatures so, and it is against the possibility of these chance happenings that the eye must be trained. On one occasion the darting in and out of the forked tongue of a cobra in a hollow tree, and on another occasion the moving of the tip of the tail of a wounded leopard lying behind a bush, warned me just in time that the cobra was on the point of striking and the leopard on the point of springing. On both these occasions I had been looking straight in front, and the movements had taken place at the extreme edge of my field of vision.

The muzzle-loader had taught me to economize ammunition and now, when I had a rifle, I considered it wasteful to practise on a fixed target, so I practised on junglefowl and on peafowl, and I can recall only one instance of having spoilt a bird for the table. I never grudged the time spent, or the trouble taken, in stalking a bird and getting a shot, and when I attained sufficient accuracy with the rifle to place the heavy ·450 bullet exactly where I wanted to, I gained confidence to hunt in those areas of the jungle into which I had previously been too frightened to go.

One of these areas, known to the family as the Farmyard, was a dense patch of tree and scrub jungle several miles in extent, and reputed to be 'crawling' with junglefowl and tigers. Crawling was not an overstatement as far as the junglefowl were concerned, for nowhere have I seen these birds in greater numbers than in those days in the Farmyard. The Kota–Kaladhungi road runs for a part of its length through the Farmyard and it was on this road that the old dak runner, some years later, told me he had seen the pug marks of the 'Bachelor of Powalgarh'.

I had skirted round the Farmyard in the bow-and-arrow and muzzle-loader days, but it was not until I was armed with the ·450 that I was able to muster sufficient courage to explore this dense tree and scrub jungle. Through the jungle ran a deep and narrow ravine, and up this ravine I was going one evening intent on shooting a bird for the pot, or a pig for our villagers, when I heard junglefowl scratching among the dead leaves in the jungle to my right. Climbing on to a rock in the ravine I sat down, and on cautiously raising my head above the bank saw some twenty to thirty junglefowl feeding towards me, led by an old cock in full plumage. Selecting the cock for my target, I was waiting with finger on trigger for his head to come in line with a tree – I never fired at a bird until I had a solid background for the bullet to go into – when I heard a heavy animal on the left of the ravine and on turning my head I saw a big leopard bounding down the hill straight towards me. The Kota road here ran across the hill, two hundred yards above me, and quite evidently the leopard had taken fright at something on the road and was now making for shelter as fast as he could go. The junglefowl had also seen the leopard and as they rose with a great flutter of wings, I slewed round on the rock to face the leopard. Failing in the general confusion to see my movement the leopard came straight on, pulling up when he arrived at the very edge of the ravine.

The ravine here was about fifteen feet wide with steep banks twelve feet high on the left, and eight feet high on the right. Near the right bank, and two feet lower than it, was the rock on which I was sitting; the leopard was, therefore, a little above, and the width of the ravine from me. When he pulled up at the edge of the ravine he turned his head to look back the way he had come, thus giving me an opportunity of raising the rifle to my shoulder without the movement being seen by him. Taking careful aim at his chest I pressed the trigger just as he was turning his head to look in my direction. A cloud of smoke from the black-powder cartridge obscured my view and I only caught a fleeting glimpse of the leopard as he passed over my head and landed on the bank behind me, leaving splashes of blood on the rock on which I was sitting, and on my clothes.

With perfect confidence in the rifle, and in my ability to put a bullet exactly where I wanted to, I had counted on killing the leopard outright and was greatly disconcerted now to find that I had only wounded him. That the leopard was badly wounded I could see from the blood, but I lacked the experience to know – from the position of the wound, and the blood – whether the wound was likely to prove fatal or not. Fearing that if I did not follow him immediately he might get away into some inaccessible cave or thicket where it would be impossible for me to find him, I reloaded the rifle and stepping from my rock on to the bank, set off to follow the blood trail.

For a hundred yards the ground was flat, with a few scattered trees and bushes, and beyond this it fell steeply away for fifty yards before again flattening out. On this steep hillside there were many bushes and big rocks, behind any one of which the leopard might have been sheltering. Moving with the utmost caution, and scanning every foot of ground, I had gone half-way down the hillside when from behind a rock, some twenty yards away, I saw the leopard's tail and one hind leg projecting. Not knowing whether the leopard was alive or dead I stood stock still until presently the leg was withdrawn, leaving only the tail visible. The leopard was alive and to get a shot at him I would have to move either to the right or to the left. Having already hit the leopard in the body, and not killed him, I now decided to try his head, so inch by inch I crept to the left until his head came into view. He was lying with his back to the rock, looking away from me. I had not made a sound but the leopard appeared to sense that I was near, and as he was turning his head to look at me I put a bullet into his ear. The range was short, and I had taken my time, and I knew now that the leopard was dead, so going up to him I caught him by the tail and pulled him away from the blood in which he was lying.

It is not possible for me to describe my feelings as I stood looking

down at my first leopard. My hands had been steady from the moment
I first saw him bounding down the steep hillside and until I pulled him
aside to prevent the blood from staining his skin. But now, not only my
hands but my whole body was trembling: trembling with fear at the
thought of what would have happened if, instead of landing on the
bank behind me, the leopard had landed on my head. Trembling with
joy at the beautiful animal I had shot, and trembling most of all with
anticipation of the pleasure I would have in carrying the news of my
great success to those at home who I knew would be as pleased and as
proud of my achievement as I was. I could have screamed, shouted,
danced and sung, all at one and the same time. But I did none of these
things, I only stood and trembled, for my feelings were too intense to be
given expression in the jungle, and could only be relieved by being
shared with others.

# 3

## *Loyalty*

The mail train was running at its maximum speed of thirty miles per hour through country that was familiar. For mile upon mile the newly risen sun had been shining on fields where people were reaping the golden wheat, for it was the month of April and the train was passing through the Gangetic valley, the most fertile land in India. During the previous year India had witnessed one of her worst famines. I had seen whole villages existing on the bark of trees; on minute grass seeds swept up with infinite labour from scorching plains; and on the wild plums that grow on waste lands too poor for the raising of crops. Mercifully the weather had changed, good winter rains had brought back fertility to the land, and the people who had starved for a year were now eagerly reaping a good harvest. Early though the hour was, the scene was one of intense activity in which every individual of the community had his, or her, allotted part. The reaping was being done by women, most of them landless labourers who move from area to area, as the crop ripens, and who for their labour – which starts at dawn and ends when there is no longer light to work by – receive one-twelfth to one-sixteenth of the crop they cut in the course of the day.

There were no hedges to obstruct the view, and from the carriage window no mechanical device of any kind was to be seen. The ploughing had been done by oxen, two to a plough; the reaping was being done by sickles with a curved blade eighteen inches long; the sheaves, tied with twisted stalks of wheat straw, were being carted to the threshing floor on ox-carts with wooden wheels; and on the threshing floor, plastered over with cowdung, oxen were treading out the corn; they were tied to a long rope, one end of which was made fast to a pole firmly fixed in the ground. As a field was cleared of the sheaves children drove cattle on to it to graze on the stubble, and amongst the cattle old and infirm women were sweeping the ground to recover any seed that had fallen from the ears when the wheat was being cut. Half of what these toilers collected would be taken by the owner of the field and the other half – which might amount to as much as a pound or two, if the ground was not too sun-cracked – they would be permitted to retain.

My journey was to last for thirty-six hours. I had the carriage to myself, and the train would stop for breakfast, lunch, and dinner. Every mile of the country through which the train was running was interesting; and yet I was not happy, for in the steel trunk under my seat was a string bag containing two hundred rupees which did not belong to me.

Eighteen months previously I had taken employment as a Fuel Inspector with the railway on which I was now travelling. I had gone straight from school to this job, and for those eighteen months I had lived in the forest cutting five hundred thousand cubic feet of timber, to be used as fuel in locomotives. After the trees had been felled and billeted, each billet not more and not less than thirty-six inches long, the fuel was carted ten miles to the nearest point of the railway, where it was stacked and measured and then loaded into fuel trains and taken to the stations where it was needed. Those eighteen months alone in the forest had been strenuous, but I had kept fit and enjoyed the work. There was plenty of game in the forest in the way of chital, four-horned antelope, pig, and peafowl, and in the river that formed one boundary of the forest there were several varieties of fish and many alligators and python. My work did not permit of my indulging in sport during daylight hours so I had to do all my shooting for the pot, and fishing, at night. Shooting by moonlight is very different from shooting in daylight, for though it is easier to stalk a deer or a rooting pig at night it is difficult to shoot accurately unless the moon can be got to shine on the foresight. The peafowl had to be shot while they were roosting, and I am not ashamed to say that I occasionally indulged in this form of murder, for the only meat I ate during that year and a half was what I shot on moonlight nights; during the dark period of the moon I had perforce to be a vegetarian.

The felling of the forest disarranged the normal life of the jungle folk and left me with the care of many waifs and orphans, all of whom had to share my small tent with me. It was when I was a bit crowded with two broods of partridges – one black and the other grey, four peafowl chicks, two leverets, and two baby four-horned antelope that could only just stand upright on their spindle legs, that Rex the python took up his quarters in the tent. I returned an hour after nightfall that day, and while I was feeding the four-footed inmates with milk I saw the lantern light glinting on something in a corner of the tent and on investigation found Rex coiled up on the straw used as a bed by the baby antelope. A hurried count revealed that none of the young inmates of the tent were missing, so I left Rex in the corner he had selected. For two months thereafter Rex left the tent each day to bask in the sun, returning to his corner at sundown, and during the whole of that period he never harmed any of the young life he shared the tent with.

Of all the waifs and orphans who were brought up in the tent, and who were returned to the forest as soon as they were able to fend for themselves, Tiddley-de-winks, a four-horned antelope, was the only one who refused to leave me. She followed me when I moved camp to be nearer to the railway line to supervise the loading of the fuel, and in doing so nearly lost her life. Having been brought up by hand she had no fear of human beings and the day after our move she approached a man who, thinking she was a wild animal, tried to kill her. When I returned to the tent that evening I found her lying near my camp bed and on picking her up saw that both her forelegs had been broken, and that the broken ends of the bones had worked through the skin. While I was getting a little milk down her throat, and trying to summon sufficient courage to do what I knew should be done, my servant came into the tent with a man who admitted to having tried to kill the poor beast. It appeared that this man had been working in his field when Tiddley-de-winks went up to him, and thinking she had strayed in from the nearby forest, he struck her with a stick and then chased her; and it was only when she entered my tent that he realized she was a tame animal. My servant had advised him to leave before I returned, but this the man had refused to do. When he had told his story he said he would return early next morning with a bone-setter from his village. There was nothing I could do for the injured animal, beyond making a soft bed for her and giving her milk at short intervals, and at daybreak next morning the man returned with the bone-setter.

It is unwise in India to judge from appearances. The bone-setter was a feeble old man, exhibiting in his person and tattered dress every sign of poverty, but he was none the less a specialist, and a man of few words. He asked me to lift up the injured animal, stood looking at her for a few minutes, and then turned and left the tent, saying over his shoulder that he would be back in two hours. I had worked week in week out for months on end so I considered I was justified in taking a morning off, and before the old man returned I had cut a number of stakes in the nearby jungle and constructed a small pen in a corner of the tent. The man brought back with him a number of dry jute stalks from which the bark had been removed, a quantity of green paste, several young castor-oil plant leaves as big as plates, and a roll of thin jute twine. When I had seated myself on the edge of the camp bed with Tiddley-de-winks across my knees, her weight partly supported by her hind legs and partly by my knees, the old man sat down on the ground in front of her with his material within reach.

The bones of both forelegs had been splintered midway between the knees and the tiny hooves, and the dangling portion of the legs had twisted round and round. Very gently the old man untwisted the legs, covered them from knee to hoof with a thick layer of green paste, laid strips of the castor-oil leaves over the paste to keep it in position, and over the leaves laid the jute stalks, binding them to the legs with jute twine. Next morning he returned with splints made of jute stalks strung together, and when they had been fitted to her legs Tiddley-de-winks was able to bend her knees and place her hooves, which extended an inch beyond the splints, on the ground.

The bone-setter's fee was one rupee, plus two annas for the ingredients he had put in the paste and the twine he had purchased in the bazaar, and not until the splints had been removed and the little antelope was able to skip about again would he accept either his fee or the little present I gratefully offered him.

My work, every day of which I had enjoyed, was over now and I was on my way to headquarters to render an account of the money I had spent and, I feared, to look for another job; for the locomotives had been converted to coal-burning and no more wood fuel would be needed. My books were all in perfect order and I had the feeling that I had rendered good service, for I had done in eighteen months what had been estimated to take two years. Yet I was uneasy, and the reason for my being so was the bag of money in my steel trunk.

I reached my destination, Samastipur, at 9 a.m. and after depositing my luggage in the waiting-room set out for the office of the head of the department I had been working for, with my account books and the bag containing two hundred rupees. At the office I was told by a very imposing doorkeeper that the master was engaged, and that I would have to wait. It was hot in the open veranda, and as the minutes dragged by my nervousness increased, for an old railway hand who had helped me to make up my books had warned me that to submit balanced accounts and then admit, as I had every intention of doing, that I had two hundred rupees in excess would land me in very great trouble. Eventually the door opened and a very harassed-looking man emerged; and before the doorkeeper could close it, a voice from inside the room bellowed at me to come in. Ryles, the head of the Locomotive Department of the Bengal & North Western Railway, was a man weighing sixteen stone, with a voice that struck terror into all who served under him, and with a heart of gold. Bidding me to sit down he drew my books towards him, summoned a clerk and very carefully checked my figures with those received from the stations to which the fuel had been sent. Then he told me he regretted my services would no longer be needed, said that discharge orders would be sent to me later in the day, and indicated that the interview was over. Having picked my hat off the floor I started to leave, but was called back and told I' had forgotten to remove what appeared to be a bag of money that I had placed on the table. It was foolish of me to have thought I could just leave the two hundred rupees and walk away, but that was what I was trying to do when Ryles called me; so I went back to the table and told him that the money belonged to the Railway, and as I did not know how to account for it in my books, I had brought it to him. 'Your books are balanced,' Ryles said, 'and if you have not faked your accounts I should like an explanation.' Tewari, the head clerk, had come into the room with a tray of papers and he stood behind Ryles's chair, with encouragement in his kindly old eyes, as I gave Ryles the following explanation.

When my work was nearing completion, fifteen cartmen, who had been engaged to cart fuel from the forest to the railway line, came to me one night and stated they had received an urgent summons to return to their village, to harvest the crops. The fuel they had carted was scattered over a wide area, and as it would take several days to stack and measure it they wanted me to make a rough calculation of the amount due to them, as it was essential for them to start on their journey that night. It was a dark night and quite impossible for me to calculate the cubic contents of the fuel, so I told them I would accept their figures. Two hours later they returned, and within a few minutes of paying them, I heard their carts creaking away into the night. They left no address with me, and several weeks later, when the fuel was stacked and measured, I found they had underestimated the amount due to them by two hundred rupees.

When I had told my story Ryles informed me that the Agent, Izat, was expected in Samastipur next day, and that he would leave him to deal with me.

Izat, Agent of three of the most flourishing railways in India, arrived next morning and at midday I received a summons to attend Ryles's office. Izat, a small dapper man with piercing eyes, was alone in the office when I entered it, and after complimenting me on having finished my job six months ahead of time, he said Ryles had shown him my books and given him a report and that he wanted to ask one question! Why had I not pocketed the two hundred rupees, and said nothing about it? My answer to this question was evidently satisfactory, for that evening, while waiting at the station in a state of uncertainty, I received two letters, one from Tewari thanking me for my contribution of two hundred rupees to the Railwaymen's Widows' and Orphans' Fund, of which he was Honorary Secretary, and the other from Izat informing me that my services were being retained, and instructing me to report to Ryles for duty.

For a year thereafter I worked up and down the railway on a variety of jobs, at times on the footplates of locomotives reporting on consumption of coal – a job I liked for I was permitted to drive the engines; at times as guard of goods trains, a tedious job, for the railway was short-handed and on many occasions I was on duty for forty-eight hours at a stretch; and at times as assistant storekeeper, or assistant station-master. And then one day I received orders to go to Mokameh Ghat and see Storrar, the Ferry Superintendent. The Bengal & North Western Railway runs through the Gangetic valley at varying distances from the Ganges river, and at several places branch lines take off from the main line and run down to the river and, by means of ferries, connect up with the broad-gauge railways on the right bank. Mokameh Ghat on the right bank of the Ganges is the most important of these connexions.

I left Samastipur in the early hours of the morning and at the branch-line terminus, Samaria Ghat, boarded the S.S. *Gorakhpur*. Storrar had been apprised of my visit but no reason had been given, and as I had not been told why I was to go to Mokameh Ghat, we spent the day partly in his house and partly in walking about the extensive sheds, in which there appeared to be a considerable congestion of goods. Two days later I was summoned to Gorakhpur, the headquarters of the railway, and informed that I had been posted to Mokameh Ghat as Transhipment Inspector, that my pay had been increased from one hundred to one hundred and fifty rupees per month, and that I was to take over the contract for handling goods a week later.

So back to Mokameh Ghat I went, arriving on this occasion at night, to take up a job about which I knew nothing, and to take on a contract without knowing where to get a single labourer, and, most important of all, with a capital of only one hundred and fifty rupees, saved during my two and a half years' service.

Storrar was not expecting me on this occasion, but he gave me dinner, and when I told him why I had returned we took our chairs on to the veranda, where a cool wind was blowing off the river, and talked late into the night. Storrar was twice my age and had been at Mokameh Ghat for several years. He was employed as Ferry Superintendent by the Bengal & North Western (metre-gauge) Railway, and was in charge of a fleet of steamers and barges that ferried passengers and metre-gauge wagons between Samaria Ghat and Mokameh Ghat. I learnt from him that eighty per cent of the long-distance traffic on the Bengal & North Western Railway passed through Mokameh Ghat; and that each year, from March to September, congestion of goods traffic took place at Mokameh Ghat and caused serious loss to the Railway.

The transfer of goods between the two railways at Mokameh Ghat, necessitated by a break of gauge, was done by a Labour Company which held the contract for handling goods throughout the length of the broad-gauge railway. In Storrar's opinion the indifference of this company to the interests of the metre-gauge railway, and the seasonal shortage of labour due to the harvesting of crops in the Gangetic valley, were the causes of the annual congestion. Having imparted this information he very pertinently asked how I, a total stranger to the locality and without any capital – he brushed aside my hard-earned savings – proposed to accomplish what the Labour Company with all their resources had failed to do. The sheds at Mokameh Ghat, he added, were stacked to the roof with goods, there were four hundred wagons in the yard waiting to be unloaded, and a thousand wagons on the far side of the river waiting to be ferried across. 'My advice to you', he concluded, 'is to catch the early steamer to Samaria Ghat and to go straight back to Gorakhpur. Tell the Railway you will have nothing to do with the handling contract.'

I was up early the next morning but I did not catch the steamer to Samaria Ghat. Instead, I went on a tour of inspection of the sheds and

of the goods yard. Storrar had not overpainted the picture: in fact the
conditions were even worse than he had said they were, for in addition
to the four hundred metre-gauge wagons there were the same number
of broad-gauge wagons waiting to be unloaded. At a rough calculation
I put the goods at Mokameh Ghat waiting to be dealt with at fifteen
thousand tons, and I had been sent to clear up the mess. Well, I was
not quite twenty-one years of age, and summer was starting, a season
when all of us are a little bit mad. By the time I met Ram Saran I had
made up my mind that I would take on the job, no matter what the
result might be.

Ram Saran was station-master at Mokameh Ghat, a post he had
held for two years. He was twenty years older than I was, had an
enormous jet black beard, and was the father of five children. He had
been advised by telegram of my arrival, but had not been told that I
was to take over the handling contract. When I gave him this bit of
news his face beamed all over and he said, 'Good, Sir. Very good. We
will manage.' My heart warmed towards Ram Saran on hearing that
'we', and up to his death, thirty-five years later, it never cooled.

When I told Storrar over breakfast that morning that I had decided
to take on the handling contract he remarked that fools never took
good advice, but added that he would do all he could to help me, a
promise he faithfully kept. In the months that followed he kept his ferry
running day and night to keep me supplied with wagons.

The journey from Gorakhpur had taken two days, so when I arrived
at Mokameh Ghat I had five days in which to learn what my duties
were, and to make arrangements for taking over the handling contract.
The first two days I spent in getting acquainted with my staff which, in
addition to Ram Saran, consisted of an assistant station-master, a
grand old man by the name of Chatterji who was old enough to be my
grandfather, sixty-five clerks, and a hundred shunters, pointsmen, and
watchmen. My duties extended across the river to Samaria Ghat where
I had a clerical and menial staff a hundred strong. The supervising of
these two staffs, and the care of the goods in transit, was in itself a
terrifying job and added to it was the responsibility of providing a
labour force sufficient to keep the five hundred thousand tons of goods
that passed through Mokameh Ghat annually flowing smoothly.

The men employed by the big Labour Company were on piece-
work, and as all work at Mokameh Ghat was practically at a standstill,
there were several hundred very discontented men sitting about the

sheds, many of whom offered me their services when they heard that I was going to do the handling for the metre-gauge railway. I was under no agreement not to employ the Labour Company's men, but thought it prudent not to do so. However, I saw no reason why I should not employ their relatives, so on the first of the three days I had in hand I selected twelve men and appointed them headmen. Eleven of these headmen undertook to provide ten men each, to start with, for the handling of goods, and the twelfth undertook to provide a mixed gang of sixty men and women for the handling of coal. The traffic to be dealt with consisted of a variety of commodities, and this meant employing different castes to deal with the different classes of goods. So of the twelve headmen, eight were Hindus, two Mohammedans, and two men of the depressed class; and as only one of the twelve was literate I employed one Hindu and one Mohammedan clerk to keep their accounts.

While one Labour Company was doing the work of both railways the interchange of goods had taken place from wagon to wagon. Now each railway was to unload its goods in the sheds, and reload from shed to wagon. For all classes of goods, excluding heavy machinery and coal, I was to be paid at the rate of Re 1-7-0 (equivalent to 1s. 11d. at the rate of exchange then current) for every thousand maunds of goods unloaded from wagons to shed or loaded from shed to wagons. Heavy machinery and coal were one-way traffic and as these two commodities were to be transhipped from wagon to wagon and only one contractor could be employed for the purpose, the work was entrusted to me, and I was to receive Re 1-4-0 (1s. 8d.) for unloading, and the same for loading, one thousand maunds. There are eighty pounds in a maund, and a thousand maunds therefore are equal to over thirty-five tons. These rates will appear incredible, but their accuracy can be verified by a reference to the records of the two railways.

A call-over on the last evening revealed that I had eleven headmen, each with a gang of ten men, and one headman with a mixed gang of sixty men and women. This, together with the two clerks, completed my force. At daybreak next morning I telegraphed to Gorakhpur that I had assumed my duties as Transhipment Inspector, and had taken over the handling contract.

Ram Saran's opposite number on the broad-gauge railway was an Irishman by the name of Tom Kelly. Kelly had been at Mokameh Ghat for some years and though he was very pessimistic of my success, he very sportingly offered to help me in every way he could. With the sheds congested with goods, and with four hundred wagons of each railway waiting to be unloaded, it was necessary to do something drastic to make room in the sheds and get the traffic moving, so I arranged with Kelly that I would take the risk of unloading a thousand tons of wheat on the ground outside the sheds and with the wagons so released clear a space in the sheds for Kelly to unload a thousand tons of salt and sugar. Kelly then with his empty wagons would clear a space in the sheds for me. This plan worked admirably. Fortunately for me it did not rain while my thousand tons of wheat were exposed to the weather, and in ten days we had not only cleared the accumulation in the sheds but also the accumulation of wagons. Kelly and I were then able to advise our respective headquarters to resume the booking of goods via Mokameh Ghat, which had been suspended for a fortnight.

I took over the contract at the beginning of the summer, the season when traffic on Indian railways is at its heaviest, and as soon as booking was opened a steady stream of downwards traffic from the Bengal & North Western Railway and an equally heavy stream from the broad-gauge railway started pouring into Mokameh Ghat. The rates on which I had been given the contract were the lowest paid to any contractor in India, and the only way in which I could hope to keep my labour was by cutting it down to the absolute minimum and making it work harder in order that it would earn as much, or possibly a little more, than other labour on similar work. All the labour at Mokameh Ghat was on piece-work, and at the end of the first week my men and I were overjoyed to find that they had earned, on paper, fifty per cent more than the Labour Company's men had earned.

When entrusting me with the contract the Railway promised to pay me weekly, and I on my part promised to pay my labour weekly. The Railway, however, when making their promise, failed to realize that by switching over from one handling contractor to another they would be raising complications for their Audit Department that would take time to resolve. For the Railway this was a small matter, but for me it was very different. My total capital on arrival at Mokameh Ghat had been one hundred and fifty rupees, and there was no one in all the world I could call on to help me with a loan, so until the Railway paid me I could not pay my men.

I have entitled this story Loyalty and I do not think that anyone has ever received greater loyalty than I did, not only from my labour, but also from the railway staff, during those first three months that I was at Mokameh Ghat. Nor do I think that men have ever worked harder. The work started every morning, weekdays and Sundays alike, at 4 a.m., and continued without interruption up to 8 p.m. The clerks whose duty it was to check and tally the goods took their meals at different hours to avoid a stoppage of work and my men ate their food, which was brought to them by wives, mothers, or daughters, in the sheds. There were no trade unions or slaves and slave-drivers in those days and every individual was at liberty to work as many, or as few, hours as he or she wished to. And everyone worked cheerfully and happily; for no matter whether it was the procuring of more and better food and clothing for the family, the buying of a new ox to replace a worn-out one, or the paying-off of a debt, the incentive, without which no man can work his best, was there. My work and Ram Saran's did not end when the men knocked off work, for there was correspondence to attend to, and the next day's work to be planned and arranged for, and during those first three months neither of us spent more than four hours in bed each night. I was not twenty-one and as hard as nails, but Ram Saran was twenty years older and soft, and at the end of the three months he had lost a stone in weight but none of his cheerfulness.

Lack of money was now a constant worry to me, and as week succeeded week the worry became a hideous nightmare that never left me. First the headmen and then the labourers pledged their cheap and pitiful bits of jewellery and now all credit had gone; and to make matters worse, the men of the Labour Company, who were jealous that my men had earned more than they did, were beginning to taunt my men. On several occasions ugly incidents were narrowly avoided, for semi-starvation had not impaired the loyalty of my men and they were willing to give battle to anyone who as much as hinted that I had tricked them into working for me, and that they would never see a pice of the money they had earned.

The monsoon was late in coming that year and the red ball in the sky, fanned by a wind from an unseen furnace, was making life a burden. At the end of a long and very trying day I received a telegram from Samaria Ghat informing me that an engine had been derailed on the slipway that fed the barges on which wagons were ferried across to Mokameh Ghat. A launch conveyed me across the river and twice within the next three hours the engine was replaced on the track, with the aid of hand jacks, only to be derailed again. It was not until the wind had died down and the powdery sand could be packed under the wooden sleepers that the engine was re-railed for the third time, and the slipway again brought into use. Tired and worn out, and with eyes swollen and sore from the wind and sand, I had just sat down to my first meal that day when my twelve headmen filed into the room, and seeing my servant placing a plate in front of me, with the innate courtesy of Indians, filed out again. I then, as I ate my dinner, heard the following conversation taking place in the veranda.

*One of the headmen.* What was on the plate you put in front of the sahib?

*My servant.* A chapati and a little dal.

*One of the headmen.* Why only one chapati and a little dal?

*My servant.* Because there is no money to buy more.

*One of the headmen.* What else does the sahib eat?

*My servant.* Nothing.

After a short silence I heard the oldest of the headmen, a Mohammedan with a great beard dyed with henna, say to his companions, 'Go home. I will stay and speak to the sahib.'

When my servant had removed the empty plate the old headman requested permission to enter the room, and standing before me spoke as follows: 'We came to tell you that our stomachs have long been empty and that after tomorrow it would be no longer possible for us to work. But we have seen tonight that your case is as bad as ours and we will carry on as long as we have the strength to stand. I will, with your permission, go now, sahib, and, for the sake of Allah, I beg you will do something to help us.'

Every day for weeks I had been appealing to headquarters at Gorakhpur for funds and the only reply I could elicit was that steps were being taken to make early payment of my bills.

After the bearded headman left me that night I walked across to the Telegraph Office, where the telegraphist on duty was sending the report I submitted each night of the work done during the day, took a form off his table and told him to clear the line for an urgent message to Gorakhpur. It was then a few minutes after midnight and the message I sent read: 'Work at Mokameh Ghat ceases at midday today unless I am assured that twelve thousand rupees has been dispatched by morning train.' The telegraphist read the message over and looking up at me said: 'If I have your permission I will tell my brother, who is on duty at this hour, to deliver the message at once and not wait until office hours in the morning.' Ten hours later, and with two hours of my ultimatum still to run, I saw a telegraph messenger hurrying towards me with a buff-coloured envelope in his hand. Each group of men he passed stopped work to stare after him, for everyone in Mokameh Ghat knew the purport of the telegram I had sent at midnight. After I had read the telegram the messenger, who was the son of my office peon, asked if the news was good; and when I told him it was good, he dashed off and his passage down the sheds was punctuated by shouts of delight. The money could not arrive until the following morning, but what did a few hours matter to those who had waited for long months?

The pay clerk who presented himself at my office next day, accompanied by some of my men carrying a cash chest slung on a bamboo pole and guarded by two policemen, was a jovial Hindu who was as broad as he was long and who exuded good humour and sweat in equal proportions. I never saw him without a pair of spectacles tied across his forehead with red tape. Having settled himself on the floor of my office he drew on a cord tied round his neck and from somewhere deep down in his person pulled up a key. He opened the cash chest, and lifted out twelve string-bags each containing one thousand freshly minted silver rupees. He licked a stamp, and stuck it to the receipt I had signed. Then, delving into a pocket that would comfortably have housed two rabbits, he produced an envelope containing bank notes to the value of four hundred and fifty rupees, my arrears of pay for three months.

I do not think anyone has ever had as great pleasure in paying out money as I had when I placed a bag containing a thousand rupees into the hands of each of the twelve headmen, nor do I think men have ever received money with greater pleasure than they did. The advent of the fat pay clerk had relieved a tension that had become almost unbearable, and the occasion called for some form of celebration, so the remainder of the day was declared a holiday – the first my men and I had indulged in for ninety-five days. I do not know how the others spent their hours of relaxation. For myself, I am not ashamed to admit that I spent mine in sound and restful sleep.

For twenty-one years my men and I worked the handling contract at Mokameh Ghat, and during the whole of that long period, and even when I was absent in France and in Waziristan during the 1914–18 war, the traffic flowed smoothly through the main outlet of the Bengal & North Western Railway with never a hitch. When we took over the contract, between four and five hundred thousand tons of goods were passing through Mokameh Ghat, and when I handed over to Ram Saran the traffic had increased to a million tons.

Those who visit India for pleasure or profit never come in contact with the real Indian – the Indian whose loyalty and devotion alone made it possible for a handful of men to administer, for close on two hundred years, a vast subcontinent with its teeming millions. To impartial historians I will leave the task of recording whether or not that administration was beneficial to those to whom I have introduced you, the poor of my India.

# 4

## *Life at Mokameh Ghat*

My men and I did not spend all our time at Mokameh Ghat working and sleeping. Work at the start had been very strenuous for all of us, and continued to be so, but as time passed and hands hardened and back-muscles developed, we settled down in our collars, and as we were pulling in the same direction with a common object – better conditions for those dependent on us – work moved smoothly and allowed of short periods for recreation. The reputation we had earned for ourselves by clearing the heavy accumulation of goods at Mokameh Ghat, and thereafter keeping the traffic moving, was something that all of us had contributed towards, and all of us took a pride in having earned this reputation and were determined to retain it. When therefore an individual absented himself to attend to private affairs, his work was cheerfully performed by his companions.

One of my first undertakings, when I had a little time to myself and a few rupees in my pocket, was to start a school for the sons of my workmen, and for the sons of the lower-paid railway staff. The idea originated with Ram Saran, who was a keen educationist, possibly because of the few opportunities he himself had had for education. Between us we rented a hut, installed a master, and the school – known ever afterwards as Ram Saran's School – started with a membership of twenty boys. Caste prejudices were the first snag we ran up against, but our master soon circumnavigated it by removing the sides of the hut. For whereas high- and low-caste boys could not sit together in the same hut, there was no objection to their sitting in the same shed. From the very start the school was a great success, thanks entirely to Ram Saran's unflagging interest. When suitable buildings had been erected, an additional seven masters employed, and the students increased to two hundred, the Government relieved us of our financial responsibilities. They raised the school to the status of a Middle School and rewarded Ram Saran, to the delight of all his friends, by conferring on him the title of Rai Sahib.

Tom Kelly, Ram Saran's opposite number on the broad-gauge railway, was a keen sportsman, and he and I started a recreation club. We cleared a plot of ground, marked out a football and a hockey ground, erected goal-posts, purchased a football and hockey-sticks, and started to train each his own football and hockey team. The training for football was comparatively easy, but not so the training for hockey, for as our means did not run to the regulation hockey-stick we purchased what at that time was known as a Khalsa stick: this was made in the Punjab from a blackthorn or small oak tree, the root being bent to a suitable angle to form the crook. The casualties at the start were considerable, for 98 per cent of the players were barefooted, the sticks were heavy and devoid of lapping, and the ball used was made of wood. When our teams had learnt the rudiments of the two games, which amounted to no more than knowing in which direction to propel the ball, we started inter-railway matches. The matches were enjoyed as much by the spectators as by us who took part in them. Kelly was stouter than he would have admitted to being and always played in goal for his side, or for our team when we combined to play out-station teams. I was thin and light and played centre forward and was greatly embarrassed when I was accidentally tripped up by foot or by hockey-stick, for when this happened all the players, with the exception of Kelly, abandoned the game to set me on my feet and dust my clothes. On one occasion while I was receiving these attentions, one of the opposing team dribbled the ball down the field and was prevented from scoring a goal by the spectators, who impounded the ball and arrested the player!

Shortly after we started the recreation club the Bengal & North Western Railway built a club house and made a tennis court for their European staff which, including myself, numbered four. Kelly was made an honorary member of the club, and a very useful member he proved, for he was good at both billiards and tennis. Kelly and I were not able to indulge in tennis more than two or three times a month, but when the day's work was done we spent many pleasant evenings together playing billiards.

The goods sheds and sidings at Mokameh Ghat were over a mile and a half long, and to save Kelly unnecessary walking his railway provided him with a rail trolly and four men to push it. This trolly was a great joy to Kelly and myself, for during the winter months, when the bar-headed and greylag geese were in, and the moon was at or near the full, we trollied down the main line for nine miles to where there were a number of small tanks. These tanks, some of which were only a few yards across while others were an acre or more in extent, were surrounded by lentil crops which gave us ample cover. We timed ourselves to arrive at the tanks as the sun was setting, and shortly after we had taken up our positions – Kelly at one of the tanks and I at another – we would see the geese coming. The geese, literally tens of thousands of them, spent the day on the islands in the Ganges and in the evening left the islands to feed on the weeds in the tanks, or on the ripening wheat and grain crops beyond. After crossing the railway line, which was half-way between our positions and the Ganges, the geese would start losing height, and they passed over our heads within easy range. Shooting by moonlight needs a little practice, for birds flighting overhead appear to be farther off than they actually are and one is apt to fire too far ahead of them. When this happened, the birds, seeing the flash of the gun and hearing the report, sprang straight up in the air and before they flattened out again were out of range of the second barrel. Those winter evenings when the full moon was rising over the palm-trees that fringed the river, and the cold brittle air throbbed and reverberated with the honking of geese and the swish of their wings as they passed overhead in flights of from ten to a hundred, are among the happiest of my recollections of the years I spent at Mokameh Ghat.

My work was never dull, and time never hung heavy on my hands, for in addition to arranging for the crossing of the Ganges, and the handling at Mokameh Ghat of a million tons of goods, I was responsible for the running of the steamers that ferried several hundred thousand passengers annually between the two banks of the river. The crossing of the river, which after heavy rains in the Himalayas was four to five miles wide, was always a pleasure to me, not only because it gave me time to rest my legs and have a quiet smoke but also because it gave me an opportunity of indulging in one of my hobbies – the study of human beings. The ferry was a link between two great systems of railways, one radiating north and the other radiating south, and among the seven hundred passengers who crossed at each trip were people from all parts of India, and from countries beyond her borders.

One morning I was leaning over the upper deck of the steamer watching the third-class passengers taking their seats on the lower deck. With me was a young man from England who had recently joined the railway and who had been sent to me to study the system of work at Mokameh Ghat. He had spent a fortnight with me and I was now accompanying him across the river to Samaria Ghat to see him off on his long railway journey to Gorakhpur. Sitting cross-legged, or tailor-wise, on a bench next to me and also looking down on the lower deck was an Indian. Crosthwaite, my young companion, was very enthusiastic about everything in the country in which he had come to serve, and as we watched the chattering crowds accommodating themselves on the open deck he remarked that he would dearly love to know who these people were, and why they were travelling from one part of India to another. The crowd, packed like sardines, had now settled down, so I said I would try to satisfy his curiosity. Let us start, I said, at the right and work round the deck, taking only the outer fringe of people who have their backs to the rail. The three men nearest to us are Brahmins, and the big copper vessels, sealed with wet clay, that they are so carefully guarding, contain Ganges water. The water on the right bank of the Ganges is considered to be more holy than the water on the left bank and these three Brahmins, servants of a well-known Maharaja, have filled the vessels on the right bank and are taking the water eighty miles by river and rail for the personal use of the Maharaja who, even when he is travelling, never uses any but Ganges water for domestic purposes. The man next to the Brahmins is a Mohammedan, a dhoonia by profession. He travels from station to station teasing the cotton in old and lumpy mattresses with the harp-like implement lying on the deck beside him. With this implement he teases old cotton until it resembles floss silk. Next to him are two Tibetan lamas who are returning from a pilgrimage to the sacred Buddhist shrine at Gaya, and who, even on this winter morning, are feeling hot, as you can see from the beads of sweat standing out on their foreheads. Next to the lamas are a group of four men returning from a pilgrimage to Benares, to their home on the foothills of Nepal. Each of the four men, as you can see, has two blown-glass jars, protected with wickerwork, slung to a short bamboo pole. These jars contain water which they have drawn from the Ganges at Benares and which they will sell drop by drop in their own and adjoining villages for religious ceremonies.

And so on round the deck until I came to the last man on the left. This man, I told Crosthwaite, was an old friend of mine, the father of one of my workmen, who was crossing the river to plough his field on the left bank.

Crosthwaite listened with great interest to all I had told him about the passengers on the lower deck, and he now asked me who the man was who was sitting on the bench near us. 'Oh', I said, 'he is a Mohammedan gentleman. A hide merchant on his way from Gaya to Muzaffarpur.' As I ceased speaking the man on the bench unfolded his legs, placed his feet on the deck and started laughing. Then turning to me he said in perfect English, 'I have been greatly entertained listening to the description you have given your friend of the men on the deck below us, and also of your description of me.' My tan hid my blushes, for I had assumed that he did not know English. 'I believe that with one exception, myself, your descriptions were right in every case. I am a Mohammedan as you say, and I am travelling from Gaya to Muzaffarpur, though how you know this I cannot think for I have not shown my railway ticket to anyone since I purchased it at Gaya. But you were wrong in describing me as a hide merchant. I do not deal in hides. I deal in tobacco.'

On occasions special trains were run for important personages, and in connexion with these trains a special ferry steamer was run, for the timings of which I was responsible. I met one afternoon one of these special trains, which was conveying the Prime Minister of Nepal, twenty ladies of his household, a Secretary, and a large retinue of servants from Katmandu, the capital of Nepal, to Calcutta. As the train came to a standstill a blond-headed giant in Nepalese national dress jumped down from the train and went to the carriage in which the Prime Minister was travelling. Here the man opened a big umbrella, put his back to the door of the carriage, lifted his right arm and placed his hand on his hip. Presently the door behind him opened and the Prime Minister appeared, carrying a gold-headed cane in his hand. With practised ease the Prime Minister took his seat on the man's arm and when he had made himself comfortable the man raised the umbrella over the Prime Minister's head and set off. He carried his burden as effortlessly as another would have carried a celluloid doll on his 300-yard walk, over loose sand, to the steamer. When I remarked to the Secretary, with whom I was acquainted, that I had never seen a greater feat of strength, he informed me that the Prime Minister always used the blond giant in the way I had just seen him being used, when other means of transport were not available. I was told that the man was a Nepalese, but my guess was that he was a national of northern Europe who for reasons best known to himself, or to his masters, had accepted service in an independent state on the borders of India.

While the Prime Minister was being conveyed to the steamer, four attendants produced a rectangular piece of black silk, some twelve feet long and eight feet wide, which they laid on the sand close to a carriage which had all its windows closed. The rectangle was fitted with loops at the four corners, and when hooks at the ends of four eight-foot silver staves had been inserted into the loops, and the staves stood on end, the rectangle revealed itself as a box-like structure without a bottom. One end of this structure was now raised to the level of the door of the closed carriage, and out of the carriage and into the silk box stepped the twenty ladies of the Prime Minister's household. With the stave-bearers walking on the outside of the box and only the twinkling patent-leather-shod feet of the ladies showing, the procession set off for the steamer. On the lower deck of the steamer one end of the box was raised and the ladies, all of whom appeared to be between sixteen and eighteen years of age, ran lightly up the stairway on to the upper deck, where I was talking to the Prime Minister. On a previous occasion I had suggested leaving the upper deck when the ladies arrived and had been told there was no necessity for me to do so and that the silk box was only intended to prevent the common men from seeing the ladies of the household. It is not possible for me to describe in detail the dress of the ladies, and all I can say is that in their gaily coloured, tight-fitting bodices and wide-spreading trousers, in the making of each of which forty yards of fine silk had been used, they looked, as they flitted from side to side of the steamer in an effort to see all that was to be seen, like rare and gorgeous butterflies. At Mokameh Ghat the same procedure was adopted to convey the Prime Minister and his ladies from the steamer to their special train, and when the whole party, and their mountain of luggage, were on board, the train steamed off on its way to Calcutta. Ten days later the party returned and I saw them off at Samaria Ghat on their way to Katmandu.

A few days later I was working on a report that had to go in that night when my friend the Secretary walked into my office. With his clothes dirty and creased, and looking as though they had been slept in for many nights, he presented a very different appearance from the spruce and well-dressed official I had last seen in company with the Prime Minister. He accepted the chair I offered him and said, without any preamble, that he was in great trouble. The following is the story he told me.

'On the last day of our visit to Calcutta the Prime Minister took the ladies of his household to the shop of Hamilton & Co., the leading jewellers in the city, and told them to select the jewels they fancied. The jewels were paid for in silver rupees for, as you know, we always take sufficient cash with us from Nepal to pay all our expenses and for everything we purchase. The selection of the jewels, the counting of the cash, the packing of the jewels into the suitcase I had taken to the shop for the purpose, and the sealing of the case by the jeweller, all took more time than we had anticipated. The result was that we had to dash back to our hotel, collect our luggage and retinue, and hurry to the station where our special train was waiting for us.

'We arrived back in Katmandu in the late evening, and the following morning the Prime Minister sent for me and asked for the suitcase containing the jewels. Every room in the palace was searched and everyone who had been on the trip to Calcutta was questioned, yet no trace of the suitcase was found, nor would anyone admit having seen it at any time. I remembered having taken it out of the motor-car that conveyed me from the shop to the hotel, but thereafter I could not remember having seen it at any stage of the journey. I am personally responsible for the case and its contents and if it is not recovered I may lose more than my job, for according to the laws of our land I have committed a great crime.

'There is in Nepal a hermit who is credited with second sight, and on the advice of my friends I went to him. I found the hermit, an old man in tattered clothing, living in a cave on the side of a great mountain, and to him I told my troubles. He listened to me in silence, asked no questions, and told me to return next morning. The following morning I again visited him and he told me that as he lay asleep the previous night he had a vision. In the vision he had seen the suitcase, with its seals intact, in a corner of a room hidden under boxes and bags of many kinds. The room was not far from a big river, had only one door leading into it, and this door was facing east. This is all the hermit could tell me, so', the Secretary concluded, with tears in his eyes and a catch in his throat, 'I obtained permission to leave Nepal for a week and I have come to see if you can help me, for it is possible that the Ganges is the river the hermit saw in his vision.'

In the Himalayas no one doubts the ability of individuals alleged to be gifted with second sight to help in recovering property lost or mislaid. That the Secretary believed what the hermit had told him there was no question, and his anxiety now was to regain possession of the suitcase, containing jewellery valued at Rs. 150,000 (£10,000), before others found and rifled it.

There were many rooms at Mokameh Ghat in which a miscellaneous assortment of goods was stored, but none of them answered to the description given by the hermit. I did, however, know of one room that answered to the description, and this room was the parcel office at Mokameh Junction, two miles from Mokameh Ghat. Having borrowed Kelly's trolly, I sent the Secretary to the Junction with Ram Saran. At the parcel office the clerk in charge denied all knowledge of the suitcase, but he raised no objection to the pile of luggage in the office being taken out on to the platform, and when this had been done, the suitcase was revealed with all its seals intact.

The question then arose as to how the case came to be in the office without the clerk's knowledge. The station-master now came on the scene and his inquiries elicited the fact that the suitcase had been put in the office by a carriage-sweeper, the lowest-paid man on the staff. This man had been ordered to sweep out the train in which the Prime Minister had travelled from Calcutta to Mokameh Ghat, and tucked away under the seat in one of the carriages he had found the suitcase. When his task was finished he carried the suitcase a distance of a quarter of a mile to the platform, and there being no one on the platform at the time to whom he could hand over the case he had put it in a corner of the parcel office. He expressed regret, and asked for forgiveness if he had done anything wrong.

Bachelors and their servants, as a rule, get into more or less set habits and my servants and I were no exception to the rule. Except when work was heavy I invariably returned to my house at 8 p.m. and when my house servant, waiting on the veranda, saw me coming he called to the waterman to lay my bath, for whether it was summer or winter I always had a hot bath. There were three rooms at the front of the house opening on to the veranda: a dining room, a sitting room, and a bedroom. Attached to the bedroom was a small bathroom, ten feet long and six wide. This bathroom had two doors and one small window. One of the doors opened on to the veranda, and the other led to the bedroom. The window was opposite the bedroom door, and set high up in the outer wall of the house. The furniture of the bathroom consisted of an egg-shaped wooden bath, long enough to sit in, a wooden bath-mat with holes in it, and two earthen vessels containing cold water.

After the waterman had laid the bath my servant would bolt the outer door of the bathroom and on his way through the bedroom pick up the shoes I had discarded and take them to the kitchen to clean. There he would remain until I called for dinner.

One night after my servant had gone to the kitchen I took a small hand-lamp off the dressing-table, went into the bathroom and there placed it on a low wall, six inches high and nine inches wide, which ran half-way across the width of the room. Then I turned and bolted the door, which like most doors in India sagged on its hinges and would not remain shut unless bolted. I had spent most of that day on the coal platform so did not spare the soap, and with a lather on my head and face that did credit to the manufacturers I opened my eyes to replace the soap on the bath-mat and, to my horror, saw the head of a snake projecting up over the end of the bath and within a few inches of my toes. My movements while soaping my head and splashing the water about had evidently annoyed the snake, a big cobra, for its hood was expanded and its long forked tongue was flicking in and out of its wicked-looking mouth. The right thing for me to have done would have been to keep my hands moving, draw my feet away from the snake, and moving very slowly stand up and step backwards to the door behind me, keeping my eyes on the snake all the time. But what I very foolishly did was to grab the sides of the bath and stand up and step backwards, all in one movement, on to the low wall. On this cemented wall my foot slipped, and while trying to regain my balance a stream of water ran off my elbow on to the wick of the lamp and extinguished it, plunging the room in pitch darkness. So here I was shut in a small dark room with one of the most deadly snakes in India. One step to the left or one step to the rear would have taken me to either of the two doors, but not knowing where the snake was I was frightened to move for fear of putting my bare foot on it. Moreover, both doors were bolted at the bottom, and even if I avoided stepping on the snake I should have to feel about for the bolts where the snake, in his efforts to get out of the room, was most likely to be.

The servants' quarters were in a corner of the compound fifty yards away on the dining-room side of the house, so shouting to them would be of no avail, and my only hope of rescue was that my servant would get tired of waiting for me to call for dinner, or that a friend would come to see me, and I devoutly hoped this would happen before the cobra bit me. The fact that the cobra was as much trapped as I was in

no way comforted me, for only a few days previously one of my men
had had a similar experience. He had gone into his house in the early
afternoon in order to put away the wages I had just paid him. While he
was opening his box he heard a hiss behind him, and turning round
saw a cobra advancing towards him from the direction of the open
door. Backing against the wall behind him, for there was only one door
to the room, the unfortunate man had tried to fend off the cobra with
his hands, and while doing so was bitten twelve times on hands and on
legs. Neighbours heard his cries and came to his rescue, but he died a
few minutes later.

I learnt that night that small things can be more nerve-racking and
terrifying than big happenings. Every drop of water that trickled down
my legs was converted in my imagination into the long forked tongue of
the cobra licking my bare skin, a prelude to the burying of his fangs in
my flesh.

How long I remained in the room with the cobra I cannot say. My
servant said later that it was only half an hour, and no sound has ever
been more welcome to me than the sounds I heard as my servant laid
the table for dinner. I called him to the bathroom door, told him of my
predicament, and instructed him to fetch a lantern and a ladder. After
another long wait I heard the babel of voices, followed by the scraping of
the ladder against the outer wall of the house. When the lantern had
been lifted to the window, ten feet above the ground, it did not illumin-
ate the room, so I told the man who was holding it to break a pane of
glass and pass the lantern through the opening. The opening was too
small for the lantern to be passed in upright. However, after it had
been relit three times it was finally inserted into the room and, feeling
that the cobra was behind me, I turned my head and saw it lying at the
bottom of the bedroom door two feet away. Leaning forward very
slowly, I picked up the heavy bath-mat, raised it high and let it fall as
the cobra was sliding over the floor towards me. Fortunately I judged
my aim accurately and the bath-mat crashed down on the cobra's neck
six inches from its head. As it bit at the wood and lashed about with its
tail I took a hasty stride to the veranda door and in a moment was
outside among a crowd of men, armed with sticks and carrying lanterns, for word had got round to the railway quarters that I was having
a life-and-death struggle with a big snake in a locked room.

The pinned-down snake was soon dispatched and it was not until the
last of the men had gone, leaving their congratulations, that I realized I

had no clothes on and that my eyes were full of soap. How the snake came to be in the bathroom I never knew. It may have entered by one of the doors, or it may have fallen from the roof, which was made of thatch and full of rats and squirrels, and tunnelled with sparrows' nests. Anyway, the servants who had laid my bath and I had much to be thankful for, for we approached that night very near the gate of the Happy Hunting Grounds.

We at Mokameh Ghat observed no Hindu or Mohammedan holidays, for no matter what the day was work had to go on. There was, however, one day in the year that all of us looked forward to with anticipation and great pleasure, and that day was Christmas. On this day custom ordained that I should remain in my house until ten o'clock, and punctually at this hour Ram Saran – dressed in his best clothes and wearing an enormous pink silk turban, specially kept for the occasion – would present himself to conduct me to my office. Our funds did not run to bunting, but we had a large stock of red and green signal flags, and with these flags and strings of marigold and jasmine flowers, Ram Saran and his band of willing helpers, working from early morning, had given the office and its surroundings a gay and festive appearance. Near the office door a table and a chair were set, and on the table stood a metal pot containing a bunch of my best roses tied round with twine as tight as twine could be tied. Ranged in front of the table were the railway staff, my headmen, and all my labourers. And all were dressed in clean clothes, for no matter how dirty we were during the rest of the year, on Christmas Day we had to be clean.

After I had taken my seat on the chair and Ram Saran had put a garland of jasmine round my neck, the proceedings started with a long speech by Ram Saran, followed by a short one by me. Sweets were then distributed to the children, and after this messy proceeding was over to the satisfaction of all concerned, the real business of the day started – the distribution of a cash bonus to Ram Saran, to the staff, and to the labourers. The rates I received for my handling contract were woefully small, but even so, by the willing co-operation of all concerned, I did make a profit, and eighty per cent of this profit was distributed on Christmas Day. Small as this bonus was – in the good years it amounted to no more than a month's pay, or a month's earnings – it was greatly appreciated, and the goodwill and willing co-operation it ensured enabled me to handle a million tons of goods a year for twenty-one years without one single unpleasant incident, and without one single day's stoppage of work.

When I hear of the labour unrest, strikes, and communal disorders that are rife today, I am thankful that my men and I served India at a time when the interest of one was the interest of all, and when Hindu, Mohammedan, Depressed Class, and Christian could live, work, and play together in perfect harmony. As could be done today if agitators were eliminated, for the poor of India have no enmity against each other.

# 5

## *Mothi*

Mothi had the delicate, finely chiselled features that are the heritage of all high-caste people in India, but he was only a young stripling, all arms and legs, when his father and mother died and left him with the responsibilities of the family. Fortunately it was a small one, consisting only of his younger brother and sister.

Mothi was at that time fourteen years of age, and had been married for six years. One of his first acts on finding himself unexpectedly the head of the family was to fetch his twelve-year-old wife – whom he had not seen since the day of their wedding – from her father's house in the Kota Dun, some dozen miles from Kaladhungi.

As the cultivation of the six acres of land Mothi inherited entailed more work than the four young people could tackle, Mothi took on a partner, locally known as a *sagee*, who in return for his day-and-night services received free board and lodging and half of the crops produced. The building of the communal hut with bamboos and grass procured from the jungles, under permit, and carried long distances on shoulder and on head, and the constant repairs to the hut necessitated by the violent storms that sweep the foothills, threw a heavy burden on Mothi and his helpers, and to relieve them of this burden I built them a masonry house, with three rooms and a wide veranda, on a four-foot plinth. For, with the exception of Mothi's wife who had come from a higher altitude, all of them were steeped in malaria.

To protect their crops the tenants used to erect a thorn fence round the entire village, but though it entailed weeks of hard labour, this flimsy fence afforded little protection against stray cattle and wild animals, and when the crops were on the ground the tenants, or members of their families, had to keep watch in the fields all night. Firearms were strictly rationed, and for our forty tenants the Government allowed us one single-barrelled muzzle-loading gun. This gun enabled one tenant in turn to protect his crops with a lethal weapon, while the others had to rely on tin cans which they beat throughout the night. Though the gun accounted for a certain number of pigs and porcupines, which were the worst offenders, the nightly damage was

considerable, for the village was isolated and surrounded by forests.
So, when my handling contract at Mokameh Ghat began paying a
dividend, I started building a masonry wall round the village. When
completed the wall was six feet high and three miles long. It took ten
years to build, for my share of the dividends was small. If today you
motor from Haldwani to Ramnagar, through Kaladhungi, you will
skirt the upper end of the wall before you cross the Boar Bridge and
enter the forest.

I was walking through the village one cold December morning, with
Robin, my dog, running ahead and putting up covey after covey of
grey partridge which no one but Robin ever disturbed – for all who
lived in the village loved to hear them calling at sunrise and at sunset –
when in the soft ground at the edge of one of the irrigation channels I
saw the tracks of a pig. This pig, with great, curved, wicked-looking
tusks, was as big as a buffalo calf and was known to everyone in the
village. As a squeaker he had wormed his way through the thorn fence
and fattened on the crops. The wall had worried him at first, but it had
a rough face and, being a determined pig, he had in time learnt to
climb it. Time and time again the watchers in the fields had fired at
him and on several occasions he had left a blood trail, but none of his
wounds had proved fatal and the only effect they had had on him was
to make him more wary.

On this December morning the pig's tracks led me towards Mothi's
holding, and as I approached the house I saw Mothi's wife standing in
front of it, her hands on her hips, surveying the ruin of their potato patch.

The pig had done a very thorough job, for the tubers were not
mature and he had been hungry, and while Robin cast round to see in
which direction the marauder had gone the woman gave vent to her
feelings. 'It is all Punwa's father's fault,' she said. 'It was his turn for
the gun last night, and instead of staying at home and looking after his
own property he must needs go and sit up in Kalu's wheat field because
he thought there was a chance of shooting a sambur there. And while
he was away, this is what the *shaitan* [devil] has done.' No woman in
our part of India ever refers to her husband, or addresses him, by
name. Before children are born he is referred to as the man of the
house, and after children come is spoken of and addressed as the father
of the first-born. Mothi now had three children, of whom the eldest was
Punwa, so to his wife he was 'Punwa's father', and his wife to everyone
in the village was 'Punwa's mother'.

Punwa's mother was not only the hardest-working woman in our village but she also had the sharpest tongue, and after telling me in no uncertain terms what she thought of Punwa's father for having absented himself the previous night, she turned on me and said I had wasted my money in building a wall over which a pig could climb to eat her potatoes, and that if I could not shoot the pig myself it was my duty to raise the wall a few feet so that no pig could climb over it. Mothi fortunately arrived while the storm was still breaking over my head, so whistling to Robin I beat a hasty retreat and left him to weather it.

That evening I picked up the tracks of the pig on the far side of the wall and followed them for two miles, at times along game paths and at times along the bank of the Boar river, until they led me to a dense patch of thorn-bushes interlaced with lantana. At the edge of this cover I took up position, as there was a fifty-fifty chance of the pig leaving the cover while there was still sufficient light for me to shoot by.

Shortly after I had taken up position behind a rock on the bank of the river, a sambur hind started belling at the upper end of the jungle in which a few years later I was to shoot the Bachelor of Powalgarh. The hind was warning the jungle folk of the presence of a tiger. A fortnight previously a party of three guns, with eight elephants, had arrived in Kaladhungi with the express purpose of shooting a tiger which, at that time, had his headquarters in the forest block for which I had a shooting pass. The Boar river formed the boundary between my block and the block taken by the party of three guns, and they had enticed the tiger to kill in their block by tying up fourteen young buffaloes on their side of the river. Two of these buffaloes had been killed by the tiger, the other twelve had died of neglect, and at about nine o'clock the previous night I had heard the report of a heavy rifle.

I sat behind the rock for two hours, listening to the belling sambur but without seeing anything of the pig, and when there was no longer any light to shoot by I crossed the river and, gaining the Kota road, loped down it, easing up and moving cautiously when passing the caves in which a big python lived, and where Bill Bailey of the Forest Department a month previously had shot a twelve-foot hamadryad. At the village gate I stopped and shouted to Mothi to be ready to accompany me at crack of dawn next morning.

Mothi had been my constant companion in the Kaladhungi jungles for many years. He was keen and intelligent, gifted with good eyesight and hearing, could move through the jungles silently, and was as brave as man could be. He was never late for an appointment, and as we walked through the dew-drenched jungle that morning, listening to the multitude of sounds of the awakening jungle folk, I told him of the belling of the sambur hind and of my suspicion that she had witnessed the killing of her young one by the tiger, and that she had stayed to watch the tiger on his kill – a not uncommon occurrence – for in no other way could I account for her sustained belling. Mothi was delighted at the prospect of our finding a fresh kill, for his means only permitted of his buying meat for his family once a month, and a sambur, chital, or pig, freshly killed by a tiger or by a leopard, was a godsend to him.

I had located the belling sambur as being due north and some fifteen hundred yards from me the previous evening, and when we arrived at this spot and found no kill we started looking on the ground for blood, hair, or a drag mark that would lead us to the kill; for I was still convinced that there was a kill to be found and that the killer was a tiger. At this spot two shallow depressions, coming down from the foot of the hill a few hundred yards away, met. The depressions ran more or less parallel to each other at a distance of about thirty yards and Mothi suggested that he should go up the right-hand depression while I went up the other. As there were only low bushes between, and we should be close to, and within sight of, each other, I agreed to the suggestion.

We had proceeded a hundred yards examining every foot of the ground, and going dead slow, when Mothi, just as I turned my head to look at him, started backwards, screaming as he did so. Then he whipped round and ran for dear life, beating the air with his hands as if warding off a swarm of bees and continuing to scream as he ran. The sudden and piercing scream of a human being in a jungle where a moment before all has been silent is terrifying to hear, and quite impossible to describe. Instinctively I knew what had happened. With his eyes fixed on the ground, looking for blood or hair, Mothi had failed to see where he was going, and had walked on to the tiger. Whether he had been badly mauled or not I could not see, for only his head and shoulders were visible above the bushes. I kept the sights of my rifle a foot behind him as he ran, intending to press the trigger if I saw any movement, but to my intense relief there was no movement as I swung round, and after he had covered a hundred yards I considered he was safe. I yelled to him to stop, adding that I was coming to him. Then, backing away for a few yards, for I did not know whether the tiger had changed his position, I hurried down the depression towards Mothi. He was standing with his back against a tree and I was greatly relieved to see that there was no blood on him or on the ground on which he was standing. As I reached him he asked what had happened, and when I told him that nothing had happened he expressed great surprise. He asked if the tiger had not sprung at him, or followed him; and when I replied that he had done everything possible to make the tiger do so, he said, 'I know, sahib. I know I should not have screamed and run, but I—could—not—help—' As his voice tailed away and his head came forward I caught him by the throat, but he slipped through my hands and slumped to the ground. Every drop of blood had drained from his face, and as he lay minute after long minute without any movement, I feared the shock had killed him.

There is little one can do in the jungles in an emergency of this kind, and that little I did. I stretched Mothi on his back, loosened his clothes, and massaged the region of his heart. Just as I was giving up hope and preparing to carry him home, he opened his eyes.

When Mothi was comfortably seated on the ground with his back to the tree and a half-smoked cigarette between his lips I asked him to tell me exactly what had happened. 'I had gone a short distance up the depression after I left you,' he said, 'closely examining the ground for traces of blood or hair, when I saw what looked like a spot of dry blood on a leaf. So I stooped down to have a closer look and, as I raised my head, I looked straight into the face of the tiger. The tiger was lying crouched down facing me at a distance of three or four paces. His head was a little raised off the ground; his mouth was wide open, and there was blood on his chin and on his chest. He looked as though he was on the point of springing at me, so I lost my head and screamed and ran away.' He had seen nothing of the sambur kill. He said the ground was open and free of bushes and there was no kill where the tiger was lying.

Telling Mothi to stay where he was I stubbed out my cigarette and set off to investigate, for I could think of no reason why a tiger with its mouth open, and blood on its chin and on its chest, should allow Mothi to approach within a few feet, over open ground, and not kill him when he screamed in its face. Going with the utmost caution to the spot where Mothi was standing when he screamed, I saw in front of me a bare patch of ground from which the tiger had swept the carpet of dead leaves as he had rolled from side to side; at the nearer edge of this bare patch of ground there was a semicircle of clotted blood. Skirting round where the tiger had been lying, to avoid disturbing the ground, I picked up on the far side of it a light and fresh blood trail, which for no apparent reason zigzagged towards the hill, and then continued along the foot of the hill for a few hundred yards and entered a deep and narrow ravine in which there was a little stream. Up this ravine, which ran deep into the foothills, the tiger had gone. I made my way back to the bare patch of ground and examined the clotted blood. There were splinters of bone and teeth in it, and these splinters provided me with the explanation I was looking for. The rifle-shot I had heard two nights previously had shattered the tiger's lower jaw, and he had made for the jungle in which he had his home. He had gone as far as his sufferings and loss of blood permitted and had then lain down on the spot where first the sambur had seen him tossing about, and where thirty hours later Mothi walked on to him. The most painful wound that can be inflicted on an animal, the shattering of the lower jaw, had quite evidently induced high fever and the poor beast had perhaps only been semi-conscious when he heard Mothi screaming in his face. He had got up quietly and staggered away, in a last effort to reach the ravine in which he knew there was water.

To make quite sure that my deductions were correct Mothi and I crossed the river into the adjoining shooting block to have a look at the ground where the fourteen buffaloes had been tied up. Here, high up in a tree, we found the machan the three guns had sat on, and the kill the tiger had been eating when fired at. From the kill a heavy blood trail led down to the river, with elephant tracks on each side of it. Leaving Mothi on the right bank I recrossed the river into my block, picked up the blood trail and the elephant tracks, and followed them for five or six hundred yards to where the blood trail led into heavy cover. At the edge of the cover the elephants had halted and, after standing about for some time, had turned to the right and gone away in the direction of Kaladhungi. I had met the returning elephants as I was starting out the previous evening to try and get a shot at the old pig, and one of the guns had asked me where I was going, and when I told him, had appeared to want to tell me something but was restrained from doing so by his companions. So, while the party of three guns went off on their elephants to the Forest Bungalow where they were staying, I had gone off on foot, without any warning, into the jungle in which they had left a wounded tiger.

The walk back to the village from where I had left Mothi was only about three miles, but it took us about as many hours to cover the distance, for Mothi was unaccountably weak and had to rest frequently. After leaving him at his house I went straight to the Forest Bungalow, where I found the party of three packed up and on the point of leaving to catch the evening train at Haldwani. We talked on the steps of the veranda for some little time, I doing most of the talking, and when I learnt that the only reason they could not spare the time to recover the tiger they had wounded was the keeping of a social engagement, I told them that if Mothi died as a result of shock or if the tiger killed any of my tenants, they would have to face a charge of manslaughter.

The party left after my talk with them, and next morning, armed with a heavy rifle, I entered the ravine up which the tiger had gone, not with the object of recovering a trophy for others, but with the object of putting the tiger out of his misery and burning his skin. The ravine, every foot of which I knew, was the last place I would have selected in which to look for a wounded tiger. However, I searched it from top to bottom, and also the hills on either side, for the whole of that day without finding any trace of the tiger, for the blood trail had stopped shortly after he entered the ravine.

Ten days later a forest guard on his rounds came on the remains of a tiger that had been eaten by vultures. In the summer of that year Government made a rule prohibiting sitting up for tigers between the hours of sunset and sunrise, and making it incumbent on sportsmen wounding tigers to make every effort to bring the wounded animal to bag, and to make an immediate report of the occurrence to the nearest Forest Officer and police outpost.

Mothi met with his experience in December, and when we left Kaladhungi in April he appeared to be little the worse for the shock. But his luck was out, for a month later he was badly mauled by a leopard he wounded one night in his field and followed next morning into heavy cover; and he had hardly recovered from his wounds when he had the misfortune of being responsible for the death of a cow – the greatest crime a Hindu can commit. The cow, an old and decrepit animal that had strayed in from an adjoining village, was grazing in Mothi's field, and as he attempted to drive it out it put its hoof in a deep rat-hole and broke its leg. For weeks Mothi attended assiduously to the cow as it lay in his field, but it died eventually, and the matter being too serious for the village priest to deal with, he ordered Mothi to make a pilgrimage to Hardwar. So, having borrowed money for the journey, to Hardwar Mothi went. Here to the head priest at the main temple Mothi confessed his crime, and after that dignitary had given the offence due consideration he ordered Mothi to make a donation to the temple: this would absolve him of his crime, but in order to show repentance he would have also to do penance. The priest then asked him from what acts he derived most pleasure and Mothi, being without guile, made answer that he derived most pleasure from shooting, and from eating meat. Mothi was then told by the priest that in future he must refrain from these two pleasures.

Mothi returned from his pilgrimage cleared of his crime, but burdened with a lifelong penance. His opportunities for shooting had been few, for besides having to share the muzzle-loading gun with others he had had to confine his shooting to the village boundaries, as no man in his position was permitted to shoot in Government forests; even so, Mothi had derived great pleasure from the old gun, and from the occasional shots I had permitted him – against all rules – to fire from my rifle. Hard as this half of his penance was the second half was even harder, and, moreover, it adversely affected his health. Though his means had only allowed him to buy a small meat ration once a month, pigs and porcupines were plentiful, and deer occasionally strayed into the fields at night. It was the custom in our village, a custom to which I also adhered, for an animal shot by one to be shared by all, so Mothi had not had to depend entirely on the meat he could buy.

It was during the winter following his pilgrimage to Hardwar that Mothi developed a hacking cough. As the remedies we tried failed to give relief, I got a doctor friend who was passing through Káladhungi to examine him, and was horrified to learn that he was suffering from tuberculosis. On the doctor's recommendation I sent Mothi to the Bhowali Sanatorium, thirty miles away. Five days later he returned with a letter from the Superintendent of the Sanatorium saying that the case was hopeless, and that for this reason the Superintendent regretted he could not admit Mothi. A medical missionary who was staying with us at the time, and who had worked for years in a sanatorium, advised us to make Mothi sleep in the open and drink a quart of milk with a few drops of paraffin in it each morning. So for the rest of that winter

Mothi slept in the open, and while sitting on our veranda, smoking a cigarette and talking to me, each morning drank a quart of milk fresh from our cows.

The poor of India are fatalists, and in addition have little stamina to fight disease. Deprived of our company, though not of our help, Mothi lost hope when we left for our summer home, and died a month later.

The women of our foothills are the hardest workers in India, and the hardest working of them all was Mothi's widow, Punwa's mother. A small compact woman, as hard as flint and a beaver for work – young enough to remarry but precluded from doing so by reasons of her caste – she bravely and resolutely faced the future, and right gallantly she fulfilled her task, ably assisted by her young children.

Of her three children, Punwa, the eldest, was now twelve, and with the assistance of neighbours was able to do the ploughing and other field jobs. Kunthi, a girl, was ten and married, and until she left the village five years later to join her husband she assisted her mother in all her thousand and one tasks, which included cooking the food and washing up the dishes; washing and mending the clothes – for Punwa's mother was very particular about her own and her children's dress, and no matter how old and patched the garments were, they always had to be clean; fetching water from the irrigation furrow or from the Boar river for domestic purposes; bringing firewood from the jungles, and grass and tender young leaves for the milch cows and their calves; weeding and cutting the crops; husking the paddy, in a hole cut in a slab of rock, with an iron-shod staff that was heavy enough to tire the muscles of any man; winnowing the wheat for Punwa to take to the watermill to be ground into atta; and making frequent visits to the bazaar two miles away to drive hard bargains for the few articles of food and clothing the family could afford to buy. Sher Singh, the youngest child, was eight, and from the moment he opened his eyes at crack of dawn each morning until he closed them when the evening meal had been eaten he did everything that a boy could do. He even gave Punwa a hand with the ploughing, though he had to be helped at the end of each furrow as he was not strong enough to turn the plough.

Sher Singh, without a care in the world, was the happiest child in the village. When he could not be seen he could always be heard, for he loved to sing. The cattle—four bullocks, twelve cows, eight calves, and Lalu the bull – were his special charge, and each morning after milking the cows he released the herd from the stakes to which he had tethered them the evening before, drove them out of the shed and through a wicket in the boundary wall, and then set to to clean up the shed. It would now be time for the morning meal, and when he heard the call from his mother, or Kunthi, he would hurry home across the fields taking the milk can with him. The frugal morning meal consisted of fresh hot chapatis and dal, liberally seasoned with green chillies and salt and cooked in mustard oil. Having breakfasted, and finished any chores about the house that he was called upon to do, Sher Singh would begin his day's real work. This was to graze the cattle in the jungle, prevent them from straying, and guard them against leopards and tigers. Having collected the four bullocks and twelve cows from the open ground beyond the boundary wall, where they would be lying basking in the sun, and left Kunthi to keep an eye on the calves, this small tousle-headed boy, his axe over his shoulder and Lalu the bull following him, would drive his charges over the Boar Bridge and into the dense jungle beyond, calling to each by name.

Lalu was a young scrub bull destined to be a plough-bullock when he had run his course but who, at the time I am writing about, was free of foot and the pride of Sher Singh his foster-brother, for Lalu had shared his mother's milk with Sher Singh. Sher Singh had christened his foster-brother *Lalu*, which means red. But Lalu was not red. He was of a light dun colour, with stronger markings on the shoulders and a dark, almost black line running down the length of his back. His horns were short, sharp, and strong, with the light and dark colourings associated with the shoehorns that adorned dressing-tables of that period.

When human beings and animals live in close association with each other under conditions in which they are daily subjected to common dangers, each infuses the other with a measure of courage and confidence which the one possesses and the other lacks. Sher Singh, whose father and grandfather had been more at home in the jungles than in the walks of men, had no fear of anything that walked, and Lalu, young and vigorous, had unbounded confidence in himself. So while Sher Singh infused Lalu with courage, Lalu in turn infused Sher Singh with confidence. In consequence Sher Singh's cattle grazed where others feared to go, and he was justly proud of the fact that they were in better condition than any others in the village, and that no leopard or tiger had ever taken toll of them.

Four miles from our village there is a valley about five miles in length, running north and south, which has no equal in beauty or richness of wild life in the five thousand square miles of forest land in the United Provinces. At the upper end of the valley a clear stream, which grows in volume as it progresses, gushes from a cave in which a python lives, from under the roots of an old jamun tree. This crystal-clear stream with its pools and runs is alive with many kinds of small fish on which live no fewer than five varieties of kingfishers. In the valley grow flowering and fruit-bearing trees and bushes that attract a multitude of nectar-drinking and fruit-eating birds and animals, which in turn attract predatory birds and carnivorous animals which find ample cover in the dense undergrowth and matted cane-brakes. In places the set of the stream has caused miniature landslides, and on these grows a reedy kind of grass, with broad lush leaves, much fancied by sambur and karker [barking deer].

The valley was a favourite haunt of mine. One winter evening, shortly after our descent to Kaladhungi from our summer home, I was standing at a point where there is a clear view into the valley when, in a clump of grass to the left, I saw a movement. After a long scrutiny the movement revealed itself as an animal feeding on the lush grass on a steep slope. The animal was too light for a sambur and too big for a karker, so I set out to stalk it, and as I did so a tiger started calling in the valley a few hundred yards lower down. My quarry also heard the tiger, and as it raised its head I saw to my surprise that it was Lalu. With head poised he stood perfectly still listening to the tiger, and when it stopped calling he unconcernedly resumed cropping the grass. This was forbidden ground for Lalu, for cattle are not permitted to graze in Government Reserved Forests, and moreover Lalu was in danger from the tiger; so I called to him by name and, after a little hesitation, he came up the steep bank and we returned to the village together. Sher Singh was tying up his cattle in the shed when we arrived, and when I told him where I had found Lalu he laughed and said, 'Don't fear for this one, sahib. The forest guard is a friend of mine and would not impound my Lalu, and as for the tiger, Lalu is well able to take care of himself.'

Not long after this incident, the Chief Conservator of Forests, Smythies, and his wife arrived on tour in Kaladhungi, and as the camels carrying their camp equipment were coming down the forest road towards the Boar Bridge, a tiger killed a cow on the road in front of them. On the approach of the camels, and the shouting of the men with them, the tiger left the cow on the road and bounded into the jungle. The Smythies were sitting on our veranda having morning coffee when the camel men brought word of the killing of the cow. Mrs Smythies was keen to shoot the tiger, so I went off with two of her men to put up a machan for her, and found that in the meantime the tiger had returned and dragged the cow twenty yards into the jungle. When the machan was ready I sent back for Mrs Smythies and, after putting her into the machan with a forest guard to keep her company, I climbed a tree on the edge of the road hoping to get a photograph of the tiger.

It was 4 p.m. We had been in position half an hour, and a karker had just started barking in the direction in which we knew the tiger was lying up, when down the road came Lalu. On reaching the spot where the cow had been killed he very carefully smelt the ground and a big pool of blood, then turned to the edge of the road and with head held high and nose stretched out started to follow the drag. When he saw the cow he circled round her, tearing up the ground with his hoofs and snorting with rage. After tying my camera to a branch I slipped off the tree and conducted a very angry and protesting Lalu to the edge of the village. Hardly had I returned to my perch on the tree, however, when up the road came Lalu to make a second demonstration round the dead cow. Mrs Smythies now sent the forest guard to drive Lalu away, and as the man passed me I told him to take the bull across the Boar Bridge and to remain there with the elephant that was coming later for Mrs Smythies. The karker had stopped barking some time previously and a covey of junglefowl now started cackling a few yards behind the machan. Getting my camera ready I looked towards Mrs Smythies, and saw she had her rifle poised, and at that moment Lalu appeared for the third time. (We learnt later that, after being taken across the bridge, he had circled round, crossed the river-bed lower down and disappeared into the jungle.) This time Lalu trotted up to the cow and, either seeing or smelling the tiger, lowered his head and charged into the bushes, bellowing loudly. Three times he did this, and after each charge he retreated backwards to his starting-point, slashing upwards with his horns as he did so.

I have seen buffaloes driving tigers away from their kills, and I have seen cattle doing the same with leopards but, with the exception of a Himalayan bear, I had never before seen a solitary animal – and a scrub bull at that – drive a tiger away from his kill.

Courageous as Lalu was he was no match for the tiger, who was now losing his temper and answering Lalu's bellows with angry growls.

Remembering a small boy back in the village whose heart would break if anything happened to his beloved companion, I was on the point of going to Lalu's help when Mrs Smythies very sportingly gave up her chance of shooting the tiger, so I shouted to the mahout to bring up the elephant. Lalu was very subdued as he followed me to the shed where Sher Singh was waiting to tie him up, and I think he was as relieved as I was that the tiger had not accepted his challenge while he was defending the dead cow.

The tiger fed on the cow that night and next evening, and while Mrs Smythies was having another unsuccessful try to get a shot at him, I took a ciné picture which some who read this story may remember having seen. In the picture the tiger is seen coming down a steep bank, and drinking at a little pool.

The jungle was Sher Singh's playground, the only playground he ever knew, just as it had been my playground as a boy, and of all whom I have known he alone enjoyed the jungles as much as I have done. Intelligent and observant, his knowledge of jungle lore was incredible. Nothing escaped his attention, and he was as fearless as the animal [tiger] whose name he bore.

Our favourite evening walk was along one of the three roads which met on the far side of the Boar Bridge – the abandoned trunk road to Moradabad, the road to Kota, and the forest road to Ramnagar. Most evenings at sundown we would hear Sher Singh before we saw him, for he sang with abandon in a clear treble voice that carried far as he drove his cattle home. Always he would greet us with a smile and a salaam, and always he would have something interesting to tell us. 'The big tiger's tracks were on the road this morning coming from the direction of Kota and going towards Naya Gaon, and at midday I heard him calling at the lower end of the Dhunigad cane-brake.' 'Near Saryapani I heard the clattering of horns, so I climbed a tree and saw two chital stags fighting. One of them has very big horns, sahib, and is very fat, and I have eaten no meat for many days.' 'What am I carrying?' – he had something wrapped in big green leaves and tied round with bark balanced on his tousled head. 'I am carrying a pig's leg. I saw some vultures on a tree, so I went to have a look and under a bush I found a pig killed by a leopard last night and partly eaten. If you want to shoot the leopard, sahib, I will take you to the kill.' 'Today I found a beehive in a hollow haldu tree,' he said one day, proudly exhibiting a large platter of leaves held together with long thorns on which the snow-white comb was resting. 'I have brought the honey for you.' Then, glancing at the rifle in my hands, he added, 'I will bring the honey to the house when I have finished my work for perchance you may meet a pig or a karker and with the honey in your hands you would not be able to shoot.' The cutting of the hive out of the haldu tree with his small axe had probably taken him two hours or more, and he had got badly stung in the process, for his hands were swollen and one eye was nearly closed, but he said nothing about this and to have commented on it would have embarrassed him. Later that night, while we were having dinner, he slipped silently into the room and as he laid the brass tray, polished till it looked like gold, on our table, he touched the elbow of his right arm with the fingers of his left hand, an old hill custom denoting respect, which is fast dying out.

After depositing such a gift on the table, leaving the tray for Kunthi to call for in the morning, Sher Singh would pause at the door and, looking down and scratching the carpet with his toes, would say, 'If you are going bird-shooting tomorrow I will send Kunthi out with the cattle and come with you, for I know where there are a lot of birds.' He was always shy in a house, and on these occasions spoke with a catch in his voice as though he had too many words in his mouth and was trying, with difficulty, to swallow the ones that were getting in his way.

Sher Singh was in his element on these bird shoots, which the boys of the village enjoyed as much as he and I did, for in addition to the excitement and the prospect of having a bird to take home at the end of the day, there was always a halt at midday at a prearranged spot to which the man sent out earlier would bring the fresh sweets and parched gram that would provide a meal for all.

When I had taken my position, Sher Singh would line up his companions and beat the selected cover towards me, shouting the loudest of them all and worming his way through the thickest cover. When a bird was put up he would yell, 'It's coming, sahib! It's coming!' Or when a heavy animal went crashing through the undergrowth, as very frequently happened, he would call to his companions not to run away, assuring them that it was only a sambur, or a chital, or maybe a sounder of pig. Ten to twelve patches of cover would be beaten in the course of the day, yielding as many peafowl and junglefowl, and two or three hares, and possibly a small pig or a porcupine. At the end of the last beat the bag would be shared out among the beaters and the gun, or if the bag was small only among the beaters, and Sher Singh was never more happy than when, at the end of the day, he made for home with a peacock in full plumage proudly draped over his shoulders.

Punwa was now married, and the day was fast approaching when Sher Singh would have to leave the home, for there was not sufficient room on the small holding of six acres for the two brothers. Knowing that it would break Sher Singh's heart to leave the village and his beloved jungles, I decided to apprentice him to a friend who had a garage at Kathgodam, and who ran a fleet of cars on the Naini Tal motor road. After his training it was my intention to employ Sher Singh to drive our car and accompany me on my shooting trips during the winter, and to look after our cottage and garden at Kaladhungi while we were in Naini Tal during the summer. Sher Singh was speechless with delight when I told him of the plans I had made for him, plans which ensured his continued residence in the village, and within sight and calling distance of the home he had never left from the day of his birth.

Plans a-many we make in life, and I am not sure there is cause for regret when some go wrong. Sher Singh was to have started his apprenticeship when we returned to Kaladhungi in November. In October he contracted malignant malaria which led to pneumonia, and a few days before we arrived he died. During his boyhood's years he had sung through life happy as the day was long and, had he lived, who can say that his life in a changing world would have been as happy, and as carefree, as those first few years?

Before leaving our home for a spell, to regain in new climes the health we lost in Hitler's war, I called together our tenants and their families as I had done on two previous occasions, to tell them the time had come for them to take over their holdings and run the village for themselves. Punwa's mother was the spokesman for the tenants on this occasion, and after I had had my say she got to her feet and, in her practical way, spoke as follows: 'You have called us away from our work to no purpose. We have told you before and we tell you again that we will not take your land from you, for to do so would imply that we were no longer your people. And now, sahib, what about the pig, the son of the *shaitan* who climbed your wall and ate my potatoes? Punwa and these others cannot shoot it and I am tired of sitting up all night and beating a tin can.'

Maggie and I were walking along the fire-track that skirts the foot-

hills with David at our heels when the pig – worthy son of the old *shaitan*
who, full of years and pellets of buckshot, had been killed in an all-
night fight with a tiger – trotted across the track. The sun had set and
the range was long – all of three hundred yards – but a shot was justifiable
for the pig was quite evidently on his way to the village. I adjusted the
sights and, resting the rifle against a tree, waited until the pig paused at
the edge of a deep depression. When I pressed the trigger, the pig
jumped into the depression, scrambled out on the far side, and made off
at top speed. 'Have you missed him?' asked Maggie, and with his eyes
David put the same question. There was no reason, except miscalcula-
tion of the range, why I should not have hit the pig, for my silver
foresight had shown up clearly on his black skin, and the tree had
assisted me to take steady aim. Anyway, it was time to make for home,
and as the cattle-track down which the pig had been going would lead
us to the Boar Bridge we set off to see the result of my shot. The pig's
feet had bitten deeply into the ground where he had taken off, and on
the far side of the depression, where he had scrambled out, there was
blood. Two hundred yards in the direction in which the pig had gone
there was a narrow strip of dense cover. I should probably find him
dead in the morning in this cover, for the blood trail was heavy; but if
he was not dead and there was trouble, Maggie would not be with me,
and there would be more light to shoot by in the morning than there
was now.

Punwa had heard my shot and was waiting on the bridge for us.
'Yes,' I said, in reply to his eager inquiry, 'it was the old pig I fired at,
and judging by the blood trail, he is hit hard.' I added that if he met
me on the bridge next morning I would show him where the pig was, so
that later he could take out a party of men to bring it in. 'May I bring
the old havildar too?' said Punwa, and I agreed. The havildar, a kindly
old man who had won the respect and affection of all, was a Gurkha
who on leaving the army had joined the police, and having retired a
year previously had settled down with his wife and two sons on a plot of
land we had given him in our village. Like all Gurkhas the havildar
had an insatiable appetite for pig's flesh, and when a pig was shot by
any of us it was an understood thing that, no matter who went short,
the ex-soldier-policeman must have his share.

Punwa and the havildar were waiting for me at the bridge next
morning. Following the cattle-track, we soon reached the spot where,
the previous evening, I had seen the blood. From here we followed the

well-defined blood trail which led us, as I had expected, to the dense cover. I left my companions at the edge of the cover, for a wounded pig is a dangerous animal, and with one exception – a bear – is the only animal in our jungles that has the unpleasant habit of savaging any human being who has the misfortune to be attacked and knocked down by him. For this reason wounded pigs, especially if they have big tusks, have to be treated with great respect. The pig had stopped where I had expected him to, but he had not died, and at daybreak he had got up from where he had been lying all night and left the cover. I whistled to Punwa and the havildar and when they rejoined me we set off to trail the animal.

The trail led us across the fire-track, and from the direction in which the wounded animal was going it was evident he was making for the heavy jungle on the far side of the hill, from which I suspected he had come the previous evening. The morning blood trail was light and continued to get lighter the farther we went, until we lost it altogether in a belt of trees, the fallen leaves of which a gust of wind had disturbed. In front of us at this spot was a tinder-dry stretch of waist-high grass. Still under the conviction that the pig was heading for the heavy jungle on the far side of the hill, I entered the grass, hoping to pick up the tracks again on the far side.

The havildar had lagged some distance behind, but Punwa was immediately behind me when, after we had gone a few yards into the grass, my woollen stockings caught on the thorns of a low bush. While I was stooping to free myself Punwa, to avoid the thorns, moved a few paces to the right and I just got free and was straightening up when out of the grass shot the pig and with an angry grunt went straight for Punwa, who was wearing a white shirt. I then did what I have always asked companions who have accompanied me into the jungles after dangerous game to do if they saw me attacked by a wounded animal. I threw the muzzle of my rifle into the air, and shouted at the top of my voice as I pressed the trigger.

If the thorns had not caught in my stockings and lost me a fraction of a second, all would have been well, for I should have killed the pig before it got to Punwa; but once the pig had reached him the only thing I could do to help him was to try to cause a diversion, for to have fired in his direction would further have endangered his life. As the bullet was leaving my rifle to land in the jungle a mile away, Punwa, with a despairing scream of 'Sahib!', was falling backwards into the grass with the pig right on top of him, but at my shout and the crack of the rifle the pig turned like a whiplash straight for me, and before I was able to eject the spent cartridge and ram a fresh one into the chamber of the ·275 rifle, he was at me. Taking my right hand from the rifle I stretched the arm out palm downwards, and as my hand came in contact with his forehead he stopped dead, and for no other reason than that my time had not come, for he was big and angry enough to have knocked over and savaged a cart-horse. The pig's body had stopped but his head was very active, and as he cut upwards with his great tusks, first on one side and then on the other, fortunately cutting only the air, he wore the skin off the palm of my hand with his rough forehead. Then, for no apparent reason, he turned away, and as he made off I put two bullets into him in quick succession and he pitched forward on his head.

After that one despairing scream Punwa had made no sound or movement, and with the awful thought of what I would say to his mother, and the still more awful thought of what she would say to me, I went with fear and trembling to where he was lying out of sight in the grass, expecting to find him ripped open from end to end. He was lying full stretch on his back, and his eyes were closed, but to my intense relief I saw no blood on his white clothes. I shook him by the shoulder and asked him how he was, and where he had been hurt. In a very weak voice he said he was dead, and that his back was broken. I straddled his body and gently raised him to a sitting position, and was overjoyed to find that he was able to retain this position when I released my hold. Passing my hand down his back I assured him that it was not broken, and after he had verified this fact with his own hand, he turned his head and looked behind him to where a dry stump was projecting two or three inches above the ground. Evidently he had fainted when the pig knocked him over and, on coming to, feeling the stump boring into his back, had jumped to the conclusion that it was broken.

And so the old pig, son of the *shaitan*, died, and in dying nearly frightened the lives out of two of us. But beyond rubbing a little skin off my hand he did us no harm, for Punwa escaped without a scratch and with a grand story to tell. The havildar, like the wise old soldier he was, had remained in the background. None the less he claimed a lion's share of the pig, for had he not stood foursquare in reserve to render assistance if assistance had been called for? And further, was it not the custom for those present at a killing to receive a double share, and what difference was there between seeing and hearing the shots that had killed the pig? So a double share was not denied him, and he too, in the course of time, had a grand story to tell of the part he took in that morning's exploit.

Punwa now reigns, and is raising a family, in the house I built for his father. Kunthi has left the village to join her husband, and Sher Singh waits in the Happy Hunting Grounds. Punwa's mother is still alive, and if you stop at the village gate and walk through the fields to Punwa's house you will find her keeping house for Punwa and his family and working as hard and as cheerfully at her thousand and one tasks as she worked when she first came to our village as Mothi's bride.

During the war years Maggie spent the winters alone in our cottage at Kaladhungi, without transport, and fourteen miles from the nearest settlement. Her safety gave me no anxiety, for I knew she was safe among my friends, the poor of India.

# 6

## *The Law of the Jungles*

Harkwar and Kunthi were married before their total ages had reached double figures. This was quite normal in the India of those days, and would possibly still have been so had Mahatma Gandhi and Miss Mayo never lived.

Harkwar and Kunthi lived in villages a few miles apart at the foot of the great Dunagiri mountain, and had never seen each other until the great day when, dressed in bright new clothes, they had for all too short a time been the centre of attraction of a vast crowd of relatives and friends. That day lived long in their memories as the wonderful occasion when they had been able to fill their small bellies to bursting-point with halwa and puris. The day also lived for long years in the memory of their respective fathers, for on it the village bania, who was their 'father and mother', realizing their great necessity had provided the few rupees that had enabled them to retain the respect of their community by marrying their children at the age that all children should be married, and on the propitious date selected by the priest of the village – and had made a fresh entry against their names in his register. True, the fifty per cent interest demanded for the accommodation was excessive, but, God willing, a part of it would be paid, for there were other children yet to be married, and who but the good bania was there to help them?

Kunthi returned to her father's home after her wedding and for the next few years performed all the duties that children are called upon to perform in the homes of the very poor. The only difference her married state made in her life was that she was no longer permitted to wear the one-piece dress that unmarried girls wear. Her new costume now consisted of three pieces, a chaddar a yard and a half long, one end of which was tucked into her skirt and the other draped over her head, a tiny sleeveless bodice, and a skirt a few inches long.

Several uneventful and carefree years went by for Kunthi until the day came when she was judged old enough to join her husband. Once again the bania came to the rescue and, arrayed in her new clothes, a very tearful girl-bride set out for the home of her boy-husband. The change from one home to another only meant for Kunthi the performing of chores for her mother-in-law which she had previously performed for her mother. There are no drones in a poor man's household in India; young and old have their allotted work to do and they do it cheerfully. Kunthi was now old enough to help with the cooking, and as soon as the morning meal had been eaten all who were capable of working for wages set out to perform their respective tasks, which, no matter how minor they were, brought grist to the family mill. Harkwar's father was a mason and was engaged on building a chapel at the American Mission School. It was Harkwar's ambition to follow in his father's profession and, until he had the strength to do so, he helped the family exchequer by carrying the materials used by his father and the other masons, earning two annas a day for his ten hours' labour. The crops on the low irrigated lands were ripening, and after Kunthi had washed and polished the metal pots and pans used for the morning meal she accompanied her mother-in-law and her numerous sisters-in-law to the fields of the headman of the village, where with other women and girls she laboured as many hours as her husband for half the wage he received. When the day's work was done the family walked back in the twilight to the hut Harkwar's father had been permitted to build on the headman's land, and with the dry sticks the younger children had collected during their elders' absence, the evening meal was cooked and eaten. Except for the fire, there had never been any other form of illumination in the hut, and when the pots and pans had been cleaned and put away, each member of the family retired to his or her allotted place, Harkwar and his brothers sleeping with their father and Kunthi sleeping with the other female members of the family.

When Harkwar was eighteen and Kunthi sixteen, they left and, carrying their few possessions, set up home in a hut placed at their disposal by an uncle of Harkwar's in a village three miles from the cantonment of Ranikhet. A number of barracks were under construction in the cantonment and Harkwar had no difficulty in finding work as a mason; nor had Kunthi any difficulty in finding work as a labourer, carrying stones from a quarry to the site of the building.

For four years the young couple worked on the barracks at Ranikhet, and during this period Kunthi had two children. In November of the fourth year the buildings were completed and Harkwar and Kunthi had to find new work, for their savings were small and would only keep them in food for a few days.

Winter set in early that year and promised to be unusually severe. The family had no warm clothes, and after a week's unsuccessful search for work Harkwar suggested that they should migrate to the foothills where he heard a canal headworks was being constructed. So, early in December, the family set out in high spirits on their long walk to the foothills. The distance between the village in which they had made their home for four years and the canal headworks at Kaladhungi, where they hoped to procure work, was roughly fifty miles. Sleeping under trees at night, toiling up and down steep and rough roads during the day, and carrying all their worldly possessions and the children by turns, Harkwar and Kunthi, tired and footsore, accomplished the journey to Kaladhungi in six days.

Other landless members of the depressed class had migrated earlier in the winter from the high hills to the foothills and built themselves communal huts capable of housing as many as thirty families. In these huts Harkwar and Kunthi were unable to find accommodation, so they had to build a hut for themselves. They chose a site at the edge of the forest where there was an abundant supply of fuel, within easy reach of the bazaar, and laboured early and late on a small hut of branches and leaves, for their supply of hard cash had dwindled to a few rupees and there was no friendly bania here to whom they could turn for help.

The forest at the edge of which Harkwar and Kunthi built their hut was a favourite hunting-ground of mine. I had first entered it carrying my old muzzle-loader to shoot red junglefowl and peafowl for the family larder, and later I had penetrated to every corner, armed with a modern rifle, in search of big game. At the time Harkwar and Kunthi and their two children, Punwa, a boy aged three, and Putli, a girl aged two, took up their residence in the hut, there were in that forest, to my certain knowledge, five tigers; eight leopards; a family of four sloth bears; two Himalayan black bears, which had come down from the high hills to feed on wild plums and honey; a number of hyenas who had their burrows in the grasslands five miles away and who visited the forest nightly to feed on the discarded portions of the tigers' and leopards' kills; a pair of wild dogs; numerous jackals and foxes and pine martens; and a variety of civet and other cats. There were also two pythons, many kinds of snakes, crested and tawny eagles, and hundreds of vultures in the forest. I have not mentioned animals such as deer, antelope, pigs, and monkeys, which are harmless to human beings, for they have no part in my story.

The day after the flimsy hut was completed, Harkwar found work as a qualified mason on a daily wage of eight annas with the contractor who was building the canal headworks, and Kunthi purchased for two rupees a permit from the Forest Department which entitled her to cut grass on the foothills, which she sold as fodder for the cattle of the shopkeepers in the bazaar. For her bundle of green grass weighing anything up to eighty pounds and which necessitated a walk of from ten to fourteen miles, mostly up and down steep hills, Kunthi received four annas, one anna of which was taken by the man who held the Government contract for sale of grass in the bazaar. On the eight annas earned by Harkwar, plus the three annas earned by Kunthi, the family of four lived in comparative comfort, for food was plentiful and cheap and for the first time in their lives they were able to afford one meat meal a month.

Two of the three months that Harkwar and Kunthi intended spending in Kaladhungi passed very peacefully. The hours of work were long, and admitted of no relaxation, but to that they had been accustomed from childhood. The weather was perfect, the children kept in good health, and except during the first few days while the hut was being built they had never gone hungry.

The children had in the beginning been an anxiety, for they were too young to accompany Harkwar to the canal headworks, or Kunthi on her long journeys in search of grass. Then a kindly old crippled woman living in the communal hut a few hundred yards away came to the rescue by offering to keep a general eye on the children while the parents were away at work. This arrangement worked satisfactorily for two months, and each evening when Harkwar returned from the canal headworks four miles away, and Kunthi returned a little later after selling her grass in the bazaar, they found Punwa and Putli eagerly awaiting their return.

Friday was fair day in Kaladhungi and on that day everyone in the surrounding villages made it a point to visit the bazaar, where open booths were erected for the display of cheap food, fruit, and vegetables. On these fair days Harkwar and Kunthi returned from work half an hour before their usual time, for if any vegetables had been left over it was possible to buy them at a reduced price before the booths closed down for the night.

One particular Friday, when Harkwar and Kunthi returned to the hut after making their modest purchases of vegetables and a pound of goat's meat, Punwa and Putli were not at the hut to welcome them. On making inquiries from the crippled woman at the communal hut, they learned that she had not seen the children since midday. The woman suggested that they had probably gone to the bazaar to see a merry-go-round that had attracted all the children from the communal hut, and as this seemed a reasonable explanation Harkwar set off to search the bazaar while Kunthi returned to the hut to prepare the evening meal. An hour later Harkwar returned with several men who had assisted him in his search to report that no trace of the children could be found, and that of all the people he had questioned, none admitted having seen them.

At that time a rumour was running through the length and breadth of India of the kidnapping of Hindu children by fakirs, for sale on the north-west frontier for immoral purposes. What truth there was in this rumour I am unable to say, but I had frequently read in the daily press of fakirs being manhandled, and on several occasions being rescued by the police from crowds intent on lynching them. It is safe to say that every parent in India had heard these rumours, and when Harkwar and the friends who had helped him in his search returned to the hut, they communicated their fears to Kunthi that the children had been kidnapped by fakirs, who had probably come to the fair for that purpose.

At the lower end of the village there was a police station in charge of a head constable and two constables. To this police station Harkwar and Kunthi repaired, with a growing crowd of well-wishers. The head constable was a kindly old man who had children of his own, and after he had listened sympathetically to the distracted parents' story, and recorded their statements in his diary, he said that nothing could be done that night, but that next morning he would send the town crier round to all the fifteen villages in Kaladhungi to announce the loss of the children. He then suggested that if the town crier could announce a reward of fifty rupees, it would greatly assist in the safe return of the children. Fifty rupees! Harkwar and Kunthi were aghast at the suggestion, for they did not know there was so much money in all the world. However, when the town crier set out on his round the following morning, he was able to announce the reward, for a man in Kaladhungi who had heard of the head constable's suggestion had offered the money.

The evening meal was eaten late that night. The children's por-

tion was laid aside, and throughout the night a small fire was kept
burning, for it was bitterly cold, and at short intervals Harkwar and
Kunthi went out into the night to call to their children, though they
knew there was no hope of receiving an answer.

At Kaladhungi two roads cross each other at right angles, one running along the foot of the hills from Haldwani to Ramnagar, and the
other running from Naini Tal to Bazpur. During that Friday night,
sitting close to the small fire to keep themselves warm, Harkwar and
Kunthi decided that if the children did not turn up by morning, they
would go along the former road and make inquiries, as this was the
most likely route for the kidnappers to have taken. At daybreak on
Saturday morning they went to the police station to tell the head
constable of their decision, and were instructed to lodge a report at the
Haldwani and Ramnagar police stations. They were greatly heartened
when the head constable told them that he was sending a letter by mail
runner to no less a person than the Inspector of Police at Haldwani,
requesting him to telegraph to all railway junctions to keep a look-out
for the children, a description of whom he was sending with his letter.

Near sunset that evening Kunthi returned from her twenty-eight-
mile walk to Haldwani and went straight to the police station to
inquire about her children and to tell the head constable that, though
her quest had been fruitless, she had lodged a report as instructed at the
Haldwani police station. Shortly afterwards Harkwar returned from his
thirty-six-mile walk to Ramnagar, and he too went straight to the
police station to make inquiries and to report that he had found no
trace of the children, but had carried out the head constable's instructions. Many friends, including a number of mothers who feared for the
safety of their own children, were waiting at the hut to express their
sympathy for Harkwar and for Punwa's mother.

Sunday was a repetition of Saturday, with the difference that instead
of going east and west, Kunthi went north to Naini Tal while Harkwar
went south to Bazpur. The former covered thirty miles, and the latter
thirty-two. Starting early and returning at nightfall, the distracted
parents traversed many miles of rough roads through dense forests,
where people do not usually go except in large parties, and where
Harkwar and Kunthi would not have dreamed of going alone had not
anxiety for their children overcome their fear of dacoits and of wild
animals.

On that Sunday evening, weary and hungry, they returned to their hut from their fruitless visit to Naini Tal and to Bazpur, to be met by the news that the town crier's visit to the villages and the police inquiries had failed to find any trace of the children. Then they lost heart and gave up all hope of ever seeing Punwa and Putli again. The anger of the gods, that had resulted in a fakir being able to steal their children in broad daylight, was not to be explained. Before starting on their long walk from the hills they had consulted the village priest, and he had selected the propitious day for them to set out on their journey. At every shrine they had passed they had made the requisite offering; at one place, a dry bit of wood, in another a small strip of cloth torn from the hem of Kunthi's chaddar, and in yet another a pice, which they could ill afford. And here, at Kaladhungi, every time they passed the temple that their low caste did not permit them to enter, they had never failed to raise their clasped hands in supplication. Why then had this great misfortune befallen them, who had done all that the gods demanded of them and who had never wronged any man?

Monday found the pair too dispirited and too tired to leave their hut. There was no food, and would be none until they resumed work. But of what use was it to work now, when the children for whom they had ungrudgingly laboured from morn to night were gone? So, while friends came and went, offering what sympathy they could, Harkwar sat at the door of the hut staring into a bleak and hopeless future, while Kunthi, her tears all gone, sat in a corner, hour after hour, rocking herself to and fro, to and fro.

On that Monday a man of my acquaintance was herding buffaloes in the jungle in which lived the wild animals and birds I have mentioned. He was a simple soul who had spent the greater part of his life in the jungles herding the buffaloes of the headman at Patabpur village. He knew the danger from tigers, and near sundown he collected the buffaloes and started to drive them to the village, along a cattle-track that ran through the densest part of the jungle. Presently he noticed that as each buffalo got to a certain spot in the track it turned its head to the right and stopped, until urged on by the horns of the animal following. When he got to this spot he also turned his head to the right, and in a little depression a few feet from the track saw two small children lying.

He had been in the jungle with his buffaloes when the town crier had made his round of the villages on Saturday, but that night, and the following night also, the kidnapping of Harkwar's children had been the topic of conversation round the village fire, as in fact it had been round every village fire in the whole of Kaladhungi. Here then were the missing children for whom a reward of fifty rupees had been offered. But why had they been murdered and brought to this remote spot? The children were naked, and were clasped in each other's arms. The herdsman descended into the depression and squatted down on his hunkers to determine, if he could, how the children had met their death. That the children were dead he was convinced, yet now as he sat closely scrutinizing them he suddenly saw that they were breathing; that in fact they were not dead, but sound asleep. He was a father himself, and very gently he touched the children and roused them. To touch them was a crime against his caste, for he was a Brahmin and they were low-caste children, but what mattered caste in an emergency like this? So, leaving his buffaloes to find their own way home, he picked up the children, who were too weak to walk, and set out for the Kaladhungi bazaar with one on each shoulder. The man was not too strong himself, for like all who live in the foothills he had suffered much from malaria. The children were an awkward load and had to be held in position. Moreover, as all the cattle-tracks and game paths in this jungle run from north to south, and his way lay from east to west, he had to make frequent detours to avoid impenetrable thickets and deep ravines. But he carried on manfully, resting every now and then in the course of his six-mile walk. Putli was beyond speech, but Punwa was able to talk a little and all the explanation he could give for their being in the jungle was that they had been playing and had got lost.

Harkwar was sitting at the door of his hut staring into the darkening night, in which points of light were beginning to appear as a lantern or cooking-fire was lit here and there, when he saw a small crowd of people appearing from the direction of the bazaar. At the head of the procession a man was walking, carrying something on his shoulders. From all sides people were converging on the procession and he could hear an excited murmur of 'Harkwar's children'. Harkwar's children! He could not believe his ears, and yet there appeared to be no mistake, for the procession was coming straight towards his hut.

Kunthi, having reached the limit of her misery and of her physical endurance, had fallen asleep curled up in a corner of the hut. Harkwar shook her awake and got her to the door just as the herdsman carrying Punwa and Putli reached it.

When the tearful greetings, and blessings and thanks for the rescuer, and the congratulations of friends had partly subsided, the question of the reward the herdsman had earned was mooted. To a poor man fifty rupees was wealth untold, and with it the herdsman could buy three buffaloes, or ten cows, and be independent for life. But the rescuer was a better man than the crowd gave him credit for. The blessings and thanks that had been showered on his head that night, he said, was reward enough for him, and he stoutly refused to touch one pice of the fifty rupees. Nor would Harkwar or Kunthi accept the reward either as a gift or a loan. They had got back the children they had lost all hope of ever seeing again, and would resume work as their strength returned. In the meantime the milk and sweets and puris[1] that one and another of the assembled people, out of the goodness of their hearts, had run to the bazaar to fetch would be amply sufficient to sustain them.

Two-year-old Putli and three-year-old Punwa were lost at midday on Friday, and were found by the herdsman at about 5 p.m. on Monday, a matter of seventy-seven hours. I have given a description of the wild life which to my knowledge was in the forest in which the children spent those seventy-seven hours, and it would be unreasonable to assume that none of the animals or birds saw, heard, or smelt the children. And yet, when the herdsman put Putli and Punwa into their parents' arms, there was not a single mark of tooth or claw on them.

I once saw a tigress stalking a month-old kid. The ground was very open and the kid saw the tigress while she was still some distance away and started bleating, whereon the tigress gave up her stalk and walked straight up to it. When the tigress had approached to within a few yards, the kid went forward to meet her, and on reaching the tigress stretched out its neck and put up its head to smell her. For the duration of a few heart beats the month-old kid and the Queen of the Forest stood nose to nose, and then the queen turned and walked off in the direction from which she had come.

When Hitler's war was nearing its end, in one week I read extracts from speeches of three of the greatest men in the British Empire, condemning war atrocities, and accusing the enemy of attempting to introduce the 'law of the jungle' into the dealings of warring man and man. Had the Creator made the same law for man as He has made for the jungle folk, there would be no wars, for the strong man would have the same consideration for the weak as is the established law of the jungles.

[1] Small rounds of unleavened bread fried in butter.

## 7

## The Muktesar Man-eater

Eighteen miles to the north-north-east of Naini Tal is a hill eight thousand feet high and twelve to fifteen miles long, running east and west. The western end of the hill rises steeply and near this end is the Muktesar Veterinary Research Institute, where lymph and vaccines are produced to fight India's cattle diseases. The laboratory and staff quarters are situated on the northern face of the hill and command one of the best views to be had anywhere of the Himalayan snowy range. This range, and all the hills that lie between it and the plains of India, runs east and west, and from a commanding point on any of the hills an uninterrupted view can be obtained not only of the snows to the north but also of the hills and valleys to the east and to the west as far as the eye can see. People who have lived at Muktesar claim that it is the most beautiful spot in Kumaon, and that its climate has no equal.

A tigress, that thought as highly of the amenities of Muktesar as human beings did, took up her residence in the extensive forests adjoining the small settlement. Here she lived very happily on sambur, karker, and wild pig, until she had the misfortune to have an encounter with a porcupine. In this encounter she lost an eye and got some fifty quills, varying in length from one to nine inches, embedded in the arm and under the pad of her right foreleg. Several of these quills after striking a bone had doubled back in the form of a U, the point and the broken-off end being close together. Suppurating sores formed where she endeavoured to extract the quills with her teeth and while she was lying up in a thick patch of grass, starving and licking her wounds, a woman selected this particular patch of grass to cut as fodder for her cattle. At first the tigress took no notice, but when the woman had cut the grass right up to where she was lying, the tigress struck once, the blow crushing in the woman's skull. Death was instantaneous, for, when found the following day, she was grasping her sickle with one hand and holding a tuft of grass, which she was about to cut when struck, with the other. Leaving the woman lying where she had fallen, the tigress limped off for a distance of over a mile and took refuge in a little hollow under a fallen tree. Two days later a man came to chip firewood off this fallen tree, and the tigress who was lying on the far side killed him also. The man fell across the tree, and as he had removed his coat and shirt and the tigress had clawed his back when killing him, it is possible that the sight of blood trickling down his body as he hung across the bole of the tree first gave her the idea that he was something that she could satisfy her hunger with. However that may be, before leaving him she ate a small portion from his back. A day later she killed her third victim deliberately, and without having received any provocation. Thereafter she became an established man-eater.

I heard of the tigress shortly after she started killing human beings, and as there were a number of sportsmen at Muktesar, all of whom were keen on bagging the tigress – who was operating right on their doorsteps – I did not consider it would be sporting of an outsider to meddle in the matter. When the toll of human beings killed by the tigress had risen to twenty-four, however, and the lives of all the people living in the settlement and neighbouring villages were endangered and work at the Institute slowed down, the veterinary officer in charge of the Institute requested Government to solicit my help.

My task, as I saw it, was not going to be an easy one, for, apart from the fact that my experience of man-eaters was very limited, the extensive ground over which the tigress was operating was not known to me and I therefore had no idea where to look for her.

Accompanied by a servant and two men carrying a roll of bedding and a suitcase, I left Naini Tal at midday and walked ten miles to the Ramgarh dak bungalow, where I spent the night. The dak bungalow *khansama* (cook, bottle-washer, and general factotum) was a friend of mine, and when he learnt that I was on my way to Muktesar to try to shoot the man-eater, he warned me to be very careful while negotiating the last two miles into Muktesar for, he said, several people had recently been killed on that stretch of road.

Leaving my men to pack up and follow me I armed myself with a double-barrelled ·500 express rifle using modified cordite, and making a very early start next morning arrived at the junction of the Naini Tal/Almora road with the Muktesar road just as it was getting light. From this point it was necessary to walk warily for I was now in the man-eater's country. Before zigzagging up the face of a very steep hill the road runs for some distance over flat ground on which grows the orange-coloured lily, the round hard seeds of which can be used as shot in a muzzle-loading gun. This was the first time I had ever climbed that hill and I was very interested to see the caves, hollowed out by wind, in the sandstone cliffs overhanging the road. In a gale I imagine these caves must produce some very weird sounds, for they are of different sizes and, while some are shallow, others appear to penetrate deep into the sandstone.

Where the road comes out on a saddle of the hill there is a small area of flat ground flanked on the far side by the Muktesar Post Office, and a small bazaar. The post office was not open at that early hour, but one of the shops was and the shopkeeper very kindly gave me directions how to find the dak bungalow, which he said was half a mile away on the northern face of the hill. There are two dak bungalows at Muktesar, one reserved for government officials and the other for the general public. I did not know this and my shopkeeper friend, mistaking me for a government official, possibly because of the size of my hat, directed me to the wrong one and the *khansama* in charge of the bungalow, and I, incurred the displeasure of the red-tape brigade, the *khansama* by providing me with breakfast, and I by partaking of it. However, of this I was at the time happily ignorant, and later I made it my business to see that the *khansama* did not suffer in any way for my mistake.

While I was admiring the superb view of the snowy range, and waiting for breakfast, a party of twelve Europeans passed me carrying service rifles, followed a few minutes later by a sergeant and two men carrying targets and flags. The sergeant, a friendly soul, informed me that the party that had just passed was on its way to the rifle range, and that it was keeping together because of the man-eater. I learnt from the sergeant that the officer in charge of the Institute had received a telegram from Government the previous day informing him that I was on my way to Muktesar. The sergeant expressed the hope that I would succeed in shooting the man-eater for, he said, conditions in the settlement had become very difficult. No one, even in daylight, cared to move about alone, and after dusk everyone had to remain behind locked doors. Many attempts had been made to shoot the man-eater but it had never returned to any of the kills that had been sat over.

After a very good breakfast I instructed the *khansama* to tell my men when they arrived that I had gone out to try to get news of the man-eater, and that I did not know when I would return. Then, picking up my rifle, I went up to the post office to send a telegram to my mother to let her know I had arrived safely.

From the flat ground in front of the post office and the bazaar the southern face of the Muktesar hill falls steeply away, and is cut up by ridges and ravines overgrown with dense brushwood, with a few trees scattered here and there. I was standing on the edge of the hill, looking down into the valley and the well-wooded Ramgarh hills beyond, when I was joined by the postmaster and several shopkeepers. The postmaster had dealt with the Government telegram of the previous day, and on seeing my signature on the form I had just handed in, he concluded I was the person referred to in the telegram and he and his friends had now come to offer me their help. I was very glad of the offer for they were in the best position to see and converse with everyone coming to Muktesar, and as the man-eater was sure to be the main topic of conversation where two or more were gathered together, they would be able to collect information that would be of great value to me. In rural India the post office and the bania's shop are to village folk what taverns and clubs are to people of other lands, and if information on any particular subject is sought, the post office and the bania's shop are the best places to seek it.

In a fold of the hill to our left front, and about two miles away and a thousand feet below us, was a patch of cultivation. This I was informed was Badri Sah's apple orchard. Badri, son of an old friend of mine, had visited me in Naini Tal some months previously and had offered to put me up in his guest house and to assist me in every way he could to shoot the man-eater. This offer, for the reason already given, I had not accepted. Now, however, as I had come to Muktesar at the request of the Government I decided I would call on Badri and accept his offer to help me, especially as I had just been informed by my companions that the last human kill had taken place in the valley below his orchard.

Thanking all the men who were standing round me, and telling them I would rely on them for further information, I set off down the Dhari road. The day was still young and before calling on Badri there was time to visit some of the villages farther along the hill to the east. There were no milestones along the road, and after I had covered what I considered was about six miles and visited two villages I turned back. I had retraced my steps for about three miles when I overtook a small girl in difficulties with a bullock. The girl, who was about eight years old, wanted the bullock to go in the direction of Muktesar, while the bullock wanted to go in the opposite direction, and when I arrived on the scene the stage had been reached when neither would do what the other wanted. The bullock was a quiet old beast, and with the girl walking in front holding the rope that was tied round his neck and I walking behind to keep him on the move he gave no further trouble. After we had proceeded a short distance I said:

'We are not stealing Kalwa, are we?' I had heard her addressing the black bullock by that name.

'N—o,' she answered indignantly, turning her big brown eyes full on me.

'To whom does he belong?' I next asked.

'To my father,' she said.

'And where are we taking him?'

'To my uncle.'

'And why does uncle want Kalwa?'

'To plough his field.'

'But Kalwa can't plough uncle's field by himself.'

'Of course not,' she said. I *was* being stupid, but then you could not expect a sahib to know anything about bullocks and ploughing.

'Has uncle only got one bullock?' I next asked.

'Yes,'she said; 'he has only got one bullock now, but he did have two.'

'Where is the other one?' I asked, thinking that it had probably been sold to satisfy a debt.

'The tiger killed it yesterday,' I was told. Here was news indeed, and while I was digesting it we walked on in silence, the girl every now and then looking back at me until she plucked up courage to ask:

'Have you come to shoot the tiger?'

'Yes,' I said, 'I have come to try to shoot the tiger.'

'Then why are you going away from the kill?'

'Because we are taking Kalwa to uncle.' My answer appeared to satisfy the girl, and we plodded on. I had got some very useful information, but I wanted more and presently I said:

'Don't you know that the tiger is a man-eater?'

'Oh, yes,' she said, 'it ate Kunthi's father and Bonshi Singh's mother, and lots of other people.'

'Then why did your father send you with Kalwa? Why did he not come himself?'

'Because he has *bhabari bokhar* [malaria].'

'Have you no brothers?'

'No. I had a brother but he died long ago.'

'A mother?'

'Yes, I have a mother; she is cooking the food.'

'A sister?'

'No, I have no sister.' So on this small girl had devolved the dangerous task of taking her father's bullock to her uncle, along a road on which men were afraid to walk except when in large parties, and on which in four hours I had not seen another human being.

We had now come to a path up which the girl went, the bullock following, and I bringing up the rear. Presently we came to a field on the far side of which was a small house. As we approached the house the girl called out and told her uncle that she had brought Kalwa.

'All right,' a man's voice answered from the house, 'tie him to the post, Putli, and go home. I am having my food.' So we tied Kalwa to the post and went back to the road. Without the connecting link of Kalwa between us, Putli ['Dolly'] was now shy, and as she would not walk by my side I walked ahead, suiting my pace to hers. We walked in silence for some time and then I said:

'I want to shoot the tiger that killed uncle's bullock but I don't know where the kill is. Will you show me?'

'Oh, yes,' she said eagerly, 'I will show you.'

'Have you seen the kill?' I asked.

'No,' she said, 'I have not seen it, but I heard uncle telling my father where it was.'

'Is it close to the road?'

'I don't know.'

'Was the bullock alone when it was killed?'

'No, it was with the village cattle.'

'Was it killed in the morning or the evening?'

'It was killed in the morning when it was going out to graze with the cows.'

While talking to the girl I was keeping a sharp look-out all round, for the road was narrow and bordered on the left by heavy tree jungle, and on the right by dense scrub. We had proceeded for about a mile when we came to a well-used cattle-track leading off into the jungle on the left. Here the girl stopped and said it was on this track that her uncle had told her father the bullock had been killed. I had now got all the particulars I needed to enable me to find the kill, and after seeing the girl safely to her home I returned to the cattle-track. This track ran across a valley and I had gone along it for about a quarter of a mile when I came on a spot where cattle had stampeded. Leaving the track, I now went through the jungle, parallel to and about fifty yards below the track. I had only gone a short distance when I came on a drag-mark. This drag-mark went straight down into the valley and after I had followed it for a few hundred yards I found the bullock, from which only a small portion of the hindquarters had been eaten. It was lying at the foot of a bank about twenty feet high, and some forty feet from the head of a deep ravine. Between the ravine and the kill was a stunted tree, smothered over by a wild rose. This was the only tree within a reasonable distance of the kill on which I could sit with any hope of bagging the tiger, for there was no moon, and if the tiger came after dark – as I felt sure it would – the nearer I was to the kill the better would be my chance of killing the tiger.

It was now 2 p.m. and there was just time for me to call on Badri and ask him for a cup of tea, of which I was in need for I had done a lot of walking since leaving Ramgarh at four o'clock that morning. The road to Badri's orchard takes off close to where the cattle-track joins the road, and runs down a steep hill for a mile through dense brushwood. Badri was near his guest house, attending to a damaged apple tree when I arrived, and on hearing the reason for my visit he took me up to the guest house which was on a little knoll overlooking the orchard. While we sat on the veranda waiting for the tea and something to eat that Badri had ordered his servant to prepare for me, I told him why I had come to Muktesar, and about the kill the young girl had enabled me to find. When I asked Badri why this kill had not been reported to the sportsmen at Muktesar, he said that owing to the repeated failures of the sportsmen to bag the tiger the village folk had lost confidence in them, and for this reason kills were no longer being reported to them. Badri attributed the failures to the elaborate preparations that had been made to sit over kills. These preparations consisted of clearing the ground near the kills of all obstructions in the way of bushes and small trees, the building of big machans, and the occupation of the machans by several men. Reasons enough for the reputation the tiger had earned of never returning to a kill. Badri was convinced that there was only one tiger in the Muktesar district and that it was slightly lame in its right foreleg, but he did not know what had caused the lameness, nor did he know whether the animal was male or female.

Sitting on the veranda with us was a big Airedale terrier. Presently the dog started growling, and looking in the direction in which the dog was facing, we saw a big langur sitting on the ground and holding down the branch of an apple tree, and eating the unripe fruit. Picking up a shot-gun that was leaning against the railing of the veranda, Badri loaded it with No. 4 shot and fired. The range was too great for the pellets, assuming any hit it, to do the langur any harm, but the shot had the effect of making it canter up the hill with the dog in hot pursuit. Frightened that the dog might come to grief, I asked Badri to call it back but he said it would be all right for the dog was always chasing this particular animal, which he said had done a lot of damage to his young trees. The dog was now gaining on the langur, and when it got to within a few yards the langur whipped round, got the dog by the ears, and bit a lump off the side of its head. The wound was a very severe one, and by the time we had finished attending to it my tea and a plate of hot puris was ready for me.

I had told Badri about the tree I intended sitting on, and when I returned to the kill he insisted on going with me accompanied by two men carrying materials for making a small machan. Badri and the two men had lived under the shadow of the man-eater for over a year and had no illusions about it, and when they saw that there were no trees near the kill – with the exception of the one I had selected – in which a machan could be built, they urged me not to sit up that night, on the assumption that the tiger would remove the kill and provide me with a more suitable place to sit up the following night. This was what I myself would have done if the tiger had not been a man-eater, but as it was I was disinclined to miss a chance which might not recur on the morrow, even if it entailed a little risk. There were bears in this forest and if one of them smelt the kill any hope I had of getting a shot at the tiger would vanish, for Himalayan bears are no respecters of tigers and do not hesitate to appropriate their kills. Climbing into the tree, smothered as it was by the rose bush, was a difficult feat, and after I had made myself as comfortable as the thorns permitted and my rifle had been handed up to me Badri and his men left, promising to return early next morning.

I was facing the hill, with the ravine behind me. I was in clear view of any animal coming down from above, but if the tiger came from below, as I expected, it would not see me until it got to the kill. The bullock, which was white, was lying on its right side with its legs towards me, and at a distance of about fifteen feet. I had taken my seat at 4 p.m. and an hour later a karker started barking on the side of the ravine two hundred yards below me. The tiger was on the move, and having seen it the karker was standing still and barking. For a long time it barked and then it started to move away, the bark growing fainter and fainter until the sound died away round the shoulder of the hill. This indicated that after coming within sight of the kill, the tiger had lain down. I had expected this to happen after having been told by Badri the reasons for the failures to shoot the tiger over a kill. I knew the tiger would now be lying somewhere near by with his eyes and ears open, to make quite sure there were no human beings near the kill, before he approached it. Minute succeeded long minute; dusk came; objects on the hill in front of me became indistinct and then faded out. I could still see the kill as a white blur when a stick snapped at the head of the ravine and stealthy steps came towards me, and then stopped immediately below. For a minute or two there was dead silence, and then the tiger lay down on the dry leaves at the foot of the tree.

Heavy clouds had rolled up near sunset and there was now a black canopy overhead blotting out the stars. When the tiger eventually got up and went to the kill, the night could best be described as pitch black. Strain my eyes as I would I could see nothing of the white bullock, and still less of the tiger. On reaching the kill the tiger started blowing on it. In the Himalayas, and especially in the summer, kills attract hornets, most of which leave as the light fades but those that are too torpid to fly remain, and a tiger – possibly after bitter experience – blows off the hornets adhering to the exposed portion of the flesh before starting to feed. There was no need for me to hurry over my shot for, close though it was, the tiger would not see me unless I attracted its attention by some movement or sound. I can see reasonably well on a dark night by the light of the stars, but there were no stars visible that night nor was there a flicker of lightning in the heavy clouds. The tiger had not moved the kill before starting to eat, so I knew he was lying broadside on to me, on the right-hand side of the kill.

Owing to the attempts that had been made to shoot the tiger I had a suspicion that it would not come before dark, and it had been my intention to take what aim I could – by the light of the stars – and then move the muzzle of my rifle sufficiently for my bullet to go a foot or two to the right of the kill. But now that the clouds had rendered my eyes useless, I would have to depend on my ears (my hearing at that time was perfect). Raising the rifle and resting my elbows on my knees, I took careful aim at the sound the tiger was making, and while holding the rifle steady, turned my right ear to the sound, and then back again. My aim was a little too high, so, lowering the muzzle a fraction of an inch, I again turned my head and listened. After I had done this a few times and satisfied myself that I was pointing at the sound, I moved the muzzle a little to the right and pressed the trigger. In two bounds the tiger was up the twenty-foot bank. At the top there was a small bit of flat ground, beyond which the hill went up steeply. I heard the tiger on the dry leaves as far as the flat ground, and then there was silence. This silence could be interpreted to mean either that the tiger had died on reaching the flat ground or that it was unwounded. Keeping the rifle to my shoulder I listened intently for three or four minutes, and as there was no further sound I lowered the rifle. This movement was greeted by a deep growl from the top of the bank. So the tiger was unwounded, and had seen me. My seat on the tree had originally been about ten feet up but, as I had nothing solid to sit on, the rose bush had sagged under my weight and I was now possibly no more than eight feet above ground, with my dangling feet considerably lower. And a little above and some twenty feet from me a tiger that I had every reason to believe was a man-eater was growling deep down in his throat.

The near proximity of a tiger in daylight, even when it has not seen you, causes a disturbance in the bloodstream. When the tiger is not an ordinary one, however, but a man-eater and the time is ten o'clock on a dark night, and you know the man-eater is watching you, the disturbance in the blood becomes a storm. I maintain that a tiger does not kill beyond its requirements, except under provocation. The tiger that was growling at me already had a kill that would last it for two or three days and there was no necessity for it to kill me. Even so, I had an uneasy feeling that on this occasion this particular tiger might prove an exception to the rule. Tigers will at times return to a kill after being fired at, but I knew this one would not do so. I also knew that in spite of my uneasy feeling I was perfectly safe so long as I did not lose my balance – I had nothing to hold on to – or go to sleep and fall off the tree. There was no longer any reason for me to deny myself a smoke, so I took out my cigarette-case and as I lit a match I heard the tiger move away from the edge of the bank. Presently it came back and again growled. I had smoked three cigarettes, and the tiger was still with me, when it came on to rain. A few big drops at first and then a heavy downpour. I had put on light clothes when I started from Ramgarh that morning and in a few minutes I was wet to the skin, for there was not a leaf above me to diffuse the raindrops. The tiger, I knew, would have hurried off to shelter under a tree or on the lee of a rock the moment the rain started. The rain came on at 11 p.m.; at 4 a.m. it stopped and the sky cleared. A wind now started to blow, to add to my discomfort, and where I had been cold before I was now frozen. When I get a twinge of rheumatism I remember that night and others like it, and am thankful that it is no more than a twinge.

Badri, good friend that he was, arrived with a man carrying a kettle of hot tea just as the sun was rising. Relieving me of my rifle the two men caught me as I slid off the tree, for my legs were too cramped to function. Then as I lay on the ground and drank the tea they massaged my legs and restored circulation. When I was able to stand, Badri sent his man off to light a fire in the guest house. I had never previously used my ears to direct a bullet and was interested to find that I had missed the tiger's head by only a few inches. The elevation had been all right but I had not moved the muzzle of the rifle far enough to the right, with the result that my bullet had struck the bullock six inches from where the tiger was eating.

The tea and the half-mile walk up to the road took all the creases out of me, and when we started down the mile-long track to Badri's orchard wet clothes and an empty stomach were my only discomfort. The track ran over red clay which the rain had made very slippery. In this clay were three tracks: Badri's and his man's tracks going up, and the man's tracks going down. For fifty yards there were only these three tracks in the wet clay, and then, where there was a bend in the track, a tigress had jumped down from the bank on the right and gone down the track on the heels of Badri's man. The footprints of the man and the pug marks of the tigress showed that both had been travelling at a fast pace. There was nothing that Badri and I could do, for the man had a twenty-minute start of us, and if he had not reached the safety of the orchard he would long ere this have been beyond any help we could give him. With uneasy thoughts assailing us we made what speed we could on the slippery ground and were very relieved to find, on coming to a footpath from where the orchard and a number of men working in it was visible, that the tigress had gone down the path while the man had carried on to the orchard. Questioned later, the man said he did not know that he had been followed by the tigress.

While drying my clothes in front of a roaring wood-fire in the guest house, I questioned Badri about the jungle into which the tigress had gone. The path which the tigress had taken, Badri told me, ran down into a deep and densely wooded ravine which extended down the face of a very steep hill, for a mile or more, to where it was met by another ravine coming down from the right. At the junction of the two ravines there was a stream and here there was an open patch of ground which, Badri said, commanded the exit of both ravines. Badri was of the opinion that the tigress would lie up for the day in the ravine into which we had every reason to believe she had gone, and as this appeared to be an ideal place for a beat, we decided to try this method of getting a shot at the tigress, provided we could muster sufficient men to carry out the beat. Govind Singh, Badri's head gardener, was summoned and our plan explained to him. Given until midday, Govind Singh said he could muster a gang of thirty men to do the beat, and in addition carry out his master's order to gather five maunds (four hundred and ten pounds) of peas. Badri had an extensive vegetable garden in addition to his apple orchard and the previous evening he had received a telegram informing him that the price of marrowfat peas on the Naini Tal market had jumped to four annas (fourpence) a pound. Badri was anxious to take advantage of this good price and his men were gathering the peas to be dispatched by pack-pony that night, to arrive in Naini Tal for the early morning market.

After cleaning my rifle and walking round the orchard, I joined Badri at his morning meal – which had been put forward an hour to suit me – and at midday Govind produced his gang of thirty men. It was essential for someone to supervise the pea-pickers, so Badri decided to remain and send Govind to carry out the beat. Govind and the thirty men were local residents and knew the danger to be apprehended from the man-eater. However, after I had told them what I wanted them to do, they expressed their willingness to carry out my instructions. Badri was to give me an hour's start to enable me to search the ravine for the tigress and, if I failed to get a shot, to take up my position on the open ground near the stream. Govind was to divide his men into two parties, take charge of one party himself, and put a reliable man in charge of the other. At the end of the hour Badri was to fire a shot and the two parties were to set off, one on either side of the ravine, rolling rocks down, and shouting and clapping their hands. It all sounded as simple as that, but I had my doubts, for I have seen many beats go wrong.

Going up the track down which I had come that morning, I followed the path that the tigress had taken, only to find after I had gone a short distance that it petered out in a vast expanse of dense brushwood. Forcing my way through for several hundred yards I found that the hillside was cut up by a series of deep ravines and ridges. Going down a ridge which I thought was the right-hand boundary of the ravine to be beaten, I came to a big drop at the bottom of which the ravine on my left met a ravine coming down from the right, and at the junction of the two ravines there was a stream. While I was looking down and wondering where the open ground was on which I was to take my stand, I heard flies buzzing near me and on following the sound found the remains of a cow that had been killed about a week before. The marks on the animal's throat showed that it had been killed by a tiger. The tiger had eaten all of the cow, except a portion of the shoulders, and the neck and head. Without having any particular reason for doing so, I dragged the carcass to the edge and sent it crashing down the steep hill. After rolling for about a hundred yards the carcass fetched up in a little hollow a short distance from the stream. Working round to the left I found an open patch of ground on a ridge about three hundred yards from the hollow into which I had rolled the remains of the cow. The ground down here was very different from what I had pictured it to be. There was no place where I could stand to overlook the hillside that was to be beaten, and the tigress might break out anywhere without my seeing her. However, it was then too late to do anything, for Badri had fired the shot that was to let me know the beat had started. Presently, away in the distance, I heard men shouting. For a time I thought the beat was coming my way and then the sounds grew fainter and fainter until they eventually died away. An hour later I again heard the beaters. They were coming down the hill to my right, and when they were on a level with me I shouted to them to stop the beat and join me on the ridge. It was no one's fault that the beat had miscarried, for without knowing the ground and without previous preparation we had tried to beat with a handful of untrained men in a vast area of dense brushwood that hundreds of trained men would have found it difficult to cope with.

The beaters had had a very strenuous time forcing their way through the brushwood, and while they sat in a bunch removing thorns from their hands and feet and smoking my cigarettes Govind and I stood facing each other, discussing his suggestion of carrying out a beat on the morrow in which every available man in Muktesar and the surrounding villages would take part. Suddenly, in the middle of a sentence, Govind stopped talking. I could see that something unusual had attracted his attention behind me, for his eyes narrowed and a look of incredulity came over his face. Swinging round I looked in the direction in which he was facing, and there, quietly walking along a field that had gone out of cultivation, was the tigress. She was about four hundred yards away on the hill on the far side of the stream, and was coming towards us.

When a tiger is approaching you in the forest – even when you are far from human habitations – thoughts course through your mind of the many things that can go wrong to spoil your chance of getting the shot, or the photograph, you are looking for. On one occasion I was sitting on a hillside overlooking a game-track, waiting for a tiger. The track led to a very sacred jungle shrine known as *Baram ka Than*. Baram is a jungle god who protects human beings and does not permit the shooting of animals in the area he watches over. The forest in the heart of which this shrine is situated is well stocked with game and is a favourite hunting-ground of poachers for miles round, and of sportsmen from all parts of India. Yet, in a lifetime's acquaintance with that forest, I do not know of a single instance of an animal having been shot in the vicinity of the shrine. When therefore I set out that day to shoot a tiger that had been taking toll of our village buffaloes, I selected a spot a mile from Baram's shrine. I was in position, behind a bush, at 4 p.m. and an hour later a sambur belled in the direction from which I was expecting the tiger. A little later and a little nearer to me a karker started barking; the tiger was coming along the track near which I was sitting. The jungle was fairly open and consisted mostly of young jamun trees, two to three feet in girth. I caught sight of the tiger – a big male – when he was two hundred yards away. He was coming slowly and had reduced the distance between us to a hundred yards when I heard the swish of leaves, and on looking up saw that one of the jamun trees whose branches were interlaced with another was beginning to lean over. Very slowly the tree heeled over until it came in contact with another tree of the same species and of about the same size. For a few moments the second tree supported the weight of the first and then it, too, started to heel over. When the two trees were at an angle of about thirty degrees from the perpendicular they fetched up against a third and smaller tree. For a moment or two there was a pause, and then all three trees crashed to the ground. While watching the trees, which were only a few yards from me, I had kept an eye on the tiger. At the first sound of the leaves he had come to a halt and when the trees crashed to the ground he turned and, without showing any sign of alarm, went back in the direction from which he had come. What made the occurrence I had witnessed so unusual was that the trees were young and vigorous; that no rain had fallen recently to loosen their roots; that not a breath of air was stirring in the forest; and, finally, that the trees had fallen across the track leading to the shrine when the tiger had only seventy yards to cover to give me the shot I was waiting for.

The chances of a shot being spoilt are greatly increased when the quarry is in an inhabited area in which parties of men may be travelling from one village to another or going to or from markets, or where shots may be fired to scare away langurs from apple orchards. The tigress still had three hundred yards to go to reach the stream, and two hundred yards of that was over open ground on which there was not a single tree or bush. The tigress was coming towards us at a slight angle and would see any movement we made, so there was nothing I could do but watch her, and no tigress had ever moved more slowly. She was known to the people of Muktesar as the lame tiger, but I could see no sign of her being lame. The plan that was forming in my head as I watched her was to wait until she entered the scrub jungle, and then run forward and try to get a shot at her either before or after she crossed the stream. Had there been sufficient cover between me and the point the tigress was making for, I would have gone forward as soon as I saw her and tried either to get a shot at her on the open ground or, failing that, intercept her at the stream. But unfortunately there was not sufficient cover to mask my movements, so I had to wait until the tigress entered the bushes between the open ground and the stream. Telling the men not to move or make a sound until I returned, I set off at a run as the tigress disappeared from view. The hill was steep and as I ran along the contour I came to a wild rose bush which extended up and down the hill for many yards. Through the middle of the bush there was a low tunnel, and as I bent down to run through it my hat was knocked off, and raising my head too soon at the end of the tunnel I was nearly dragged off my feet by the thorns that entered my head. The thorns of these wild roses are curved and very strong and as I was not able to stop myself some embedded themselves and broke off in my head – where my sister Maggie had difficulty in removing them when I got home – while others tore through the flesh. With little trickles of blood running down my face I continued to run until I approached the hollow into which I had rolled the partly-eaten kill from the hill above. This hollow was about forty yards long and thirty yards wide. The upper end of it where the kill was lying, the hill above the kill, and the further bank, were overgrown with dense brushwood. The lower half of the hollow and the bank on my side were free of bushes. As I reached the edge of the hollow and peered over, I heard a bone crack. The tigress had reached the hollow before me and, on finding the old kill, was trying to make up for the meal she had been deprived of the previous night.

If after leaving the kill, on which there was very little flesh, the tigress came out on to the open ground I would get a shot at her, but if she went up the hill or up the far bank I would not see her. From the dense brushwood in which I could hear the tigress a narrow path ran up the bank on my side and passed within a yard to my left, and a yard beyond the path there was a sheer drop of fifty feet into the stream below. I was considering the possibility of driving the tigress out of the brushwood on to the open ground by throwing a stone on to the hill above her, when I heard a sound behind me. On looking round I saw Govind standing behind me with my hat in his hand. At that time no European in India went about without a hat, and having seen mine knocked off by the rose bush Govind had retrieved it and brought it to me. Near us there was a hole in the hill. Putting my finger to my lips I got Govind by the arm and pressed him into the hole. Sitting on his hunkers with his chin resting on his drawn-up knees, hugging my hat, he just fitted into the hole and looked a very miserable object, for he could hear the tigress crunching bones a few yards away. As I straightened up and resumed my position on the edge of the bank, the tigress stopped eating. She had either seen me or, what was more probable, she had not found the old kill to her liking. For a long minute there was no movement or sound, and then I caught sight of her. She had climbed up the opposite bank, and was now going along the top of it towards the hill. At this point there were a number of six-inch-thick poplar saplings, and I could only see the outline of the tigress as she went through them. With the forlorn hope that my bullet would miss the saplings and find the tigress I threw up my rifle and took a hurried shot. At my shot the tigress whipped round, came down the bank, across the hollow, and up the path on my side, as hard as she could go. I did not know, at the time, that my bullet had struck a sapling near her head, and that she was blind of one eye. So what looked like a very determined charge might only have been a frightened animal running away from danger, for in that restricted space she would not have known from what direction the report of my rifle had come. Be that as it may, what I took to be a wounded and a very angry tigress was coming straight at me; so, waiting until she was two yards away, I leant forward and with great good luck managed to put the remaining bullet in the rifle into the hollow where her neck joined her shoulder. The impact of the heavy ·500 bullet deflected her just sufficiently for her to miss my left shoulder, and her impetus carried her over the fifty-foot drop into the stream below, where she landed with a great splash. Taking a step forward I looked over the edge and saw the tigress lying submerged in a pool with her feet in the air, while the water in the pool reddened with her blood.

Govind was still sitting in the hole, and at a sign he joined me. On seeing the tigress he turned and shouted to the men on the ridge, 'The tiger is dead! The tiger is dead!' The thirty men on the ridge now started shouting, and Badri on hearing them got hold of his shot-gun and fired off ten rounds. These shots were heard at Muktesar and in the surrounding villages, and presently men from all sides were converging on the stream. Willing hands drew the tigress from the pool, lashed her to a sapling and carried her in triumph to Badri's orchard. Here she was put down on a bed of straw for all to see, while I went to the guest house for a cup of tea. An hour later by the light of hand lanterns, and with a great crowd of men standing round, among whom were several sportsmen from Muktesar, I skinned the tigress. It was then that I found she was blind of one eye and that she had some fifty porcupine quills, varying in length from one to nine inches, embedded in the arm and under the pad of her right foreleg. By ten o'clock my job was finished, and declining Badri's very kind invitation to spend the night with him I climbed the hill in company with the people who had come down from Muktesar, among whom were my two men carrying the skin. On the open ground in front of the post office the skin was spread out for the postmaster and his friends to see. At midnight I lay down in the dak bungalow reserved for the public, for a few hours' sleep. Four hours later I was on the move again and at midday I was back in my home at Naini Tal after an absence of seventy-two hours.

The shooting of a man-eater gives one a feeling of satisfaction. Satisfaction at having done a job that badly needed doing. Satisfaction at having out-manœuvred, on his own ground, a very worthy antagonist. And, greatest satisfaction of all, at having made a small portion of the earth safe for a brave little girl to walk on.

# 8

## *The Panar Leopard*

I

While I was hunting the Champawat man-eater in 1907 I heard of a
man-eating leopard that was terrorizing the inhabitants of villages on
the eastern border of the Almora district. This leopard, about which
questions were asked in the House of Commons, was known under
several names and was credited with having killed four hundred human
beings. I knew the animal under the name of the Panar man-eater,
and I shall therefore use this name for the purpose of my story.

No mention is made in Government records of man-eaters prior to
the year 1905 and it would appear that until the advent of the
Champawat tiger and the Panar leopard, man-eaters in Kumaon were
unknown. When therefore these two animals – who between them
killed eight hundred and thirty-six human beings – made their appearance Government was faced with a difficult situation for it had no
machinery to put in action against them and had to rely on personal
appeals to sportsmen. Unfortunately there were very few sportsmen in
Kumaon at that time who had any inclination for this new form of
sport which, rightly or wrongly, was considered as hazardous as
Wilson's solo attempt – made a few years later – to conquer Everest. I
myself was as ignorant of man-eaters as Wilson was of Everest and that I
succeeded in my attempt, where he apparently failed in his, was due
entirely to luck.

When I returned to my home in Naini Tal after killing the
Champawat tiger I was asked by Government to undertake the shooting of the Panar leopard. I was working hard for a living at the time
and several weeks elapsed before I was able to spare the time to undertake this task, and then just as I was ready to start for the outlying area
of the Almora district in which the leopard was operating I received an
urgent request from Berthoud, the Deputy Commissioner of Naini Tal,
to go to the help of the people of Muktesar where a man-eating tiger had
established a reign of terror. After hunting down the tiger, an account of
which I have given, I went in pursuit of the Panar leopard.

As I had not previously visited the vast area over which this leopard was operating, I went via Almora to learn all I could about the leopard from Stiffe, the Deputy Commissioner of Almora. He kindly invited me to lunch, provided me with maps, and then gave me a bit of a jolt when wishing me goodbye by asking me if I had considered all the risks and prepared for them by making my will.

My maps showed that there were two approaches to the affected area, one via Panwanaula on the Pithoragarh road, and the other via Lamgara on the Dabidhura road. I selected the latter route and after lunch set out in good heart – despite the reference to a will – accompanied by one servant and four men carrying my luggage. My men and I had already done a stiff march of fourteen miles from Khairna, but being young and fit we were prepared to do another long march before calling it a day.

As the full moon was rising we arrived at a small isolated building which, from the scribbling on the walls and the torn bits of paper lying about, we assumed was used as a school. I had no tent with me and as the door of the building was locked I decided to spend the night in the courtyard with my men, a perfectly safe proceeding for we were still many miles from the man-eater's hunting-grounds. This courtyard, which was about twenty feet square, abutted on the public road and was surrounded on three sides by a two-foot-high wall. On the fourth side it was bounded by the school building.

There was plenty of fuel in the jungle behind the school and my men soon had a fire burning in a corner of the courtyard for my servant to cook my dinner on. I was sitting with my back to the locked door, smoking, and my servant had just laid a leg of mutton on the low wall nearest the road and turned to attend to the fire, when I saw the head of a leopard appear over the wall close to the leg of mutton. Fascinated, I sat motionless and watched – for the leopard was facing me – and when the man had moved away a few feet the leopard grabbed the meat and bounded across the road into the jungle beyond. The meat had been put down on a big sheet of paper, which had stuck to it, and when my servant heard the rustle of paper and saw what he thought was a dog running away with it he dashed forward shouting, but on realizing that he was dealing with a leopard and not with a mere dog he changed direction and dashed towards me with even greater speed. All white people in the East are credited with being a little mad – for other reasons than walking about in the midday sun – and I am afraid my good servant thought I was a little more mad than most of my kind when he found I was laughing, for he said in a very aggrieved voice, 'It was your dinner that the leopard carried away and I have nothing else for you to eat.' However, he duly produced a meal that did him credit, and to which I did as much justice as I am sure the hungry leopard did to his leg of prime mutton.

Making an early start next morning, we halted at Lamgara for a meal, and by evening reached the Dol dak bungalow on the border of the man-eater's domain. Leaving my men at the bungalow I set out the following morning to try to get news of the man-eater. Going from village to village, and examining the connecting footpaths for leopard pug marks, I arrived in the late evening at an isolated homestead consisting of a single stone-built slate-roofed house, situated in a few acres of cultivated land and surrounded by scrub jungle. On the footpath leading to this homestead I found the pug marks of a big male leopard.

As I approached the house a man appeared on the narrow balcony and, climbing down a few wooden steps, came across the courtyard to meet me. He was a young man, possibly twenty-two years of age, and in great distress. It appeared that the previous night while he and his wife were sleeping on the floor of the single room that comprised the house, with the door open for it was April and very hot, the man-eater climbed on to the balcony and getting a grip of his wife's throat started to pull her head-foremost out of the room. With a strangled scream the woman flung an arm round her husband who, realizing in a flash what was happening, seized her arm with one hand and, placing the other against the lintel of the door, for leverage, jerked her away from the leopard and closed the door. For the rest of the night the man and his wife cowered in a corner of the room, while the leopard tried to tear down the door. In the hot unventilated room the woman's wounds started to turn septic and by morning her suffering and fear had rendered her unconscious.

Throughout the day the man remained with his wife, too frightened to leave her for fear the leopard should return and carry her away, and too frightened to face the miles of scrub jungle that lay between him and his nearest neighbour. As day was closing down and the unfortunate man was facing another night of terror he saw me coming towards the house, and when I had heard his story I was no longer surprised that he had run towards me and thrown himself sobbing at my feet.

A difficult situation faced me. I had not up to that time approached Government to provide people living in areas in which a man-eater was operating with first-aid sets, so there was no medical or any other kind of aid nearer than Almora, and Almora was twenty-five miles away. To get help for the woman I would have to go for it myself and that would mean condemning the man to lunacy, for he had already stood as much as any man could stand and another night in that room, with the prospect of the leopard returning and trying to gain entrance, would of a certainty have landed him in a madhouse.

The man's wife, a girl of about eighteen, was lying on her back when the leopard clamped its teeth into her throat, and when the man got a grip of her arm and started to pull her back the leopard – to get a better purchase – drove the claws of one paw into her breast. In the final struggle the claws ripped through the flesh, making four deep cuts. In the heat of the small room, which had only one door and no windows and in which a swarm of flies were buzzing, all the wounds in the girl's throat and on her breast had turned septic, and whether medical aid could be procured or not the chances of her surviving were very slight; so, instead of going for help, I decided to stay the night with the man. I very sincerely hope that no one who reads this story will ever be condemned to seeing and hearing the sufferings of a human being, or of an animal, that has had the misfortune of being caught by the throat by either a leopard or a tiger and not having the means – other than a bullet – of alleviating or of ending the suffering.

The balcony which ran the length of the house, and which was boarded up at both ends, was about fifteen feet long and four feet wide, accessible by steps hewn in a pine sapling. Opposite these steps was the one door of the house, and under the balcony was an open recess four feet wide and four feet high, used for storing firewood.

The man begged me to stay in the room with him and his wife but it was not possible for me to do this, for, though I am not squeamish, the smell in the room was overpowering and more than I could stand. So between us we moved the firewood from one end of the recess under the balcony, clearing a small space where I could sit with my back to the wall. Night was now closing in, so after a wash and a drink at a nearby spring I settled down in my corner and told the man to go up to his wife and keep the door of the room open. As he climbed the steps the man said, 'The leopard will surely kill you, sahib, and then what will I do?' 'Close the door,' I answered, 'and wait for morning.'

The moon was two nights off the full and there would be a short period of darkness. It was this period of darkness that was worrying me. If the leopard had remained scratching at the door until daylight, as the man said, it would not have gone far and even now it might be lurking in the bushes watching me. I had been in position for half an hour, straining my eyes into the darkening night and praying for the moon to top the hills to the east, when a jackal gave its alarm-call. This call, which is given with the full force of the animal's lungs, can be heard for a very long distance and can be described as *pheaon, pheaon,* repeated over and over again as long as the danger that has alarmed the jackal is in sight. Leopards when hunting or when approaching a kill move very slowly, and it would be many minutes before this one – assuming it was the man-eater – covered the half-mile between us, and even if in the meantime the moon had not risen it would be giving sufficient light to shoot by, so I was able to relax and breathe more freely.

Minutes dragged by. The jackal stopped calling. The moon rose over the hills, flooding the ground in front of me with brilliant light. No movement to be seen anywhere, and the only sound to be heard in all the world the agonized fight for breath of the unfortunate girl above me. Minutes gave way to hours. The moon climbed the heavens and then started to go down in the west, casting the shadow of the house on the ground I was watching. Another period of danger, for if the leopard had seen me he would, with a leopard's patience, be waiting for these lengthening shadows to mask his movements. Nothing happened, and one of the longest nights I have ever watched through came to an end when the light from the sun lit up the sky where, twelve hours earlier, the moon had risen.

The man, after his vigil of the previous night, had slept soundly and as I left my corner and eased my aching bones – only those who have sat motionless on hard ground for hours know how bones can ache – he came down the steps. Except for a few wild raspberries I had eaten nothing for twenty-four hours, and as no useful purpose would have been served by my remaining any longer, I bade the man goodbye and set off to rejoin my men at the Dol dak bungalow, eight miles away, and summon aid for the girl. I had only gone a few miles when I met my men. Alarmed at my long absence they had packed up my belongings, paid my dues at the dak bungalow, and then set out to look for me. While I was talking to them the Road Overseer, whom I have mentioned in my story of the Temple Tiger, came along. He was well mounted on a sturdy Bhutia pony, and as he was on his way to Almora he gladly undertook to carry a letter from me to Stiffe. Immediately on receipt of my letter Stiffe dispatched medical aid for the girl, but her sufferings were over when it arrived.

It was this Road Overseer who informed me about the human kill that took me to Dabidhura, where I met with one of the most interesting and the most exciting shikar experiences I have ever had. After that experience I asked the old priest of the Dabidhura temple if the man-eater had as effective protection from his temple as the tiger I had failed to shoot, and he answered, 'No, no, sahib. This *shaitan* has killed many people who worshipped at my temple and when you come back to shoot him, as you say you will, I shall offer up prayers for your success morning and evening.'

2

No matter how full of happiness our life may have been, there are periods in it that we look back to with special pleasure. Such a period for me was the year 1910, for in that year I shot the Muktesar man-eating tiger and the Panar man-eating leopard, and in between these two – for me – great events, my men and I set up an all-time record at Mokameh Ghat by handling, without any mechanical means, five thousand five hundred tons of goods in a single working day.

My first attempt to shoot the Panar leopard was made in April 1910, and it was not until September of the same year that I was able to spare the time to make a second attempt. I have no idea how many human beings were killed by the leopard between April and September, for no bulletins were issued by Government and beyond a reference to questions asked in the House of Commons no mention of the leopard – as far as I am aware – was made in the Indian press. The Panar leopard was credited with having killed four hundred human beings, against one hundred and twenty-five killed by the Rudraprayag leopard, and the fact that the former received such scant publicity while the latter was headline news throughout India was due entirely to the fact that the Panar leopard operated in a remote area far from the beaten track, whereas the Rudraprayag leopard operated in an area visited each year by sixty thousand pilgrims ranging from the humblest in the land to the highest, all of whom had to run the gauntlet of the man-eater. It was these pilgrims, and the daily bulletins issued by Government, that made the Rudraprayag leopard so famous, though it caused far less human suffering than the Panar leopard.

Accompanied by a servant and four men carrying my camp kit and provisions, I set out from Naini Tal on 10 September on my second attempt to shoot the Panar leopard. The sky was overcast when we left home at 4 a.m. and we had only gone a few miles when a deluge of rain came on. Throughout the day it rained and we arrived at Almora, after a twenty-eight-mile march, wet to the bone. I was to have spent the night with Stiffe, but not having a stitch of dry clothing to put on I excused myself and spent the night at the dak bungalow. There were no other travellers there and the man in charge very kindly put two rooms at my disposal, with a big wood fire in each, and by morning my kit was dry enough for me to continue my journey.

It had been my intention to follow the same route from Almora that I had followed in April, and start my hunt for the leopard from the house in which the girl had died of her wounds. While I was having breakfast a mason by the name of Panwa, who did odd jobs for us in Naini Tal, presented himself. Panwa's home was in the Panar valley, and on learning from my men that I was on my way to try to shoot the man-eater he asked for permission to join our party, for he wanted to visit his home and was frightened to undertake the journey alone. Panwa knew the country and on his advice I altered my plans and instead of taking the road to Dabidhura via the school where the leopard had eaten my dinner, I took the road leading to Pithoragarh. Spending the night at Panwa Naula dak bungalow, we made an early start next morning and after proceeding a few miles left the Pithoragarh road for a track leading off to the right. We were now in the man-eater's territory where there were no roads, and where the only communication was along footpaths running from village to village.

Progress was slow, for the villages were widely scattered over many hundreds of square miles of country, and as the exact whereabouts of the man-eater were not known it was necessary to visit each village to make inquiries. Going through Salan and Rangot *pattis* (*patti* is a group of villages), I arrived late on the evening of the fourth day at Chakati, where I was informed by the headman that a human being had been killed a few days previously at a village called Sanouli on the far side of the Panar river. Owing to the recent heavy rain the Panar was in flood and the headman advised me to spend the night in his village, promising to give me a guide next morning to show me the only safe ford over the river, for the Panar was not bridged.

The headman and I had carried on our conversation at one end of a long row of double-storeyed buildings and when, on his advice, I elected to stay the night in the village, he said he would have two rooms vacated in the upper storey for myself and my men. I had noticed while talking to him that the end room on the ground floor was untenanted, so I told him I would stay in it and that he need only have one room vacated in the upper storey for my men. The room I had elected to spend the night in had no door, but this did not matter for I had been told that the last kill had taken place on the far side of the river and I knew the man-eater would not attempt to cross the river while it was in flood.

The room had no furniture of any kind, and after my men had swept all the straw and bits of rags out of it, complaining as they did so that the last tenant must have been a very dirty person, they spread my groundsheet on the mud floor and made up my bed. I ate my dinner – which my servant cooked on an open fire in the courtyard – sitting on my bed, and as I had done a lot of walking during the twelve hours I had been on my feet it did not take me long to get to sleep. The sun was just rising next morning, flooding the room with light, when on hearing a slight sound in the room I opened my eyes and saw a man sitting on the floor near my bed. He was about fifty years of age, and *in the last stage of leprosy*. On seeing that I was awake this unfortunate living death said he hoped I had spent a comfortable night in his room. He went on to say that he had been on a two-days' visit to friends in an adjoining village, and finding me asleep in his room on his return had sat near my bed and waited for me to awake.

Leprosy, the most terrible and the most contagious of all diseases in the East, is very prevalent throughout Kumaon, and especially bad in the Almora district. Being fatalists the people look upon the disease as a visitation from God, and neither segregate the afflicted nor take any precautions against infection. So, quite evidently, the headman did not think it necessary to warn me that the room I had selected to stay in had for years been the home of a leper. It did not take me long to dress that morning, and as soon as our guide was ready we left the village.

Moving about as I have done in Kumaon I have always gone in dread of leprosy, and I have never felt as unclean as I did after my night in that poor unfortunate's room. At the first stream we came to I called a halt, for my servant to get breakfast ready for me and for my men to have their food. Then, telling my men to wash my groundsheet and lay my bedding out in the sun, I took a bar of carbolic soap and went down the stream to where there was a little pool surrounded by great slabs of rock. Taking off every stitch of clothing I had worn in that room, I washed it all in the pool and, after laying it out on the slabs of rock, I used the remainder of the soap to scrub myself as I had never scrubbed myself before. Two hours later, in garments that had shrunk a little from the rough treatment they had received, I returned to my men feeling clean once again, and with a hunter's appetite for breakfast.

Our guide was a man about four foot six inches tall with a big head crowned with a mop of long hair; a great barrel of a body, short legs, and few words. When I asked him if we had any stiff climbing to do, he stretched out his open hand, and answered, 'Flat as that.' Having said this he led us down a very steep hill into a deep valley. Here I expected him to turn and follow the valley down to its junction with the river. But no. Without saying a word or even turning his head he crossed the open ground and went straight up the hill on the far side. This hill, in addition to being very steep and overgrown with thorn-bushes, had loose gravel on it which made the going difficult, and as the sun was now overhead and very hot, we reached the top in a bath of sweat. Our guide, whose legs appeared to have been made for climbing hills, had not turned a hair.

There was an extensive view from the top of the hill, and when our guide informed us that we still had the two high hills in the foreground to climb before reaching the Panar river Panwa, the mason, who was carrying a bundle containing presents for his family and a greatcoat made of heavy dark material, handed the coat to the guide and said that as he was making us climb all the hills in Kumaon he could carry the coat for the rest of the way. Unwinding a length of goathair cord from round his body the guide folded up the coat and strapped it securely to his back. Down and up we went and down and up again, and then away down in a deep valley we saw the river. So far we had been going over trackless ground, without a village in sight, but now we came on a narrow path running straight down to the river. The nearer we got to the river the less I liked the look of it. The path leading to the water and up the far side showed that there was a ford here, but the river was in flood and the crossing appeared to me to be a very hazardous one. The guide assured us, however, that it was perfectly safe to cross, so removing my shoes and stockings I linked arms with Panwa and stepped into the water. The river was about forty yards wide and from its broken surface I judged it was running over a very rough bed. In this I was right, and after stubbing my toes a few times and narrowly avoiding being washed off our feet we struggled out on the far bank.

Our guide had followed us into the river and, on looking back, I saw that the little man was in difficulties. The water which for us had been thigh deep was for him waist deep and on reaching the main stream, instead of bracing his back against it and walking crab fashion, he very foolishly faced upstream with the result that he was swept over backwards and submerged under the fast-running current. I was barefoot and helpless on the sharp stones, but Panwa – to whom sharp stones were no obstacle – threw down the bundle he was carrying and without a moment's hesitation sprinted along the bank to where, fifty yards farther down, a big slab of rock jutted into the river at the head of a terrifying rapid. Running out on to this wet and slippery rock Panwa lay down, and as the drowning man was swept past, grabbed him by his long hair and after a desperate struggle drew him on to the rock. When the two men rejoined me – the guide looking like a drowned rat – I complimented Panwa on his noble and brave act in having saved the little man's life, at great risk to his own. After looking at me in some surprise Panwa said, 'Oh, it was not his life that I wanted to save, but my new coat that was strapped to his back.' Anyway, whatever the motive, a tragedy had been averted, and after my men had linked arms and crossed safely I decided to call it a day and spend the night on the river bank. Panwa, whose village was five miles farther up the river, now left me, taking with him the guide, who was frightened to attempt a second crossing of the river.

### 3

Next morning we set out to find Sanouli, where the last human kill had taken place. Late in the evening of that day we found ourselves in a wide open valley, and as there were no human habitations in sight, we decided to spend the night on the open ground. We were now in the heart of the man-eater's country and after a very unrestful night, spent on cold wet ground, arrived about midday at Sanouli. The inhabitants of this small village were overjoyed to see us and they very gladly put a room at the disposal of my men, and gave me the use of an open platform with a thatched roof.

The village was built on the side of a hill overlooking a valley in which there were terraced fields, from which a paddy crop had recently been harvested. The hill on the far side of the valley sloped up gradually, and a hundred yards from the cultivated land there was a dense patch of brushwood, some twenty acres in extent. On the brow of the hill, above this patch of brushwood, there was a village, and on the shoulder of the hill to the right another village. To the left of the terraced fields the valley was closed in by a steep grassy hill. So, in effect, the patch of brushwood was surrounded on three sides by cultivated land, and on the fourth by open grass land.

While breakfast was being got ready, the men of the village sat round me and talked. During the second half of March and the first half of April, four human beings had been killed in this area by the man-eater. The first kill had taken place in the village on the shoulder of the hill, the second and third in the village on the brow of the hill, and the fourth in Sanouli. All four victims had been killed at night and carried some five hundred yards into the patch of brushwood, where the leopard had eaten them at his leisure, for – having no firearms – the inhabitants of the three villages were too frightened to make any attempt to recover the bodies. The last kill had taken place six days before, and my informants were convinced that the leopard was still in the patch of brushwood.

I had purchased two young male goats in a village we passed through earlier that day, and towards evening I took the smaller one and tied it at the edge of the patch of brushwood to test the villagers' assertion that the leopard was still in the cover. I did not sit over the goat, because there were no suitable trees near by and also because clouds were banking up and it looked as though there might be rain during the night. The platform that had been placed at my disposal was open all round, so I tied the second goat near it in the hope that if the leopard visited the village during the night it would prefer a tender goat to a tough human being. Long into the night I listened to the two goats calling to each other. This convinced me that the leopard was not within hearing distance. However, there was no reason why he should not return to the locality, so I went to sleep hoping for the best.

There was a light shower during the night and when the sun rose in a cloudless sky every leaf and blade of grass was sparkling with rain-drops and every bird that had a song to sing was singing a joyful welcome to the day. The goat near my platform was contentedly browsing off a bush and bleating occasionally, while the one across the valley was silent. Telling my servant to keep my breakfast warm, I crossed the valley and went to the spot where I had tied up the smaller goat. Here I found that, some time before the rain came on, a leopard had killed the goat, broken the rope, and carried away the kill. The rain had washed out the drag-mark, but this did not matter for there was only one place to which the leopard could have taken his kill, and that was into the dense patch of brushwood.

Stalking a leopard, or a tiger, on its kill is one of the most interesting forms of sport I know of, but it can only be indulged in with any hope of success when the conditions are favourable. Here the conditions were not favourable, for the brushwood was too dense to permit of a noiseless approach. Returning to the village, I had breakfast and then called the villagers together, as I wanted to consult them about the surrounding country. It was necessary to visit the kill to see if the leopard had left sufficient for me to sit over and, while doing so, I would not be able to avoid disturbing the leopard. What I wanted to learn from the villagers was whether there was any other heavy cover, within a reasonable distance, to which the leopard could retire on being disturbed by me. I was told that there was no such cover nearer than two miles, and that to get to it the leopard would have to cross a wide stretch of cultivated land.

At midday I returned to the patch of brushwood and, a hundred yards from where he had killed it, I found all that the leopard had left of the goat – its hooves, horns, and part of its stomach. As there was no fear of the leopard leaving its cover at that time of day for the jungle two miles away, I tried for several hours to stalk it, helped by bulbuls, drongos, thrushes, and scimitar babblers, all of whom kept me informed of the leopard's every movement. In case any should question why I did not collect the men of the three villages and get them to drive the leopard out on to the open ground, where I could have shot it, it is necessary to say that this could not have been attempted without grave danger to the beaters. As soon as the leopard found he was being driven towards open ground, he would have broken back and attacked anyone who got in his way.

On my return to the village after my unsuccessful attempt to get a shot at the leopard, I went down with a bad attack of malaria and for the next twenty-four hours I lay on the platform in a stupor. By the evening of the following day the fever had left me and I was able to continue the hunt. On their own initiative the previous night my men had tied out the second goat where the first had been killed, but the leopard had not touched it. This was all to the good, for the leopard would now be hungry, and I set out on that third evening full of hope.

On the near side of the patch of brushwood, and about a hundred yards from where the goat had been killed two nights previously, there was an old oak tree. This tree was growing out of a six-foot-high bank between two terraced fields and was leaning away from the hill at an angle that made it possible for me to walk up the trunk in my rubber-soled shoes. On the underside of the trunk and about fifteen feet from the ground there was a branch jutting out over the lower field. This branch, which was about a foot thick, offered a very uncomfortable and a very unsafe seat for it was hollow and rotten. However, as it was the only branch on the tree, and as there were no other trees within a radius of several hundred yards, I decided to risk the branch.

As I had every reason to believe – from the similarity of the pug marks I had found in the brushwood to those I had seen in April on the path leading to the homestead where the girl was killed – that the leopard I was dealing with was the Panar man-eater, I made my men cut a number of long blackthorn shoots. After I had taken my seat with my back to the tree and my legs stretched out along the branch, I made the men tie the shoots into bundles and lay them on the trunk of the tree and lash them to it securely with strong rope. To the efficient carrying out of these small details I am convinced I owe my life.

Several of the blackthorn shoots, which were from ten to twenty feet long, projected on either side of the tree; and as I had nothing to hold on to, to maintain my balance, I gathered the shoots on either side of me and held them firmly pressed between my arms and my body. By five o'clock my preparations were complete. I was firmly seated on the branch with my coat collar pulled up well in front to protect my throat, and my soft hat pulled down well behind to protect the back of my neck. The goat was tied to a stake driven into the field thirty yards in front of me, and my men were sitting out in the field smoking and talking loudly.

Up to this point all had been quiet in the patch of brushwood, but now a scimitar babbler gave its piercing alarm-call followed a minute or two later by the chattering of several whitethroated laughing thrushes. These two species of birds are the most reliable informants in the hills, and on hearing them I signalled to my men to return to the village. This they appeared to be very glad to do, and as they walked away, still talking loudly, the goat started bleating. Nothing happened for the next half-hour and then, as the sun was fading off the hill above the village, two drongos that had been sitting on the tree above me, flew off and started to bait some animal on the open ground between me and the patch of brushwood. The goat while calling had been facing in the direction of the village, and it now turned round, facing me, and stopped calling. By watching the goat I could follow the movements of the animal that the drongos were baiting and that the goat was interested in, and this animal could only be a leopard.

The moon was in her third quarter and there would be several hours of darkness. In anticipation of the leopard's coming when light conditions were not favourable, I had armed myself with a 12-bore double-barrelled shot-gun loaded with slugs, for there was a better chance of my hitting the leopard with eight slugs than with a single rifle bullet. Aids to night shooting, in the way of electric lights and torches, were not used in India at the time I am writing about, and all that one had to rely on for accuracy of aim was a strip of white cloth tied round the muzzle of the weapon.

Again nothing happened for many minutes, and then I felt a gentle pull on the blackthorn shoots I was holding and blessed my forethought in having had the shoots tied to the leaning tree, for I could not turn round to defend myself and at best the collar of my coat and my hat were poor protection. No question now that I was dealing with a man-eater, and a very determined man-eater at that. Finding that he could not climb over the thorns, the leopard, after his initial pull, had now got the butt ends of the shoots between his teeth and was jerking them violently, pulling me hard against the trunk of the tree. And now the last of the daylight faded out of the sky and the leopard, who did all his human killing in the dark, was in his element and I was out of mine, for in the dark a human being is the most helpless of all animals and – speaking for myself – his courage is at its lowest ebb. Having killed four hundred human beings at night, the leopard was quite unafraid of me, as was evident from the fact that while tugging at the shoots, he was growling loud enough to be heard by the men anxiously listening in the village. While this growling terrified the men, as they told me later, it had the opposite effect on me, for it let me know where the leopard was and what he was doing. It was when he was silent that I was most terrified, for I did not know what his next move would be. Several times he had nearly unseated me by pulling on the shoots vigorously and then suddenly letting them go, and now that it was dark and I had nothing stable to hold on to I felt sure that if he sprang up he would only need to touch me to send me crashing to the ground.

After one of these nerve-racking periods of silence the leopard jumped down off the high bank and dashed towards the goat. In the hope that the leopard would come while there was still sufficient light to shoot by, I had tied the goat thirty yards from the tree to give me time to kill the leopard before it got to the goat. But now, in the dark, I could not save the goat – which, being white, I could only just see as an indistinct blur – so I waited until it had stopped struggling and then aimed where I thought the leopard would be and pressed the trigger. My shot was greeted with an angry grunt and I saw a white flash as the leopard went over backwards, and disappeared down another high bank into the field beyond.

For ten or fifteen minutes I listened anxiously for further sounds from the leopard, and then my men called out and asked if they should come to me. It was now quite safe for them to do so, provided they kept to the high ground. So I told them to light pine torches, and thereafter carry out my instructions. These torches, made of 12- to 18-inch-long splinters of resin-impregnated pinewood cut from a living tree, give a brilliant light and provide the remote villages in Kumaon with the only illumination they have ever known.

After a lot of shouting and running about, some twenty men each carrying a torch left the village and, following my instructions, circled round above the terraced fields and approached my tree from behind. The knots in the ropes securing the blackthorn shoots to the tree had been pulled so tight by the leopard that they had to be cut. After the thorns had been removed men climbed the tree and helped me down, for the uncomfortable seat had given me cramp in my legs.

The combined light from the torches lit up the field on which the dead goat was lying, but the terraced field beyond was in shadow. When cigarettes had been handed round I told the men I had wounded the leopard but did not know how badly, and that we would return to the village now and I would look for the wounded animal in the morning. At this, great disappointment was expressed. 'If you have wounded the leopard it must surely be dead by now.' 'There are many of us, and you have a gun, so there is no danger.' 'At least let us go as far as the edge of the field and see if the leopard has left a blood trail.' After all arguments for and against going to look for the leopard immediately had been exhausted I consented against my better judgement to go as far as the edge of the field, from where we could look down on the terraced field below.

Having acceded to their request, I made the men promise that they would walk in line behind me, hold their torches high, and not run away and leave me in the dark if the leopard charged. This promise they very willingly gave, and after the torches had been replenished and were burning brightly we set off, I walking in front and the men following five yards behind.

Thirty yards to the goat, and another twenty yards to the edge of the field. Very slowly, and in silence, we moved forward. When we reached the goat – no time now to look for a blood trail – the farther end of the lower field came into view. The nearer we approached the edge, the more of this field became visible, and then, when only a narrow strip remained in shadow from the torches, the leopard, with a succession of angry grunts, sprang up the bank and into full view.

There is something very terrifying in the angry grunt of a charging leopard, and I have seen a line of elephants that were staunch to tiger turn and stampede from a charging leopard; so I was not surprised when my companions, all of whom were unarmed, turned as one man and bolted. Fortunately for me, in their anxiety to get away they collided with each other and some of the burning splinters of pine – held loosely in their hands – fell to the ground and continued to flicker, giving me sufficient light to put a charge of slugs into the leopard's chest.

On hearing my shot the men stopped running, and then I heard one of them say, '*Oh, no.* He won't be angry with us, for he knows that this devil has turned our courage to water.' Yes, I knew, from my recent experience on the tree, that fear of a man-eater robs a man of courage. As for running away, had I been one of the torch-bearers I would have run with the best. So there was nothing for me to be angry about. Presently, while I was making believe to examine the leopard, to ease their embarrassment, the men returned in twos and threes. When they were assembled, I asked, without looking up, 'Did you bring a bamboo pole and a rope to carry the leopard back to the village?' 'Yes,' they answered eagerly, 'we left them at the foot of the tree.' 'Go and fetch them,' I said, 'for I want to get back to the village for a cup of hot tea.' The cold night-wind blowing down from the north had brought on another attack of malaria, and now that all the excitement was over I was finding it difficult to remain on my feet.

That night, for the first time in years, the people of Sanouli slept, and have continued to sleep, free from fear.

# 9

## *Goongi*

On the motor road connecting Almora and Ranikhet with Kathgodam, and not far from Ratighat, a gang of men were working one day when on the hill above the road they saw what appeared to be some strange animal, moving from one patch of cover to another. Dropping their picks and shovels the men surrounded the patch of cover and on closing in saw a naked human being cowering under a bush who, on their near approach, broke through the ring of men and made off at great speed on all fours. After a long chase, the human being was run down, overpowered, roped hand and foot, and sent to Naini Tal in a *kandi,* a large conical basket which hill-men use for carrying their wares.

I was at Mokameh Ghat at the time, and reading in the press of the finding near Naini Tal of what was alleged to be a wolf-child I telegraphed to Lawrie, a professional photographer, to take a series of photographs of the child for me. Lawrie visited the hospital to which the child had been taken but was unfortunately unable to get any photographs as he was not able to coax the child to leave the shelter of the straw under which she had concealed herself in a corner of the room in which she had been confined. For the next few weeks the child was news, and speculation was rife as to whether she was a wolf-child or a monkey-child, until eventually interest died down, and she was forgotten.

When I visited Naini Tal some months later I received a letter which had been addressed to the Government of India by an association in England, of which Sir Bampfylde Fuller[1] was president, asking for full information about the Naini Tal wolf-child. On receipt of this letter I sent Mothi Singh, a friend who had been with me for twenty years, to Ratighat, to make inquiries if any child had been lost from any of the villages within ten miles of Ratighat during the preceding fifteen years, and also to find out if anyone in that area had at any time seen anything answering to the description of the wolf-child. While Mothi

[1] Sir Bampfylde Fuller, I.C.S., was Director of Timber Supplies at the War Office in 1917 and had probably met Corbett at Mokameh Ghat.

Singh was making these inquiries I visited the Tahsildar's office at
Naini Tal, where all records are kept, and with the help of the
Tahsildar searched his records over a period of fifteen years to ascertain
if any report had been lodged of the loss of a child in the Naini Tal
District. Neither Mothi Singh's inquiries, nor mine, established the fact
that a child had been lost, or that anything resembling a child had
been seen in the jungles in that area.

I then went to the Crosthwaite Hospital, to which the child had been
admitted. The lady doctor in charge, Miss Misra, was an old and
valued friend of our family and when I told her my errand she very
kindly offered to assist me in every way she could. In addition to Miss
Misra, a nurse and a ward attendant had ministered to the child and
from these three ladies, and from the records of the hospital, I gathered
the following information.

On 15 July 1914 a girl aged about fourteen years was admitted to the
hospital, and was entered in the register under the name of Goongi.
The girl was brought to the hospital roped up in a *kandi* carried on the
back of a hill-man, and was accompanied by a policeman and by a
large crowd of people. The girl, who appeared to be terrified of human
beings, was carried into an empty room and as the rope with which she
was secured was being untied she bit the nurse, and terrified the three
women by growling fiercely. On being released the girl ran across the
room on all fours, and cowered in a corner.

From Miss Misra, the nurse, and the ward attendant, I obtained the
following particulars:

1. The girl was named Goongi ['dumb'] by Miss Misra because she
could not speak.

2. Age about fourteen years.

3. Strong and healthy. Showing no signs of undernourishment.

4. Body very dirty and covered over with thick growth of hair.

5. Hair on head short and matted.

6. Nails of hands long and claw-like.

7. Shoulders and upper part of body exhibiting a number of deep
scratches, some comparatively fresh, some in process of healing, and
others again just scars.

8. Tore up, using her teeth to do so, clothes that were thrown to her,

but welcomed a bundle of straw which she pushed into a corner of the room and thereafter remained concealed under it.

9. Refused all cooked food but ate raw meat, fruit and vegetables.

10. Showed her pleasure by making a cooing sound, and her displeasure by growling.

11. Did not use her hands, as human beings and monkeys do, to convey the raw meat, fruit, or vegetables that were thrown into the room, to her mouth but gathered them in front of her with the back of her hands and then picked them up with her teeth and carried them into the corner in which she had made her nest.

12. Moved with great agility on all fours, i.e. on her hands and feet and not on her elbows and knees.

13. Was very dirty in her habits – not house-trained. When room needed washing she was roped round the middle and dragged into the veranda, the roof of which was supported on wooden pillars. On the rope being made fast to one of these pillars she immediately, and without any apparent effort, shinned up to the top of the pillar where she remained until pulled down again.

14. Miss Misra, the nurse, and the ward attendant, all three of whom were hill-women, were convinced – from the girl's colouring, features and build – that she was a hill-girl. And they were definite in their opinion that, apart from being timid and wild, in the sense that all wild animals are, the girl was perfectly sane and very intelligent.

Towards the end of her stay at the Crosthwaite Hospital Goongi responded to kind treatment to the extent that she no longer tried to bite her attendants; allowed herself to be washed, her hair to be brushed and her nails cut, and to don – for a few hours at a time – a loose one-piece garment. She refused however to have anything to do with a bed or blankets, spent all her time under the straw in the corner, and varied her cooing sounds to express different degrees of pleasure.

On 25 July 1914 Goongi was sent under escort to the Lunatic Asylum at Bareilly, where she died of heat-stroke shortly after admission. And so Goongi the wolf-child passed on, after her brief contact with civilization, leaving only speculation as to who she was and whence she had come.

Goongi's advent very naturally aroused great interest not only in Naini Tal and the surrounding hills but also throughout India, and many theories were advanced to account for her. The white population were of the opinion that she was a wolf-child or alternatively a monkey-child, whereas the Indian opinion was that she was a wolf-child. From the facts that the girl did not use her hands to convey food to her mouth; that she ate raw meat; and that she had never been seen in company with monkeys (as she would undoubtedly have been had she lived with them over a long period of years, for monkeys in the hills are never far from cultivated lands, and owing to their habits are very noticeable), the theory that Goongi was a monkey-child can be discounted. Remains the theory that she was a wolf-child. The age-old belief, dating back to the days of Romulus and Remus, that wolves rear children is current throughout the length and breadth of India even in those areas in which wolves have been extinct for centuries. In view of this universal belief I know I shall expose myself to ridicule when I state that I do not believe there has ever been an authentic case of a wolf stealing and rearing a child. Cases have been reported, even in recent years, of children being dug out of holes in the ground, alleged to be wolf dens, but in every case I have heard of the child has been found to be insane, and presence of an insane child in the ground is no proof that the child was placed in the hole by a wolf or was being fed by a wolf. The reasons why I do not believe these stories of wolf-children are:

*a*. The Indian wolf is a timid animal and for such an animal to enter a human habitation and carry off a child it would have to be in the extreme of starvation. This being so, it is inconceivable that the starving animal, instead of satisfying its hunger, would present the child to its cubs or, if it had no cubs, retain it as a pet. Life in the wild, as I know it, is far too strenuous a business for animals to indulge in play-things or in pets, and further, no child would survive on the food it would have, under these conditions, to eat.

*b*. The poorer class of Indian children – and it is always the children of the poorer class that wolves are alleged to carry off – sleep with their parents, and I cannot credit that a child in process of being carried off *alive* by the insertion of a wolf's teeth in its flesh would be silent, and that the parents of the child, or the neighbours, or the pye-dogs that swarm in every Indian village would be unaware of the proceedings.

*c*. The Indian wolf is little bigger than a jackal, and though it might be able to drag a child over the ground for a short distance, I do not give it credit for having the strength to lift a child off the ground and convey it alive, for possibly miles, to its distant den.

*d.* And finally, and here I may be exhibiting my ignorance, if wolf-children occur in India where wolves are scarce and small, why do they not occur in Russia and Canada where wolves are plentiful and large?

Had Goongi been insane and in the physical condition that children dug out of holes in the vicinity of human habitations are said to be found in, I would unhesitatingly have said – even in the face of Mothi Singh's inquiries, and the Tahsildar's registers – that she was just one of India's unwanted girls who had been cast away to fend for herself as best she could. But Goongi was not insane; her physical condition left nothing to be desired; and she had been captured far from human habitations. Her timidity, wildness, and terror of human beings can be accounted for by her long estrangement from human beings, and the reactions she had seen in animals to human beings.

If monkeys and wolves are ruled out, for the reasons given and also because there are no wolves within a hundred miles of where Goongi was found, remains the very remote possibility of her having associated with – I will not go to the extent of saying reared by – wild dogs or bears, both of which occur in the locality in which she was found, and both of which would have taught her to eat raw meat.

It is greatly to be regretted that when Goongi was captured by the road gang no inquiries – other than those subsequently made by me – were made to establish her identity. And it is also greatly to be regretted that Goongi, a hill-girl who had run wild in a cold climate, was sent to a hot plains station to be confined within four walls. For this the lady doctor in charge of the Crosthwaite Hospital was in no way to blame. Goongi was not in need of medical treatment and her presence attracted hundreds of people who hindered the normal work of the hospital, and Miss Misra was justified in asking for her removal. Nevertheless an opportunity that may never occur again was lost, of establishing whether Goongi had associated with any of the animals in Kumaon, which could have been done by confronting her with these animals at the nearest zoo. Further, the fact that Goongi could not speak did not necessarily mean that she was permanently dumb. Quite possibly she could have been taught to speak and in any case she could have been taught to write, and her story would have established once and for all whether wild animals do in fact undertake the care of children, or permit children to live in close association with them. For according to the testimony of the three highly trained women who attended on her, Goongi was quite sane, and very intelligent, and her experiences prior to capture would have been indelibly etched on her young memory to be recorded later when she had been taught to speak or to write. Had such a record been made I would have expected Goongi to have said that she had associated with bears, for the following reasons:

Bears spend much of their time in trees: Goongi could climb a wooden pillar without apparent effort, and it is reasonable to assume that she could have climbed trees.

Bears shuffle their food towards them with their front paws and lift it off the ground with their teeth: Goongi did the same.

Bears eat raw meat, fruit, and vegetables: these were the only articles of food Goongi ate when first admitted to hospital.

Bears throughout the Himalayas have the reputation of molesting women, and so strong is this belief that when certain fruits are in season women refrain from going into the forests adjoining the villages. The scratches on Goongi's shoulders and on the upper portion of her body need explanation. If she had acquired these scratches in her passage through thorns she would also have had scratches on the lower portion of her body, and on her arms and legs.

A forest guard set a rumour afloat that Goongi had been seen walking on all fours on the heels of a bear a Forest Officer shot. The Forest Officer in question, Smythies, told me that he had indeed shot a bear in the locality in which Goongi was found but that as far as he was aware the bear was not accompanied by a child.

And so the story of who Goongi was, who her associates had been, and how she managed to exist in the jungles until she attained the age of fourteen years, will remain a mystery.

## *The Pipal Pani Tiger*

Beyond the fact that he was born in a ravine running deep into the foothills and was one of a family of three, I know nothing of his early history.

He was about a year old when, attracted by the calling of a chital hind early one November morning, I found his pug marks in the sandy bed of a little stream known locally as Pipal Pani. I thought at first that he had strayed from his mother's care, but, as week succeeded week, and his single tracks showed on the game paths of the forest, I came to the conclusion that the near approach of the breeding season was an all-sufficient reason for his being alone. Jealously guarded one day, protected at the cost of the parent life if necessary, and set adrift the next, is the lot of all jungle folk; nature's method of preventing inbreeding.

That winter he lived on peafowl, karker, small pig, and an occasional chital hind, making his home in a prostrate giant of the forest felled for no apparent reason and hollowed out by time and porcupines. Here he brought most of his kills, basking, when the days were cold, on the smooth bole of the tree, where many a leopard had basked before him.

It was not until January was well advanced that I saw the cub at close quarters. I was out one evening without any definite object in view, when I saw a crow rise from the ground and wipe its beak as it lit on the branch of a tree. Crows, vultures, and magpies always interest me in the jungle, and many are the kills I have found both in India and in Africa with the help of these birds. On the present occasion the crow led me to the scene of an overnight tragedy. A chital had been killed and partly eaten and, attracted to the spot probably as I had been, a party of men passing along the road, distant some fifty yards, had cut up and removed the remains. All that was left of the chital were a few splinters of bone and a little congealed blood off which the crow had lately made his meal. The absence of thick cover and the proximity of the road convinced me that the animal responsible for the kill had not witnessed the removal and that it would return in due course; so I decided to sit up, and made myself as comfortable in a plum tree as the thorns permitted.

I make no apology to you, my reader, if you differ with me on the ethics of the much-debated subject of sitting up over kills. Some of my most pleasant shikar memories centre round the hour or two before sunset that I have spent in a tree over a natural kill, ranging from the time when, armed with a muzzle-loader whipped round with brass wire to prevent the cracked barrel from bursting, I sat over a langur killed by a leopard, to a few days ago when, with the most modern rifle across my knees, I watched a tigress and her two full-grown cubs eat up the sambur stag they had killed, and counted myself no poorer for not having secured a trophy.

True, on the present occasion there is no kill below me, but, for the reasons given, that will not affect my chance of a shot; scent to interest the jungle folk there is in plenty in the blood-soaked ground, as witness the old grey-whiskered boar who has been quietly rooting along for the past ten minutes, and who suddenly stiffens to attention as he comes into the line of the blood-tainted wind. His snout held high, and worked as only a pig can work that member, tells him more than I was able to glean from the ground which showed no tracks; his method of approach, a short excursion to the right and back into the wind, and then a short excursion to the left and again back into the wind, each manœuvre bringing him a few yards nearer, indicates the chital was killed by a tiger. Making sure once and again that nothing worth eating has been left, he finally trots off and disappears from view.

Two chital, both with horns in velvet, now appear, and from the fact that they are coming downwind, and making straight for the blood-soaked spot, it is evident they were witnesses to the overnight tragedy. Alternately snuffing the ground or standing rigid with every muscle tensed for instant flight, they satisfy their curiosity and return the way they came.

Curiosity is not a human monopoly: many an animal's life is cut short by indulging in it. A dog leaves the veranda to bark at a shadow, a deer leaves the herd to investigate a tuft of grass that no wind agitated, and the waiting leopard is provided with a meal.

The sun is nearing the winter line when a movement to the right front attracts attention. An animal has crossed an opening between two bushes at the far end of a wedge of scrub that terminates thirty yards from my tree. Presently the bushes at my end part, and out into the open, with never a look to right or left, steps the cub. Straight up to the spot where his kill had been he goes, his look of expectancy giving place to one of disappointment as he realizes that his chital, killed, possibly, after hours of patient stalking, is gone. The splinters of bone and congealed blood are rejected, and his interest centres on a tree stump lately used as a butcher's block, to which some shreds of flesh are adhering. I was not the only one who carried fire-arms in these jungles and, if the cub was to grow into a tiger, it was necessary he should be taught the danger of carelessly approaching kills in daylight. A scatter-gun and dust-shot would have served my purpose better, but the rifle will have to do this time; and, as he raises his head to smell the stump, my bullet crashes into the hard wood an inch from his nose. Only once in the years that followed did the cub forget that lesson.

The following winter I saw him several times. His ears did not look so big now and he had changed his baby hair for a coat of rich tawny red with well-defined stripes. The hollow tree had been given up to its rightful owners, a pair of leopards, new quarters found in a thick belt of scrub skirting the foothills, and young sambur added to his menu.

On my annual descent from the hills next winter, the familiar pug marks no longer showed on the game paths and at the drinking places, and for several weeks I thought the cub had abandoned his old haunts and gone further afield. Then one morning his absence was explained for, side by side with his tracks, were the smaller and more elongated tracks of the mate he had gone to find. I only once saw the tigers, for the cub was a tiger now, together. I had been out before dawn to try to bag a serow that lived on the foothills, and returning along a fire-track my attention was arrested by a vulture, perched on the dead limb of a sal tree.

The bird had his back towards me and was facing a short stretch of scrub with dense jungle beyond. Dew was still heavy on the ground, and without a sound I reached the tree and peered round. One antler of a dead sambur, for no living deer would lie in that position, projected above the low bushes. A convenient moss-covered rock afforded my rubber-shod feet silent and safe hold, and as I drew myself erect the sambur came into full view. The hindquarters had been eaten away and, lying on either side of the kill, were the pair, the tiger being on the far side with only his hind legs showing. Both tigers were asleep. Ten feet straight in front, to avoid a dead branch, and thirty feet to the left would give me a shot at the tiger's neck, but in planning the stalk I had forgotten the silent spectator. Where I stood I was invisible to him, but before the ten feet had been covered I came into view and, alarmed at my near proximity, he flapped off his perch, omitting as he did so to notice a thin creeper dependent from a branch above him against which he collided, and came ignominiously to ground. The tigress was up and away in an instant, clearing at a bound the kill and her mate, the tiger not being slow to follow; a possible shot, but too risky with thick jungle ahead, where a wounded animal would have all the advantages. To those who have never tried it, I can recommend the stalking of leopards and tigers on their kills as a most pleasant form of sport. Great care should, however, be taken over the shot, for if the animal is not killed outright, or anchored, trouble is bound to follow.

A week later the tiger resumed his bachelor existence. A change had now come over his nature. Hitherto he had not objected to my visiting his kills but, after his mate left, at the first drag I followed up I was given very clearly to understand that no liberties would in future be permitted. The angry growl of a tiger at close quarters, than which there is no more terrifying sound in the jungles, has to be heard to be appreciated.

Early in March the tiger killed his first full-grown buffalo. I was near the foothills one evening when the agonized bellowing of a buffalo, mingled with the angry roar of a tiger, rang through the forest. I located the sound as coming from a ravine about six hundred yards away. The going was bad, mostly over loose rocks and through thorn bushes, and when I crawled up a steep bluff commanding a view of the ravine the buffalo's struggles were over, and the tiger nowhere to be seen. For an hour I lay with finger on trigger without seeing anything of the tiger. At dawn next morning I again crawled up the bluff, to find the buffalo lying just as I had left her. The soft ground, torn up by hoof and claw, testified to the desperate nature of the struggle, and it was not until the buffalo had been hamstrung that the tiger had finally succeeded in pulling her down, in a fight which had lasted from ten to fifteen minutes. The tiger's tracks led across the ravine and, on following them up, I found a long smear of blood on a rock, and, a hundred yards further on, another smear on a fallen tree. The wound inflicted by the buffalo's horns was in the tiger's head and sufficiently severe to make the tiger lose all interest in the kill, for he never returned to it.

Three years later the tiger, disregarding the lesson received when a cub (his excuse may have been that it was the close season for tigers), incautiously returned to a kill, over which a zamindar and some of his tenants were sitting at night, and received a bullet in the shoulder which fractured the bone. No attempt was made to follow him up, and thirty-six hours later, his shoulder covered with a swarm of flies, he limped through the compound of the Inspection Bungalow, crossed a bridge flanked on the far side by a double row of tenanted houses, the occupants of which stood at their doors to watch him pass, entered the gate of a walled-in compound and took possession of a vacant godown. Twenty-four hours later, possibly alarmed by the number of people who had collected from neighbouring villages to see him, he left the compound the way he had entered it, passed our gate, and made his way to the lower end of our village. A bullock belonging to one of our tenants had died the previous night and had been dragged into some bushes at the edge of the village; this the tiger found, and here he remained a few days, quenching his thirst at an irrigation furrow.

When we came down from the hills two months later the tiger was living on small animals (calves, sheep, goats, etc.) that he was able to catch on the outskirts of the village. By March his wound had healed, leaving his right foot turned inwards. Returning to the forest where he had been wounded, he levied heavy toll of the village cattle, taking, for safety's sake, but one meal off each, and in this way killing five times as many as he would ordinarily have done. The zamindar who had wounded him and who had a herd of some four hundred head of cows and buffaloes was the chief sufferer.

In the succeeding years he gained as much in size as in reputation, and many were the attempts made by sportsmen, and others, to bag him.

One November evening a villager, armed with a single-barrel muzzle-loading gun, set out to try to bag a pig, selecting for his ground machan an isolated bush growing in a twenty-yard-wide *rowkah* [dry watercourse] running down the centre of some broken ground. This ground was rectangular, flanked on the long sides by cultivated land and on the short sides by a road, and by a ten-foot canal that formed the boundary between our cultivation and the forest. In front of the man was a four-foot-high bank with a cattle-track running along the upper edge; behind him a patch of dense scrub. At 8 p.m. an animal appeared on the track and, taking what aim he could, he fired. On receiving the shot the animal fell off the bank and passed within a few feet of the man, grunting as it entered the scrub behind. Casting aside his blanket, the man ran to his hut two hundred yards away. Neighbours soon collected and, on hearing the man's account, came to the conclusion that a pig had been hard hit. It would be a pity, they said, to leave the pig for hyenas and jackals to eat, so a lantern was lit and as a party of six bold spirits set out to retrieve the bag, one of my tenants (who declined to join the expedition, and who confessed to me later that he had no stomach for looking for wounded pig in dense scrub in the dark) suggested that the gun should be loaded and taken.

His suggestion was accepted and, as a liberal charge of powder was being rammed home, the wooden ramrod jammed and broke inside the barrel. A trivial accident which undoubtedly saved the lives of six men. The broken rod was eventually, and after great trouble, extracted, the gun loaded, and the party set off.

Arrived at the spot where the animal had entered the bushes, a careful search was made and, on blood being found, every effort to find the 'pig' was made; it was not until the whole area had been combed out that the quest for that night was finally abandoned. Early next morning the search was resumed, with the addition of my informant of weak stomach, who was a better woodsman than his companions and who, examining the ground under a bush where there was a lot of blood, collected and brought some bloodstained hairs to me which I recognized as tiger's hairs. A brother sportsman was with me for the day, and together we went to have a look at the ground.

The reconstruction of jungle events from signs on the ground has always held great interest for me. True, one's deductions are sometimes wrong, but they are also sometimes right. In the present instance I was right in placing the wound in the inner forearm of the right foreleg, but was wrong in assuming the leg had been broken and that the tiger was a young animal and a stranger to the locality.

There was no blood beyond the point where the hairs had been found and, as tracking on the hard ground was impossible, I crossed the canal to where the cattle-track ran through a bed of sand. Here, from the pug marks, I found that the wounded animal was not a young tiger but my old friend the Pipal Pani tiger who, taking a short cut through the village, had in the dark been mistaken for a pig.

Once before when badly wounded he had passed through the settlement without harming man or beast, but he was older now, and if driven by pain and hunger might do considerable damage. A disconcerting prospect, for the locality was thickly populated, and I was due to leave within the week, to keep an engagement that could not be put off.

For three days I searched every bit of the jungle between the canal and the foothills, an area of about four square miles, without finding any trace of the tiger. On the fourth afternoon, as I was setting out to continue the search, I met an old woman and her son hurriedly leaving the jungle. From them I learnt that the tiger was calling near the foothills and that all the cattle in the jungle had stampeded. When out with a rifle I invariably go alone; it is safer in a mix-up, and one can get through the jungle more silently. However, I stretched a point on this occasion, and let the boy accompany me since he was very keen on showing me where he had heard the tiger.

Arrived at the foothills, the boy pointed to a dense bit of cover, bounded on the far side by the fire-track to which I have already referred, and on the near side by the Pipal Pani stream. Running parallel to and about a hundred yards from the stream was a shallow depression some twenty feet wide, more or less open on my side and fringed with bushes on the side nearer the stream. A well-used path crossed the depression at right angles. Twenty yards from the path, and on the open side of the depression, was a small tree. If the tiger came down the path he would in all likelihood stand for a shot on clearing the bushes. Here I decided to take my stand and, putting the boy into the tree with his feet on a level with my head and instructing him to signal with his toes if from his raised position he saw the tiger before I did, I put my back to the tree and called.

Those who have spent as many years in the jungle as I have, need no description of the call of a tigress in search of a mate, and to the less fortunate ones I can only say that the call, to acquire which necessitates close observation and the liberal use of throat salve, cannot be described in words.

To my great relief, for I had crawled through the jungle for three days with finger on trigger, I was immediately answered from a distance of about five hundred yards, and for half an hour thereafter – it may have been less and certainly appeared more – the call was tossed back and forth. On the one side the urgent summons of the king, and on the other the subdued and coaxing answer of his handmaiden. Twice the boy signalled, but I had as yet seen nothing of the tiger, and it was not until the setting sun was flooding the forest with golden light that he suddenly appeared, coming down the path at a fast walk with never a pause as he cleared the bushes. When half-way across the depression, and just as I was raising the rifle, he turned to the right and came straight towards me.

This manœuvre, unforeseen when selecting my stand, brought him nearer than I had intended he should come and, moreover, presented me with a head shot which at that short range I was not prepared to take. Resorting to an old device, learned long years ago and successfully used on similar occasions, the tiger was brought to a stand without being alarmed. With one paw poised, he slowly raised his head, exposing as he did so his chest and throat. After the impact of the heavy bullet, he struggled to his feet and tore blindly through the forest, coming down with a crash within a few yards of where, attracted by the calling of a chital hind one November morning, I had first seen his pug marks.

It was only then that I found he had been shot under a misapprehension, for the wound which I feared might make him dangerous proved on examination to be almost healed and caused by a pellet of lead having severed a small vein in his right forearm.

Pleasure at having secured a magnificent trophy – he measured ten feet three inches over curves and his winter coat was in perfect condition – was not unmixed with regret, for never again would the jungle folk and I listen with held breath to his deep-throated call resounding through the foothills, and never again would his familiar pug marks show on the game-paths that he and I had trodden for fifteen years.

## 11

## The Pilgrim Road

If you are a Hindu, from the sun-scorched plains of India, and you desire – as all good Hindus do – to perform the pilgrimage to the age-old shrines of Kedarnath and Badrinath, you must start on your pilgrimage from Hardwar and, in order to acquire a full measure of the merits vouchsafed to you for the correct performance of the pilgrimage, you must walk every step of the way from Hardwar to Kedarnath, and thence over the mountain track to Badrinath, barefoot.

Having purified yourself by immersion in the sacred Har-ki-pauri pool, and done *darshan* at the many shrines and temples in Hardwar and added your mite to their coffers, you must not omit to toss a coin within reach of the festering stumps – which once were hands – of the lepers who line the narrowest part of the pilgrim road above the sacred pool, for if you make this omission, they will call down curses on your head. What matter if these unfortunate ones have wealth beyond your dreams secreted in their filthy rags, or in the rock caves they call their homes? The curses of such as they were best avoided, and immunity will cost you but a few coppers.

You have now done all that custom and religion require of a good Hindu and are at liberty to start on your long and hard pilgrimage.

The first place of interest you will come to after leaving Hardwar is Rikikesh. Here you will make your first acquaintance with the Kalakamli Wallahs, so called because of the black blanket their founder wore – and which many of his disciples still wear – in the form of a habit or loose cloak bound round the middle with a cord of goat's hair; and who are renowned throughout the land for their good deeds. I do not know if any of the other religious brotherhoods you will meet on your pilgrimage have any claim to renown, but I do know that the Kalakamli Wallahas have such a claim, and justly so, for out of the offerings they receive at their many shrines and temples, they have built – and they maintain – hospitals, dispensaries, and pilgrim shelters, and they feed the poor and the needy.

With Rikikesh behind you, you will come next to Lachman Jhula, where the pilgrim road crosses from the right to the left bank of the Ganges on a suspension bridge. Here beware of the red monkeys who infest the bridge, for they are even more importunate than the lepers of Hardwar, and if you omit to propitiate them with offerings of sweets, or parched gram, your passage across the long and narrow bridge is likely to be both difficult and painful.

Three days' journey up the left bank of the Ganges and you have reached the ancient capital of Garhwal, Shreenagar, an historic, religious, and trading centre of considerable importance and of great beauty, nestling in a wide, open valley surrounded by high mountains. It was here, in the year 1805, that the forebears of the Garhwali soldiers who have fought so gallantly in two world wars made their last, and unsuccessful, stand against the Gurkha invaders, and it is a matter of great regret to the people of Garhwal that their ancient city of Shreenagar, together with the palaces of their kings, was swept away, to the last stone, by the bursting of the Gohna Lake dam in 1894. This dam, caused by a landslide in the valley of the Birehi Ganga, a tributary of the Ganges, was 11,000 feet wide at the base, 2,000 feet wide at the summit, and 900 feet high, and when it burst, ten billion cubic feet of water were released in the short space of six hours. So well was the bursting of the dam timed that, though the flood devastated the valley of the Ganges right down to Hardwar and swept away every bridge, only one family was lost, the members of which had returned to the danger-zone after having been forcibly removed from it.

From Shreenagar you have to face a stiff climb to Chatikhal, which is compensated for by the magnificent views you will get of the Ganges valley and of the eternal snows above Kedarnath.

A day's march from Chatikhal and you see in front of you Golabrai with its row of grass-thatched pilgrim shelters, a one-roomed stone-built house, and its drinking trough. This big and imposing drinking trough is fed by a tiny crystal-clear stream which, in summer, is sedately conducted down the mountainside by a series of channels rough-hewn from pine saplings. At other seasons of the year the water cascades unconfined and merrily over rocks draped with moss and maidenhair fern, through luxuriant beds of vivid green watercress and sky-blue strobilanthes.

Another two miles, along the last flat bit of ground you will see for many a day, and you have reached Rudraprayag, where you and I, my pilgrim friend, must part, for your way lies across the Alaknanda and up the left bank of the Mandakini to Kedarnath, while mine lies over the mountains to my home in Naini Tal.

## 12

## *Terror*

The word 'terror' is so generally and universally used in connexion with everyday trivial matters that it is apt to fail to convey, when intended to do so, its real meaning. I should like therefore to give you some idea of what terror – real terror – meant to the fifty thousand inhabitants living in the five hundred square miles of Garhwal in which the man-eater was operating, and to the sixty thousand pilgrims who annually passed through that area between the years 1918 and 1926. And I will give you a few instances to show you what grounds the inhabitants, and the pilgrims, had for that terror.

No curfew order has ever been more strictly enforced, and more implicitly obeyed, than the curfew imposed by the man-eating leopard of Rudraprayag.

During the hours of sunlight life in that area carried on in a normal way. Men went long distances to the bazaars to transact business, or to outlying villages to visit relatives or friends; women went up the mountainsides to cut grass for thatching or for cattle-fodder; children went to school or into the jungles to graze goats or to collect dry sticks, and, if it was summer, pilgrims either singly or in large numbers toiled along the pilgrim routes on their way to and from the sacred shrines of Kedarnath and Badrinath.

As the sun approached the western horizon and the shadows lengthened, the behaviour of the entire population of the area underwent a very sudden and a very noticeable change. Men who had sauntered to the bazaars or to outlying villages were hurrying home; women carrying great bundles of grass were stumbling down the steep mountainsides; children who had loitered on their way from school, or who were late in bringing in their flocks of goats or the dry sticks they had been sent out to collect, were being called to by anxious mothers, and the weary pilgrims were being urged by any local inhabitant who passed them to hurry to shelter.

When night came an ominous silence brooded over the whole area – no movement and no sound anywhere. The entire local population were behind fast-closed doors, and in many cases they had sought further protection by building additional doors. Those of the pilgrims who had not been fortunate enough to find accommodation inside houses were huddled close together in pilgrim shelters. And all, whether in house or shelter, were silent for fear of attracting the dread man-eater.

This is what terror meant to the people of Garhwal, and to the pilgrims, for eight long years.

I will now give a few instances to show you what grounds there were for that terror.

A boy, an orphan aged fourteen, was employed to look after a flock of forty goats. He was of the depressed – untouchable – class, and each evening when he returned with his charges he was given his food and then shut into a small room with the goats. The room was on the ground floor of a long row of double-storeyed buildings and was immediately below the room occupied by the boy's master, the owner of the goats. To prevent the goats crowding in on him as he slept, the boy had fenced off the far left-hand corner of the room.

This room had no windows and only the one door, and when the boy and the goats were safely inside, the boy's master pulled the door to, and fastened it by passing the hasp, which was attached by a short length of chain to the door, over the staple fixed in the lintel. A piece of wood was then inserted in the staple to keep the hasp in place, and on his side of the door the boy, for his better safety, rolled a stone against it.

On the night that the orphan was gathered to his fathers his master asserts the door was fastened as usual, and I have no reason to question the truth of his assertion. In support of it, the door showed many deep claw-marks, and it is possible that in his attempts to claw open the door the leopard displaced the piece of wood that was keeping the hasp in place, after which it would have been easy for him to push the stone aside and enter the room.

Forty goats packed into a small room, one corner of which was fenced off, could not have left the intruder much space to manœuvre in, and it is left to conjecture whether the leopard covered the distance from the door to the boy's corner of the room over the backs of the goats or under their bellies, for at this stage of the proceedings all the goats must have been on their feet.

It were best to assume that the boy slept through all the noise the leopard must have made when trying to force open the door, and that the goats must have made when the leopard had entered the room, and that he did not cry for help to deaf ears, only screened from him and the danger that menaced him by a thin plank.

After killing the boy in the fenced-off corner, the leopard carried him across the empty room – the goats had escaped into the night – down a steep hillside, and then over some terraced fields to a deep boulder-strewn ravine. It was here, after the sun had been up a few hours, that the master found all that the leopard had left of his servant.

Incredible as it may seem, not one of the forty goats had received so much as a scratch.

A neighbour had dropped in to spend the period of a long smoke with a friend. The room was L-shaped and the only door in it was not visible from where the two men sat on the floor with their backs to the wall, smoking. The door was shut but not fastened, for up to that night there had been no human kills in the village.

The room was in darkness and the owner of it had just passed the hookah to his friend when it fell to the ground, scattering a shower of burning charcoal and tobacco. Telling his friend to be more careful or he would set the blanket on which they were sitting on fire, the man bent forward to gather up the embers and, as he did so, the door came into view. A young moon was near setting and, silhouetted against it, the man saw a leopard carrying his friend through the door.

When recounting the incident to me a few days later the man said: 'I am speaking the truth, sahib, when I tell you I never heard even so much as the intake of a breath, or any other sound, from my friend who was sitting only an arm's-length from me, either when the leopard was killing him, or when it was carrying him away. There was nothing I could do for my friend, so I waited until the leopard had been gone some little while, and then I crept up to the door and hastily shut and secured it.'

The wife of the headman of a village was ill of a fever, and two friends had been called in to nurse her.

There were two rooms in the house. The outer room had two doors, one opening on to a small flagged courtyard, and the other leading into the inner room. This outer room also had a narrow slip of a window set some four feet above floor level, and in this window, which was open, stood a large brass vessel containing drinking-water for the sick woman.

Except for the one door giving access to the outer room, the inner room had no other opening in any of its four walls.

The door leading out on to the courtyard was shut and securely fastened, and the door between the two rooms was wide open.

The three women in the inner room were lying on the ground, the sick woman in the middle with a friend on either side of her. The husband in the outer room was on a bed on the side of the room nearest the window, and on the floor beside his bed, where its light would shine into the inner room, was a lantern, turned down low to conserve oil.

Round about midnight, when the occupants of both the rooms were asleep, the leopard entered by way of the narrow slip of a window, avoiding in some miraculous way knocking over the brass vessel which nearly filled it, skirted round the man's low bed and, entering the inner room, killed the sick woman. It was only when the heavy brass vessel crashed to the floor as the leopard attempted to lift its victim through the window that the sleepers awoke.

When the lantern had been turned up the woman who had been sick was discovered lying huddled up under the window, and in her throat were four great teeth-marks.

A neighbour, whose wife had been one of the nurses on that night, when relating the occurrence to me said, 'The woman was very ill of her fever and was like to have died in any case, so it was fortunate that the leopard selected her.'

Two Gujars were moving their herd of thirty buffaloes from one grazing-ground to another, and accompanying them was the twelve-year-old daughter of the older of the two men, who were brothers.

They were strangers to the locality and either had not heard of the man-eater or, which is more probable, thought the buffaloes would give them all the protection they needed.

Near the road and at an elevation of eight thousand feet was a narrow strip of flat ground below which was a sickle-shaped terraced field, some quarter of an acre in extent, which had long been out of cultivation. The men selected this for their camp and having cut stakes from the jungle which surrounded them on all sides they drove them deep into the field and tethered their buffaloes in a long row.

After the evening meal prepared by the girl had been eaten, the party of three laid their blankets on the narrow strip of ground between the road and the buffaloes and went to sleep.

It was a dark night, and some time towards the early hours of the morning the men were awakened by the booming of their buffalo-bells and by the snorting of the frightened animals. Knowing from long experience that these sounds indicated the presence of carnivora, the men lit a lantern and went among the buffaloes to quieten them, and to see that none had broken the ropes tethering them to the stakes.

The men were absent only a few minutes. When they returned to their sleeping-place they found that the girl whom they had left asleep was missing. On the blanket on which she had been lying were big splashes of blood.

When daylight came the father and the uncle followed the blood trail. After skirting round the row of tethered buffaloes, it went across the narrow field and down the steep hillside for a few yards, to where the leopard had eaten his kill.

'My brother was born under an unlucky star, sahib, for he has no son, and he had only this one daughter who was to have been married shortly, and to whom he looked in the fullness of time to provide him with an heir, and now the leopard has come and eaten her.'

I could go on and on, for there were many kills, and each one has its own tragic story, but I think I have said enough to convince you that the people of Garhwal had ample reason to be terrified of the man-eating leopard of Rudraprayag, especially when it is remembered that Garhwalis are intensely superstitious and that, added to their fear of physical contact with the leopard, was their even greater fear of the supernatural.

## 13

## *Vigil on a Pine-tree*

The following morning [during the hunt for the Rudraprayag leopard] I found the tracks of the man-eater on a path leading out of a village in which the previous night he had tried to break open the door of a house in which there was a child suffering from a bad cough. On following the tracks for a couple of miles they led me to the shoulder of the mountain where, some days previously, Ibbotson and I had sat up over the calling goat which the leopard later had killed.

It was still quite early, and as there was a chance of finding the leopard basking on one of the rocks in this considerable area of broken ground, I lay on a projecting rock that commanded an extensive view. It had rained the previous evening – thus enabling me to track the leopard – and washed the haze out of the atmosphere. Visibility was at its best and the view from the projecting rock was as good as could be seen in any part of the world where mountains rise to a height of twenty-three thousand feet. Immediately below me was the beautiful valley of the Alaknanda, with the river showing as a gleaming silver ribbon winding in and out of it. On the hill beyond the river, villages were dotted about, some with only a single thatched hut, and others with long rows of slate-roofed houses. These rows of buildings are in fact individual homesteads, built one against the other to save expense and to economize space, for the people are poor, and every foot of workable land in Garhwal is needed for agriculture.

Beyond the hills were rugged rock cliffs, down which avalanches roar in winter and early spring, and beyond and above the cliffs were the eternal snows, showing up against the intense blue sky as clear as if cut out of white cardboard. No more beautiful or peaceful scene could be imagined, and yet when the sun, now shining on the back of my head, set on the far side of the snow mountains, terror – terror which it is not possible to imagine until experienced – would grip, as it had done for eight long years, the area I was now overlooking.

I had been lying on the rock for an hour when two men came down the hill, on their way to the bazaar. They were from a village about a mile farther up the hill that I had visited the previous day, and they informed me that a little before sunrise they had heard a leopard calling in this direction. We discussed the possibilities of my getting a shot at the leopard over a goat, and as at that time I had no goats of my own, they offered to bring me one from their village and promised to meet me where we were standing, two hours before sunset.

When the men had gone I looked round for a place where I could sit. The only tree on the whole of this part of the mountain was a solitary pine. It was growing on the ridge close to the path down which the men had come, and from under it a second path took off and ran across the face of the mountain skirting the upper edge of the broken ground, where I had recently been looking for the leopard. The tree commanded an extensive view, but it could be difficult to climb, and would afford little cover. However, as it was the only tree in the area, I had no choice, so decided I would try it.

The men were waiting for me with a goat when I returned at about 4 p.m., and when, in reply to their question where I intended sitting, I pointed to the pine, they started laughing. Without a rope ladder, they said, it would not be possible to climb the tree; and further, if I succeeded in climbing the tree without a ladder, and carried out my intention of remaining out all night, I should have no protection against the man-eater, to whom the tree would offer no obstacle. There were two white men in Garhwal – Ibbotson was one of them – who had collected birds' eggs when boys, and both of whom could climb the tree; and as there is no exact equivalent in Hindustani for 'waiting until you come to a bridge before crossing it', I let the second part of the men's objection go unanswered, contenting myself by pointing to my rifle.

The pine was not easy to climb, for there were no branches for twenty feet, but once having reached the lowest branch, the rest was easy. I had provided myself with a long length of cotton cord, and when the men had tied my rifle to one end of it, I drew it up and climbed to the top of the tree, where the pine-needles afforded most cover.

The men had assured me that the goat was a good caller, and after they had tied it to an exposed root of the tree they set off for their village promising to return early next morning. The goat watched the men out of sight, and then started to nibble the short grass at the foot of the tree. The fact that it had not up to then called once did not worry me, for I felt sure that it would presently feel lonely and that it would then do its share of the business of the evening, and if it did it while it was still light, from my elevated position I should able to kill the leopard long before it got anywhere near the goat.

When I climbed the tree the shadows cast by the snow mountains had reached the Alaknanda. Slowly these shadows crept up the hill and passed me, until only the top of the mountain glowed with red light. As this glow faded, long streamers of light shot up from the snow mountains where the rays of the setting sun were caught and held on a bank of clouds as soft and as light as thistledown. Everyone who has eyes to see a sunset – and the number, as you might have observed, is regrettably few – thinks that the sunsets in his particular part of the world are the best ever. I am no exception, for I too think that there are no sunsets in all the world to compare with ours, and a good second are the sunsets in northern Tanganyika, where some quality in the atmosphere makes snow-capped Kilimanjaro, and the clouds that are invariably above it, glow like molten gold in the rays of the setting sun. Our sunsets in the Himalayas are mostly red, pink, or gold. The one I was looking at that evening from my seat on the pine-tree was rose-pink, and the white shafts of light, starting as spear-points from valleys in the cardboard snows, shot through the pink clouds and, broadening, faded out in the sky overhead.

The goat, like many human beings, had no interest in sunsets, and after nibbling the grass within reach, scratched a shallow hole for itself, lay down, curled up, and went to sleep. Here was a dilemma. I had counted on the animal now placidly sleeping below me to call up the leopard, and not once since I had first seen it had it opened its mouth, except to nibble grass, and now, having made itself comfortable, it would probably sleep throughout the night. To have left the tree at that hour in an attempt to return to the bungalow would have added one more to the number who deliberately commit suicide, and as I had to be doing something to kill the man-eater, and as – in the absence of a kill – one place was as good as another, I decided to stay where I was, and try to call up the leopard myself.

If I were asked what had contributed most to my pleasure during all the years that I have spent in Indian jungles, I would unhesitatingly say that I had derived most pleasure from a knowledge of the language, and the habits, of the jungle folk. There is no universal language in the jungles; each species has its own language, and though the vocabulary of some is limited, as in the case of porcupines and vultures, the language of each species is understood by all the jungle folk. The vocal chords of human beings are more adaptable than the vocal chords of any of the jungle folk, with the one exception of the crested wire-tailed drongo, and for this reason it is possible for human beings to hold commune with quite a big range of birds and animals. The ability to speak the language of the jungle folk, apart from adding an hundredfold to one's pleasure in the jungle, can, if so desired, be put to great use. One example will suffice.

Lionel Fortescue – up till recently a housemaster at Eton – and I were on a photographing and fishing tour in the Himalayas shortly after 1918, and we arrived one evening at a Forest Bungalow at the foot of a great mountain, on the far side of which was our objective, the Vale of Kashmir. We had been marching over hard ground for many days, and as the men carrying our luggage needed a rest, we decided to halt for a day at the bungalow. Next day, while Fortescue wrote up his notes, I set out to explore the mountain and try for a Kashmir stag. I had been informed by friends who had shot in Kashmir that it was not possible to shoot one of these stags without the help of an experienced shikari, and this was confirmed by the chowkidar in charge of the Forest Bungalow. With the whole day before me I set out alone, after breakfast, without having the least idea at what elevation the red deer lived, or the kind of ground on which they were likely to be found. The mountain, over which there is a pass into Kashmir, is about twelve thousand feet high, and after I had climbed to a height of eight thousand a storm came on.

From the colour of the clouds I knew I was in for a hailstorm, so I selected with care a tree under which to shelter. I have seen both human beings and animals killed by hail, and by the lightning that invariably accompanies hailstorms, so rejecting the big fir-trees with tapering tops I selected a small tree with a rounded top and dense foliage, and collecting a supply of dead wood and fir-cones, I built a fire, and for the hour that the thunder roared overhead and the hail lashed down, I sat at the foot of my tree safe and warm.

The moment the hail stopped the sun came out, and from the shelter of the tree I stepped into fairyland, for the hail that carpeted the ground gave off a million points of light to which every glistening leaf and blade of grass added its quota. Continuing up for another two or three thousand feet, I came on an outcrop of rock, at the foot of which was a bed of blue mountain poppies. The stalks of many of these, the most beautiful of all wild flowers in the Himalayas, were broken; even so these sky-blue flowers standing in a bed of spotless white were a never-to-be-forgotten sight.

The rocks were too slippery to climb, and there appeared to be no object in going to the top of the hill, so keeping to the contours I went to the left, and after half a mile through a forest of giant fir-trees I came to a grassy slope which, starting from the top of the hill, extended several thousand feet down into the forest. As I came through the trees towards this grassy slope I saw on the far side of it an animal standing on a little knoll, with its tail towards me. From illustrations seen in game books I knew the animal was a red Kashmir deer, and when it raised its head, I saw it was a hind.

On my side of the grassy slope, and about thirty yards from the edge of the forest, there was a big isolated rock some four feet high; the distance between this rock and the knoll was about forty yards. Moving only when the deer was cropping the grass, and remaining still each time she raised her head, I crept up to the shelter of the rock. The hind was quite obviously a sentinel, and from the way she looked to her right each time she raised her head, I knew she had companions, and the exact direction in which these companions were. To approach any nearer over the grass without being seen was not possible. To re-enter the forest and work down from above would not have been difficult but would have defeated my purpose, for the wind was blowing down the hill. There remained the alternative of re-entering the forest and skirting round the lower end of the grass slope, but this would take time and entail a stiff climb. I therefore finally decided to remain where I was and see if these deer – which I was seeing for the first time – would react in the same way as chital and sambur do to the call of a leopard, of which I knew there was at least one on the mountain, for I had seen its scratch-marks earlier in the day. With only one eye showing, I waited until the hind was cropping the grass, and then gave the call of a leopard.

At the first sound of my voice the hind swung round and, facing me, started to strike the ground with her forefeet. This was a warning to her companions to be on the alert, but those companions whom I wanted to see would not move until the hind called, and this she would not do until she saw the leopard. I was wearing a brown tweed coat, and projecting a few inches of my left shoulder beyond the rock I moved it up and down. The movement was immediately detected by the hind, who, taking a few quick steps forward, started to call; the danger she had warned her companions of was in sight, and it was now safe for them to join her. The first to come was a yearling, which, stepping daintily over the hail-covered ground, ranged itself alongside the hind; the yearling was followed by three stags, who in turn were followed by an old hind. The entire herd, numbering six in all, were now in full view at a range of thirty-five yards. The hind was still calling, while the others, with ears alternately held rigid or feeling forward and backward for sound and wind direction, were standing perfectly still and gazing into the forest behind me. My seat on the melting hail was uncomfortable and wet, and to remain inactive longer would possibly result in a cold. I had seen a representative herd of the much-famed Kashmir deer, and I had heard a hind call, but there was one thing more that I wanted. That was, to hear a stag call; so I again projected a few inches of my shoulder beyond the rock, and had the satisfaction of hearing the stags, the hinds, and the yearling calling in different pitched keys.

My pass permitted me to shoot one stag, and for all I knew one of the stags might have carried a record head, but though I had set out that morning to look for a stag, and procure meat for the camp, I now realized that I was in no urgent need of a trophy. In any case the stag's meat would probably be tough so, instead of using the rifle, I stood up, and six of the most surprised deer in Kashmir vanished out of sight, and a moment later I heard them crashing through the undergrowth on the far side of the knoll.

It was now time for me to retrace my steps to the bungalow, and I decided to go down the grassy slope and work through the lighter forest at the foot of the mountain. The slope was at an angle that lent itself to an easy lope, provided care was taken to see that every step was correctly placed. I was running in the middle of the hundred-yard open ground and had gone about six hundred yards when I caught sight of a white object, standing on a rock at the edge of the forest on the left-hand side of the slope, and about three hundred yards below me. A hurried glance convinced me that the white object was a goat, that had probably been lost in the forest. We had been without meat for a fortnight and I had promised Fortescue that I would bring something back with me, and here was my opportunity. The goat had seen me, and if I could disarm suspicion would possibly let me pass close enough to catch it by the legs; so as I loped along I edged to the left, keeping the animal in sight out of the corner of my eyes. Provided the animal stayed where it was, no better place on all the mountain could have been found on which to catch it, for the flat rock, at the very edge of which it was standing, jutted out into the slope, and was about five feet high. Without looking directly at it, and keeping up a steady pace, I ran past the rock and, as I did so, made a sweep with my left hand for its forelegs. With a sneeze of alarm the animal reared up, avoiding my grasp, and when I pulled up clear of the rock and turned round, I saw to my amazement that the animal I had mistaken for a white goat was an albino musk-deer. With only some ten feet between us the game little animal was standing its ground and sneezing defiance at me. Turning away I walked down the hill for fifty yards, and when I looked back, the deer was still standing on the rock, possibly congratulating itself on having frightened me away. When some weeks later I related the occurrence to the Game Warden of Kashmir he expressed great regret at my not having shot the deer, and was very anxious to know the exact locality in which I had seen it, but as my memory for places, and my description of localities, is regrettably faulty, I do not think that particular albino musk-deer is gracing any museum.

Male leopards are very resentful of others of their kind in the area they consider to be their own. True, the man-eater's territory extended over an area of five hundred square miles in which there were possibly many other male leopards; still, he had been in this particular area for several weeks, and might very reasonably consider it his own. And again, the mating season was only just over, and the leopard might mistake my call for the call of a female in search of a mate, so waiting until it was quite dark I called and, to my surprise and delight, was immediately answered by a leopard some four hundred yards below and a little to the right.

The ground between us was strewn with great rocks and overgrown with matted thorn-bushes, and I knew the leopard would not come in a straight line towards me, and that he would probably skirt round the broken ground and come up a subsidiary ridge to the one my tree was on; this I found, when next he called, that he was doing. Five minutes later I located his call as coming from the path that, starting from my tree, ran across the face of the hill, about two hundred yards away. This call I answered, to give the leopard direction. Three, or it may have been four, minutes later, he called again from a distance of a hundred yards.

It was a dark night and I had an electric torch lashed to the side of my rifle, and my thumb on the push button. From the root of the tree the path ran in a straight line for fifty yards, to where there was a sharp bend in it. It would not be possible for me to know when or where to direct the beam of the torch on this part of the path, so I should have to wait until the leopard was on the goat.

Just beyond the bend, and only sixty yards away, the leopard again called, and was answered by another leopard far up the mountainside. A complication as unexpected as it was unfortunate, for my leopard was too close now for me to call, and as he had last heard me from a distance of two hundred yards he would naturally assume that the coy female had removed herself farther up the hill and was calling to him to join her there. There was, however, just a possibility of his continuing along the path to its junction with the path coming down the hill, in which case he would be sure to kill the goat, even if he had no use for it. But the goat's luck was in, and mine out, for the leopard cut across the angle formed by the two paths, and the next time he called he was a hundred yards farther from me, and a hundred yards nearer his prospective coaxing mate. The calling of the two leopards drew nearer and nearer together, and finally stopped. After a long period of silence the caterwauling of these two giant cats came floating down to me from where I judged the grassland ended and the dense forest began.

The leopard's luck too was unfortunately in, in more ways than one, not least of all because it was dark, for leopards when courting are very easy to shoot. The same can be said of tigers, but the sportsman who goes on foot to look for courting tigers should be quite sure that he wants to see them, for a tigress – never a tiger – is very sensitive at these times, and quite understandably so, for males of the cat tribe are rough in their courting, and do not know how sharp their claws are.

The leopard had not died, nor would he die that night, but maybe he would die the next day, or the day after, for his sands were running out; and so for a long moment I thought were mine, for without any warning a sudden blast of wind struck the tree, and my heels and my head changed their relative position with the land of Garhwal. For seconds I thought it impossible for the tree to regain its upright position, or for me to retain contact with it. When the pressure eased, the tree and I got back to where we were before the wind struck us, and fearing that worse might follow, I hurriedly tied the rifle to a branch, to have the use of both hands. The pine had possibly withstood many windstorms equally bad, if not worse, but never with a human being on it to add weight and increase wind-pressure. When the rifle was safe, I climbed out on to one branch after another, and broke off all the tassels of pine-needles that I could reach. It may only have been my imagination, but after I had lightened the tree it did not appear to heel over as dangerously as it had at first done. Fortunately the pine was comparatively young and supple, and its roots firm set, for it was tossed about like a blade of grass for an hour and then, as suddenly as it had started, the wind died down. There was no possibility of the leopard returning, so, after I had smoked a cigarette, I followed the goat into the land of dreams.

As the sun was rising a cooee brought me back to within fifty feet of earth, and under the tree were my two companions of the previous evening, reinforced by two youths from their village. When they saw that I was awake they asked whether I had heard the leopards during the night, and what had happened to the tree, and were hugely amused when I told them I had had a friendly conversation with the leopards, and that having nothing else to do I had amused myself by breaking the branches of the tree. I then asked them if by chance they had noticed that there had been some little wind during the night, on which one of the youths answered, 'A little wind, sahib! Such a big wind has never been known, and it has blown away my hut!' To which his companion rejoined, 'That is no matter for regret, sahib, for Sher Singh has long been threatening to rebuild his hut, and the wind has saved him the trouble of dismantling the old one.'

## 14

## *The Chowgarh Tigers*

I

The map of Eastern Kumaon that hangs on the wall before me is marked with a number of crosses, and below each cross is a date. These crosses indicate the locality, and the date, of the officially recorded human victims of the man-eating tiger of Chowgarh. There are sixty-four crosses on the map. I do not claim this as being a correct tally, for the map was posted up by me for two years, and during this period not all kills were reported to me; further, victims who were only mauled, and who died subsequently, have not been awarded a cross and a date.

The first cross is dated 15 December 1925, and the last 21 March 1930. The distance between the extreme crosses, north to south, is fifty miles, and east to west, thirty miles, an area of 1,500 square miles of mountain and vale where the snow lies deep during winter, and the valleys are scorching hot in summer. Over this area the Chowgarh tiger had established a reign of terror. Villages of varying size, some with a population of a hundred or more, and others with only a small family or two, are scattered throughout the area. Footpaths, beaten hard by bare feet, connect the villages. Some of these paths pass through thick forests, and when a man-eater renders their passage dangerous inter-village communication is carried on by shouting. Standing on a commanding point, maybe a big rock or the roof of a house, a man cooees to attract the attention of the people in a neighbouring village, and when the cooee is answered, the message is shouted across in a high-pitched voice. From village to village the message is tossed, and is broadcast throughout large areas in an incredibly short space of time.

It was at a District Conference in February 1929 that I found myself committed to have a try for this tiger. There were at that time three man-eaters in the Kumaon Division, and as the Chowgarh tiger had done most damage I promised to go in pursuit of it first.

The map with the crosses and dates, furnished to me by Government, showed that the man-eater was most active in the villages on the north and east face of the Kala Agar ridge. This ridge, some forty miles in length, rises to a height of 8,500 feet and is thickly wooded along the crest. A forest road runs along the north face of the ridge, in some places passing for miles through dense forests of oak and rhododendron, and in others forming a boundary between the forest and cultivated land. In one place the road forms a loop, and in this loop is situated the Kala Agar Forest Bungalow. This bungalow was my objective, and after a four-days' march, culminating in a stiff climb of 4,000 feet, I arrived at it one evening in April 1929. The last human victim in this area was a young man of twenty-two, who had been killed while out grazing cattle, and while I was having breakfast, the morning after my arrival, the grandmother of the young man came to see me.

She informed me that the man-eater had, without any provocation, killed the only relative she had in the world. After giving me her grandson's history from the day he was born, and extolling his virtues, she pressed me to accept her three milch buffaloes to use as bait for the tiger, saying that if I killed the tiger with the help of her buffaloes she would have the satisfaction of feeling that she had assisted in avenging her grandson. These full-grown animals were of no use to me, but knowing that refusal to accept them would give offence, I thanked the old lady and assured her I would draw on her for bait as soon as I had used up the four young male buffaloes I had brought with me from Naini Tal. The Headmen of nearby villages had now assembled, and from them I learned that the tiger had last been seen ten days previously in a village twenty miles away, on the eastern slope of the ridge, where it had killed and eaten a man and his wife.

A trail ten days old was not worth following up, and after a long discussion with the Headmen I decided to make for Dalkania village on the eastern side of the ridge. Dalkania is ten miles from Kala Agar, and about the same distance from the village where the man and his wife had been killed.

From the number of crosses Dalkania and the villages adjoining it had earned, it appeared that the tiger had its headquarters in the vicinity of these villages.

After breakfast next morning I left Kala Agar and followed the forest road, which I was informed would take me to the end of the ridge, where I should have to leave the road and take a path two miles downhill to Dalkania. This road, running right to the end of the ridge through dense forest, was very little used, and, examining it for tracks as I went along, I arrived at about 2 p.m. at the point where the path took off. Here I met a number of men from Dalkania. They had heard – via the cooee method of communication – of my intention of camping at their village and had come up to the ridge to inform me that the tiger had that morning attacked a party of women, while they had been cutting their crops in a village ten miles to the north of Dalkania.

The men carrying my camp equipment had done eight miles and were quite willing to carry on, but on learning from the villagers that the path to this village, ten miles away, was very rough and ran through dense forest I decided to send my men with the villagers to Dalkania, and visit the scene of the tiger's attack alone. My servant immediately set about preparing a substantial meal for me, and at 3 p.m., having fortified myself, I set out on my ten-mile walk. Ten miles under favourable conditions is a comfortable two-and-a-half-hours' walk, but here the conditions were anything but favourable. The track running along the east face of the hill wound in and out through deep ravines and was bordered alternately by rocks, dense undergrowth, and trees; and when every obstruction capable of concealing sudden death, in the form of a hungry man-eater, had to be approached with caution, progress was of necessity slow. I was still several miles from my objective when the declining day warned me it was time to call a halt.

In any other area, sleeping under the stars on a bed of dry leaves would have ensured a restful night, but here, to sleep on the ground would have been to court death in a very unpleasant form. Long practice in selecting a suitable tree, and the ability to dispose myself comfortably in it, has made sleeping up aloft a simple matter. On this occasion I selected an oak tree, and, with the rifle tied securely to a branch, had been asleep for some hours when I was awakened by the rustling of several animals under the tree. The sound moved on, and presently I heard the scraping of claws on bark and realized that a family of bears were climbing some *karphal*[1] trees I had noticed growing a little way down the hillside. Bears are very quarrelsome when feeding, and sleep was impossible until they had eaten their fill and moved on.

The sun had been up a couple of hours when I arrived at the village, which consisted of two huts and a cattle-shed, in a clearing of five acres surrounded by forest. The small community were in a state of terror and were overjoyed to see me. The wheat-field, a few yards from the

[1] *Karphal* is found on our hills at an elevation of 6,000 feet. The tree grows to a height of about forty feet and produces a small red and very sweet berry, which is greatly fancied by both human beings and bears.

huts, where the tiger, with belly to ground, had been detected only just in time, stalking the three women cutting the crop, was eagerly pointed out to me. The man who had seen the tiger, and given the alarm, told me the tiger had retreated into the jungle, where it had been joined by a second tiger, and that the two animals had gone down the hillside into the valley below. The occupants of the two huts had had no sleep, for the tigers, baulked of their prey, had called at short intervals throughout the night, and had only ceased calling a little before my arrival. This statement, that there were two tigers, confirmed the reports I had already received that the man-eater was accompanied by a full-grown cub.

Our hill folk are very hospitable, and when the villagers learned that I had spent the night in the jungle, and that my camp was at Dalkania, they offered to prepare a meal for me. This I knew would strain the resources of the small community, so I asked for a dish of tea, but as there was no tea in the village I was given a drink of fresh milk sweetened to excess with jaggery, a very satisfying and not unpleasant drink – when one gets used to it. At the request of my hosts I mounted guard while the remaining portion of the wheat crop was cut; and at midday, taking the good wishes of the people with me, I went down into the valley in the direction in which the tigers had been heard calling.

The valley, starting from the watershed of the three rivers, Ladhya, Nandhour, and Eastern Goula, runs south-west for twenty miles and is densely wooded. Tracking was impossible, and my only hope of seeing the tigers was to attract them to myself, or, helped by the jungle folk, to stalk them.

To those of you who may be inclined to indulge in the sport of man-eater hunting on foot, it will be of interest to know that the birds and animals of the jungle, and the four winds of heaven, play a very important part in this form of sport. This is not the place to give the names of the jungle folk on whose alarm-calls the sportsman depends, to a great extent, for his safety and knowledge of his quarry's movements; for, in a country in which a walk up or down hill of three or four miles might mean a difference in altitude of as many thousand feet, the variation in fauna, in a well-stocked area, is considerable. The wind, however, at all altitudes, remains a constant factor, and a few words relevant to its importance in connexion with man-eater hunting on foot will not be out of place.

Tigers do not know that human beings have no sense of smell, and when a tiger becomes a man-eater it treats human beings exactly as it treats wild animals; that is, it approaches its intended victims upwind, or lies up in wait for them downwind.

The significance of this will be apparent when it is realized that, while the sportsman is trying to get a sight of the tiger, the tiger in all probability is trying to stalk the sportsman, or is lying up in wait for him. The contest, owing to the tiger's height, colouring, and ability to move without making a sound, would be very unequal were it not for the wind factor operating in favour of the sportsman.

In all cases where killing is done by stalking or stealth, the victim is approached from behind. This being so, it would be suicidal for the sportsman to enter dense jungle, in which he had every reason to believe a man-eater was lurking, unless he was capable of making full use of the currents of air. For example, assuming that the sportsman has to proceed, owing to the nature of the ground, in the direction from which the wind is blowing, the danger would lie behind him, where he would be least able to deal with it, but by frequently tacking across the wind he could keep the danger alternately to right and left of him. In print this scheme may not appear very attractive, but in practice it works; and, short of walking backwards, I do not know of a better or safer method of going upwind through dense cover in which a hungry man-eater is lurking.

By evening I had reached the upper end of the valley, without having seen the tigers and without having received any indication from bird or animal of their presence in the jungle. The only habitation then in sight was a cattle-shed, high up on the north side of the valley.

I was careful in the selection of a tree on this second night, and was rewarded by an undisturbed night's rest. Not long after dark the tigers called, and a few minutes later two shots from a muzzle-loader came echoing down the valley, followed by a lot of shouting from the graziers at the cattle station. Thereafter the night was silent.

By the afternoon of the following day I had explored every bit of the valley, and I was making my way up a grassy slope intent on rejoining my men at Dalkania when I heard a long-drawn-out cooee from the direction of the cattle-shed. The cooee was repeated, and on my sending back an answering call I saw a man climb on a projecting rock, and from this vantage point he shouted across the valley to ask if I was the sahib who had come from Naini Tal to shoot the man-eater. On my telling him I was that sahib, he informed me that his cattle had stampeded out of a ravine on my side of the valley at about midday, and that when he counted them on arrival at the cattle station he found that one – a white cow – was missing.

He suspected that the cow had been killed by the tigers he had heard calling the previous night, half a mile to the west of where I was standing. Thanking him for his information, I set off to investigate the ravine. I had gone but a short distance along the edge of the ravine when I came on the tracks of the stampeding cattle, and following these tracks back I had no difficulty in finding the spot where the cow had been killed. After killing the cow the tigers had taken it down the steep hillside into the ravine. An approach along the drag was not advisable, so going down into the valley I made a wide detour, and approached the spot where I expected the kill to be from the other side of the ravine. This side of the ravine was less steep than the side down which the kill had been taken, and was deep in young bracken – ideal ground for stalking over. Step by step, and as silently as a shadow, I made my way through the bracken, which reached above my waist, and when I was some thirty yards from the bed of the ravine a movement in front of me caught my eye. A white leg was suddenly thrust up into the air and violently agitated, and next moment there was a deep-throated growl – the tigers were on the kill and were having a difference of opinion over some toothsome morsel.

For several minutes I stood perfectly still; the leg continued to be agitated, but the growl was not repeated. A nearer approach was not advisable, for even if I succeeded in covering the thirty yards without being seen, and managed to kill one of the tigers, the other, as likely as not, would blunder into me, and the ground I was on would give me no chance of defending myself. Twenty yards to my left front, and about the same distance from the tigers, there was an outcrop of rock, some ten to fifteen feet high. If I could reach this rock without being seen, I should in all probability get an easy shot at the tigers. Dropping on hands and knees, and pushing the rifle before me, I crawled through the bracken to the shelter of the rock, paused a minute to regain my breath and make quite sure the rifle was loaded, and then climbed the rock. When my eyes were level with the top I looked over and saw the two tigers.

One was eating the hindquarters of the cow, while the other was lying nearby licking its paws. Both tigers appeared to be about the same size, but the one that was licking its paws was several shades lighter than the other; and concluding that her light colouring was due to age and that she was the old man-eater, I aligned the sights very carefully on her, and fired. At my shot she reared up and fell backwards, while the other bounded down the ravine and was out of sight before I could press the second trigger. The tiger I had shot did not move again, and after pelting it with stones to make sure it was dead, I approached and met with a great disappointment; for a glance at close quarters showed me I had made a mistake and shot the cub – a mistake that during the ensuing twelve months cost the district fifteen lives and incidentally nearly cost me my own life.

Disappointment was to a certain extent mitigated by the thought that this young tigress, even if she had not actually killed any human beings herself, had probably assisted her old mother to kill (this assumption I later found to be correct), and in any case, having been nurtured on human flesh, she could – to salve my feelings – be classed as a potential man-eater.

Skinning a tiger with assistance on open ground and with the requisite appliances is an easy job, but here the job was anything but easy, for I was alone, surrounded by thick cover, and my only appliance was a penknife; and though there was no actual danger to be apprehended from the man-eater, for tigers never kill in excess of their requirements, there was the uneasy feeling in the back of my mind that the tigress had returned and was watching my every movement.

The sun was near setting before the arduous task was completed, and as I should have to spend yet another night in the jungle I decided to remain where I was. The tigress was a very old animal, as I could see from her pug marks, and having lived all her life in a district in which there are nearly as many fire-arms as men to use them, had nothing to learn about men and their ways. Even so, there was just a chance that she might return to the kill some time during the night, and remain in the vicinity until light came in the morning.

My selection of a tree was of necessity limited, and the one I spent that night in proved, by morning, to be the most uncomfortable tree I have ever spent twelve hours in. The tigress called at intervals throughout the night, and as morning drew near the calling became fainter and fainter, and eventually died away on the ridge above me.

Cramped, and stiff, and hungry – I had been without food for sixty-four hours – and with my clothes clinging to me – it had rained for an hour during the night – I descended from the tree when objects were clearly visible, and, after tying the tiger's skin up in my coat, set off for Dalkania.

I have never weighed a tiger's skin when green, and if the skin, plus the head and paws, which I carried for fifteen miles that day, weighed 40 pounds at the start, I would have taken my oath it weighed 200 pounds before I reached my destination.

In a courtyard, flagged with great slabs of blue slate, and common to a dozen houses, I found my men in conference with a hundred or more villagers. My approach, along a yard-wide lane between two houses, had not been observed, and the welcome I received when, bedraggled and covered with blood, I staggered into the circle of squatting men will live in my memory as long as memory lasts.

My 40-pound tent had been pitched in a field of stubble a hundred yards from the village, and I had hardly reached it before tea was laid out for me on a table improvised out of a couple of suitcases and planks borrowed from the village. I was told later by the villagers that my men, who had been with me for years and had accompanied me on several similar expeditions, refusing to believe that the man-eater had claimed me as a victim, had kept a kettle on the boil night and day in anticipation of my return, and, further, had stoutly opposed the Headmen of Dalkania and the adjoining villages sending a report to Almora and Naini Tal that I was missing.

A hot bath, taken of necessity in the open and in full view of the village – I was too dirty and too tired to care who saw me – was followed by an ample dinner, and I was thinking of turning in for the night when a flash of lightning, succeeded by a loud peal of thunder, heralded the approach of a storm. Tent-pegs are of little use in a field, so long stakes were hurriedly procured and securely driven into the ground, and to these stakes the tent-ropes were tied. For further safety all the available ropes in camp were criss-crossed over the tent and lashed to the stakes. The storm of wind and rain lasted an hour and was one of the worst the little tent had ever weathered. Several of the guy-ropes were torn from the canvas, but the stakes and criss-cross ropes held. Most of my things were soaked through, and a little stream several inches deep was running from end to end of the tent; my bed, however, was comparatively dry, and by 10 o'clock my men were safely lodged behind locked doors in the house the villagers had placed at their disposal, while I, with a loaded rifle for company, settled down to a sleep which lasted for twelve hours.

The following day was occupied in drying my kit and in cleaning and pegging out the tiger's skin. While these operations were in progress the villagers, who had taken a holiday from their field work, crowded round to hear my experiences and to tell me theirs. Every man present had lost one or more relatives, and several bore tooth and claw marks, inflicted by the man-eater, which they will carry to their graves. My regret at having lost an opportunity of killing the man-eater was not endorsed by the assembled men. True, there had originally been only one man-eater; but, of recent months, rescue parties who had gone out to recover the remains of human victims had found two tigers on the kills, and only a fortnight previously a man and his wife had been killed simultaneously, which was proof sufficient for them that both tigers were established man-eaters.

My tent was on a spur of the hill, and commanded an extensive view. Immediately below me was the valley of the Nandhour river, with a hill, devoid of any cultivation, rising to a height of 9,000 feet on the far side. As I sat on the edge of the terraced fields that evening, with a pair of good binoculars in my hand and the Government map spread out beside me, the villagers pointed out the exact positions where twenty human beings had been killed during the past three years. These kills were more or less evenly distributed over an area of forty square miles.

The forests in this area were open to grazing, and on the cattle-paths leading to them I decided to tie up my four young buffaloes.

During the following ten days no news was received of the tigress, and I spent the time in visiting the buffaloes in the morning, searching the forests in the day, and tying out the buffaloes in the evening. On the eleventh day my hopes were raised by the report that a cow had been killed in a ravine on the hill above my tent. A visit to the kill, however, satisfied me the cow had been killed by an old leopard, whose pug marks I had repeatedly seen. The villagers complained that the leopard had for several years been taking heavy toll of their cattle and goats, so I decided to sit up for him. A shallow cave close to the dead cow gave me the cover I needed. I had not been long in the cave when I caught sight of the leopard coming down the opposite side of the ravine, and I was raising my rifle for a shot when I heard a very agitated voice from the direction of the village calling to me.

There could be but one reason for this urgent call, and grabbing up my hat I dashed out of the cave, much to the consternation of the leopard, who first flattened himself out on the ground and then, with an angry woof, went bounding back the way he had come, while I scrambled up my side of the ravine; and, arriving at the top, shouted to the man that I was coming, and set off at top speed to join him.

The man had run all the way uphill from the village, and when he regained his breath he informed me that a woman had just been killed by the man-eater, about half a mile on the far side of the village. As we ran down the hillside I saw a crowd of people collected in the court-yard already alluded to. Once again my approach through the narrow lane was not observed, and looking over the heads of the assembled men I saw a girl sitting on the ground

The upper part of her clothing had been torn off her young body, and, with head thrown back and hands resting on the ground behind to support her, she sat without sound or movement, other than the heaving up and down of her breast, in the hollow of which the blood that was flowing down her face and neck was collecting in a sticky congealed mass.

My presence was soon detected and a way made for me to approach the girl. While I was examining her wounds, a score of people, all talking at the same time, informed me that the attack on the girl had been made on comparatively open ground in full view of a number of people, including the girl's husband; that, alarmed at their combined shouts, the tiger had left the girl and gone off in the direction of the forest; that, leaving the girl for dead where she had fallen, her compan-ions had run back to the village to inform me; that subsequently the girl had regained consciousness and returned to the village; that she would without doubt die of her injuries in a few minutes; and that they would then carry her back to the scene of the attack, and I could sit up over her corpse and shoot the tiger.

While this information was being imparted to me the girl's eyes never left my face and followed my every movement with the liquid pleading gaze of a wounded and frightened animal. Room to move unhampered, quiet to collect my wits, and clean air for the girl to breathe were necessary, and I am afraid the methods I employed to gain them were not as gentle as they might have been. When the last of the men had left in a hurry I set the women, who up to now had remained in the background, to warming water and to tearing my shirt, which was comparatively clean and dry, into bandages, while one girl, who appeared to be on the point of getting hysterics, was bundled off to scour the village for a pair of scissors. The water and bandages were ready before the girl I had sent for the scissors returned with the only pair, she said, the village could produce. They had been found in the house of a tailor, long since dead, and had been used by the widow for digging up potatoes. The rusty blades, some eight inches long, could not be made to meet at any point, and after a vain attempt I decided to leave the thick coils of blood-caked hair alone.

The major wounds consisted of two claw cuts, one starting between the eyes and extending right over the head and down to the nape of the neck, leaving the scalp hanging in two halves, and the other, starting near the first, running across the forehead up to the right ear. In addition to these ugly gaping wounds there were a number of deep scratches on the right breast, right shoulder and neck, and one deep cut on the back of the right hand, evidently inflicted when the girl had put up her hand in a vain attempt to shield her head.

A doctor friend whom I had once taken out tiger-shooting on foot had, on our return after an exciting morning, presented me with a two-ounce bottle of yellow fluid which he advised me to carry whenever I went out shooting. I had carried the bottle in the inner pocket of my shooting jacket for over a year and a portion of the fluid had evaporated; but the bottle was still three-parts full, and after I had washed the girl's head and body I knocked the neck off the bottle and poured the contents, to the last drop, into the wounds. This done, I bandaged the head, to try to keep the scalp in position, and then picked up the girl and carried her to her home – a single room combining living quarters, kitchen, and nursery – with the women following behind.

Dependent from a rafter near the door was an open basket, the occupant of which was now clamouring to be fed. This was a complication with which I could not deal, so I left the solution of it to the assembled women. Ten days later, when on the eve of my departure I visited the girl for the last time, I found her sitting on the doorstep of her home with the baby asleep in her lap.

Her wounds, except for a sore at the nape of her neck where the tiger's claws had sunk deepest into the flesh, were all healed, and when parting her great wealth of raven-black hair to show me where the scalp had made a perfect join, she said, with a smile, that she was very glad her young sister had – quite by mistake – borrowed the wrong pair of scissors from the tailor's widow (for a shorn head here is the sign of widowhood). If these lines should ever be read by my friend the doctor, I should like him to know that the little bottle of yellow fluid he so thoughtfully provided for me saved the life of a very brave young mother.

While I had been attending to the girl my men had procured a goat. Following back the blood trail made by the girl I found the spot where the attack had taken place, and tying the goat to a bush I climbed into a stunted oak, the only tree in the vicinity, and prepared for an all-night vigil. Sleep, even in snatches, was not possible, for my seat was only a few feet from the ground, and the tigress was still without her dinner. However, I neither saw nor heard anything throughout the night.

On examining the ground in the morning – I had not had time to do this the previous evening – I found that the tigress, after attacking the girl, had gone up the valley for half a mile to where a cattle-track crossed the Nandhour river. This track it had followed for two miles, to its junction with the forest road on the ridge above Dalkania. Here on the hard ground I lost the tracks.

For two days the people in all the surrounding villages kept as close to their habitations as the want of sanitary conveniences permitted, and then on the third day news was brought to me by four runners that the man-eater had claimed a victim at Lohali, a village five miles to the south of Dalkania. The runners stated that the distance by the forest road was ten miles, but only five by a short cut by which they proposed taking me back. My preparations were soon made, and a little after midday I set off with my four guides.

A very stiff climb of two miles brought us to the crest of the long ridge south of Dalkania and in view of the valley three miles below, where the 'kill' was reported to have taken place. My guides could give me no particulars. They lived in a small village a mile on the near side of Lohali, and at 10 a.m. a message had come to them – in the manner already described – that a woman of Lohali had been killed by the man-eater, and they were instructed to convey this information to me at Dalkania.

The top of the hill on which we were standing was bare of trees, and, while I regained my breath and had a smoke, my companions pointed out the landmarks. Close to where we were resting, and under the shelter of a great rock, there was a small ruined hut, with a circular thorn enclosure near by. Questioned about this hut, the men told me the following story. Four years previously a Bhutia (a man from across the border), who had all the winter been sending packages of gur, salt, and other commodities from the bazaars at the foothills into the interior of the district, had built the hut with the object of resting and fattening his flock of goats through the summer and rains, and getting them fit for the next winter's work. After a few weeks the goats wandered down the hill and damaged my informants' crops, and when they came up to lodge a protest, they found the hut empty, and the fierce sheep-dog these men invariably keep with them to guard their camps at night, chained to an iron stake and dead. Foul play was suspected, and next day men were collected from adjoining villages and a search organized. Pointing to an oak tree scored by lightning and distant some four hundred yards, my informants said that under it the remains of the man – his skull and a few splinters of bone – and his clothes had been found. This was the Chowgarh man-eater's first human victim.

There was no way of descending the precipitous hill from where we were sitting, and the men informed me we should have to proceed half a mile along the ridge to where we should find a very steep and rough track which would take us straight down, past their village, to Lohali, which we could see in the valley below. We had covered about half the distance we had to go along the ridge, when all at once, and without being able to ascribe any reason for it, I felt we were being followed. Arguing with myself against this feeling was of no avail; there was only one man-eater in all this area and she had procured a kill three miles away, which she was not likely to leave. However, the uneasy feeling persisted, and as we were now at the widest part of the grassy ridge I made the men sit down, instructing them not to move until I returned, and myself set out on a tour of investigation. Retracing my steps to where we had first come out on the ridge, I entered the jungle and carefully worked round the open ground and back to where the men were sitting. No alarm-call of animal or bird indicated that a tiger was anywhere in the vicinity, but from there on I made the four men walk in front of me, while I brought up the rear, with thumb on safety-catch and a constant look-out behind.

When we arrived at the little village my companions had started from, they asked for permission to leave me. I was very glad of this request, for I had a mile of dense scrub jungle to go through, and though the feeling that I was being followed had long since left me, I felt safer and more comfortable with only my own life to guard. A little below the outlying terraced fields, and where the dense scrub started, there was a crystal-clear spring of water, from which the village drew its water supply. Here, in the soft, wet ground, I found the fresh pug marks of the man-eater.

These pug marks, coming from the direction of the village I was making for, coupled with the uneasy feeling I had experienced on the ridge above, convinced me that something had gone wrong with the 'kill' and that my quest would be fruitless. As I emerged from the scrub jungle I came in view of Lohali, which consisted of five or six small houses. Near the door of one of these houses a group of people were collected.

My approach over the steep, open ground and narrow terraced fields was observed, and a few men detached themselves from the group near the door and advanced to meet me. One of the number, an old man, bent down to touch my feet, and with tears streaming down his cheeks implored me to save the life of his daughter. His story was as short as it was tragic. His daughter, who was a widow and the only relative he had in the world, had gone out at about ten o'clock to collect dry sticks with which to cook their midday meal. A small stream flows through the valley, and on the far side of the stream from the village the hill goes steeply up. On the lower slope of this hill there are a few terraced fields. At the edge of the lowest field, and distant about 150 yards from the home, the woman had started to collect sticks. A little later some women, who were washing their clothes in the stream, heard a scream, and on looking up saw the woman and a tiger disappearing together into the dense thorn-bushes, which extended from the edge of the field right down to the stream. Dashing back to the village, the women raised an alarm. The frightened villagers made no attempt at a rescue, and a message for help was shouted to a village higher up the valley, from where it was tossed back to the village from which the four men had set out to find me. Half an hour after the message had been sent the wounded woman crawled home. Her story was that she had seen the tiger just as it was about to spring on her, and as there was no time to run, she had jumped down the almost perpendicular hillside and while she was in the air the tiger had caught her and they had gone down the hill together. She remembered nothing further until she regained consciousness and found herself near the stream; and, being unable to call for help, she had crawled back to the village on her hands and knees.

We had reached the door of the house while this tale was being told. Making the people stand back from the door – the only opening in the four walls of the room – I drew the blood-stained sheet off the woman, whose pitiful condition I am not going to attempt to describe. Had I been a qualified doctor, armed with modern appliances, instead of just a mere man with a little permanganate of potash in his pocket, I do not think it would have been possible to save the woman's life; for the deep tooth and claw wounds in her face, neck, and other parts of her body had, in that hot unventilated room, already turned septic. Mercifully, she was only semi-conscious. The old father had followed me into the room, and, more for his satisfaction than for any good I thought it would do, I washed the caked blood from the woman's head and body, and cleaned out the wounds as best I could with my handkerchief and a strong solution of permanganate.

It was now too late to think of returning to my camp, and a place would have to be found in which to pass the night. A little way up the stream, and not far from where the women had been washing their clothes, there was a giant pipal tree, with a foot-high masonry platform round it, used by the villagers for religious ceremonies.

I undressed on the platform and bathed in the stream; and when the wind had carried out the functions of a towel, dressed again, put my back to the tree and, laying the loaded rifle by my side, prepared to see the night out. Admittedly, it was an unsuitable place in which to spend the night, but any place was preferable to the village, and that dark room, with its hot fetid atmosphere and swarm of buzzing flies, where a woman in torment fought desperately for breath.

During the night the wailing of women announced that the sufferer's troubles were over, and when I passed through the village at daybreak preparations for the funeral were well advanced.

From the experience of this unfortunate woman, and that of the girl at Dalkania, it was now evident that the old tigress had depended, to a very great extent, on her cub to kill the human beings she attacked. Usually only one out of every hundred people attacked by man-eating tigers escapes, but in the case of this man-eater it was apparent that more people would be mauled than killed outright, and as the nearest hospital was fifty miles away, when I returned to Naini Tal I appealed to Government to send a supply of disinfectants and dressings to all the

Headmen of villages in the area in which the man-eater was operating. On my subsequent visit I was glad to learn that the request had been complied with and that the disinfectants had saved the lives of a number of people.

I stayed at Dalkania for another week and announced on a Saturday that I would leave for home the following Monday. I had now been in the man-eater's domain for close on a month, and the constant strain of sleeping in an open tent and of walking endless miles during the day, with the prospect of every step being the last, was beginning to tell on my nerves. The villagers received my announcement with consternation and only desisted from trying to make me change my decision when I promised them I would return at the first opportunity.

After breakfast on Sunday morning the Headmen of Dalkania paid me a visit and requested me to shoot them some game before I left. The request was gladly acceded to, and half an hour later, accompanied by four villagers and one of my own men, and armed with a ·275 rifle and a clip of cartridges, I set off for the hill on the far slope of the Nandhour river, on the upper slopes of which I had, from my camp, frequently seen ghooral feeding.

One of the villagers accompanying me was a tall, gaunt man with a terribly disfigured face. He had been a constant visitor to my camp, and finding in me a good listener had told and retold his encounter with the man-eater so often that I could, without effort, repeat the whole story in my sleep. The encounter had taken place four years previously and is best told in his own words.

'Do you see that pine-tree, sahib, at the bottom of the grassy slope on the shoulder of the hill? Yes, the pine-tree with a big white rock to the east of it. Well, it was at the upper edge of the grassy slope that the man-eater attacked me. The grassy slope is as perpendicular as the wall of a house, and none but a hill-man could find foothold on it. My son, who was eight years of age at the time, and I had cut grass on that slope on the day of my misfortune, carrying the grass up in armfuls to the belt of trees where the ground is level.

'I was stooping down at the very edge of the slope, tying the grass into a big bundle, when the tiger sprang at me and buried its teeth, one under my right eye, one in my chin, and the other two here at the back of my neck. The tiger's mouth struck me with a great blow and I fell over on my back, while the tiger lay on top of me, chest to chest, with its stomach between my legs. When falling backwards I had flung out my arms and my right hand had come in contact with an oak sapling. As my fingers grasped the sapling, an idea came to me. My legs were free, and if I could draw them up and insert my feet under and against the tiger's belly, I might be able to push the tiger off, and run away. The pain, as the tiger crushed all the bones on the right side of my face, was terrible; but I did not lose consciousness, for you see, sahib, at that time I was a young man, and in all the hills there was no one to compare with me in strength. Very slowly, so as not to anger the tiger, I drew my legs up on either side of it, and gently, very gently, inserted my bare feet against its belly. Then placing my left hand against its chest and pushing and kicking upwards with all my might, I lifted the tiger right off the ground and, we being on the very edge of the perpendicular hillside, the tiger went crashing down and belike would have taken me with him had my hold on the sapling not been a good one.

'My son had been too frightened to run away, and when the tiger had gone, I took his loincloth from him and wrapped it round my head, and, holding his hand, I walked back to the village. Arrived at my home, I told my wife to call all my friends together, for I wished to see their faces before I died. When my friends were assembled and saw my condition they wanted to put me on a charpoy and carry me fifty miles to the Almora hospital, but this I would not consent to; for my suffering was great, and being assured that my time had come I wanted to die where I had been born, and where I had lived all my life. Water was brought, for I was thirsty and my head was on fire, but when it was poured into my mouth, it all flowed out through the holes in my neck. Thereafter, for a period beyond measure, there was great confusion in my mind, and much pain in my head and in my neck, and while I waited and longed for death to end my sufferings my wounds healed of themselves, and I became well.

'And now, sahib, I am, as you see me, old and thin and with white hair, and a face that no man can look on without repulsion. My enemy lives and continues to claim victims; but do not be deceived into thinking it is a tiger, for it is no tiger but an evil spirit who, when it craves for human flesh and blood, takes on for a little while the semblance of a tiger. But they say you are a sadhu, sahib, and the spirits that guard sadhus are more powerful than this evil spirit, as is proved by the fact that you spent three days and three nights alone in the jungle, and came out – as your men said you would – alive and unhurt.'

Looking at the great frame of the man, it was easy to picture him as having been a veritable giant. And a giant in strength he must have been, for no man, unless he had been endowed with strength far above the average, could have lifted the tigress into the air, torn its hold from the side of his head, carrying away, as it did, half his face with it, and hurled it down the precipitous hill.

My gaunt friend constituted himself our guide and, with a beautifully polished axe, with long tapering handle, over his shoulder, led us by devious steep paths to the valley below. Fording the Nandhour river, we crossed several wide terraced fields, now gone out of cultivation for fear of the man-eater, and on reaching the foot of the hill started what proved to be a very stiff climb, through forest, to the grass slopes above. Gaunt my friend may have been, but he lacked nothing in wind, and tough as I was it was only by calling frequent halts – to admire the view – that I was able to keep up with him.

Emerging from the tree forest, we went diagonally across the grassy slope, in the direction of a rock cliff that extended upwards for a thousand feet or more. It was on this cliff, sprinkled over with tufts of short grass, that I had seen ghooral feeding from my tent. We had covered a few hundred yards when one of these small mountain goats started up out of the ravine, and at my shot crumpled up and slipped back out of sight. Alarmed by the report of the rifle, another ghooral, that had evidently been lying asleep at the foot of the cliff, sprang to his feet and went up the rock face, as only he or his big brother, the tahr, could have done. As he climbed upwards I lay down and, putting the sight to 200 yards, waited for him to stop. This he presently did, coming out on a projecting rock to look down on us. At my shot he staggered, regained his footing, and very slowly continued his climb. At the second shot he fell, hung for a second or two on a narrow ledge, and then fell through space to the grassy slope from whence he had started. Striking the ground he rolled over and over, passing within a hundred yards of us, and eventually came to rest on a cattle-track a hundred and fifty yards below.

I have only once, in all the years I have been shooting, witnessed a similar sight to the one we saw during the next few minutes, and on that occasion the marauder was a leopard.

The ghooral had hardly come to rest when a big Himalayan bear came lumbering out of a ravine on the far side of the grassy slope and, with never a pause or backward look, came at a fast trot along the cattle-track. On reaching the dead goat he sat down and took it into his lap, and as he started nosing the goat, I fired. Maybe I hurried over my shot, or allowed too much for refraction; anyway, the bullet went low and struck the bear in the stomach instead of in the chest. To the six of us who were intently watching, it appeared that the bear took the smack of the bullet as an assault from the ghooral, for, rearing up, he flung the animal from him and came galloping along the track, emitting angry grunts. As he passed a hundred yards below us I fired my fifth and last cartridge, the bullet, as I found later, going through the fleshy part of his hindquarters.

While the men retrieved the two ghooral, I descended to examine the blood trail. The blood on the track showed the bear to be hard hit, but even so there was danger in following it up with an empty rifle, for bears are bad tempered at the best of times and are very ugly customers to deal with when wounded.

When the men rejoined me a short council of war was held. Camp was three and a half miles away, and as it was now 2 p.m. it would not be possible to fetch more ammunition, track down and kill the bear and get back home by dark; so it was unanimously decided that we should follow up the wounded animal and try to finish it off with stones and the axe.

The hill was steep and fairly free of undergrowth, and by keeping above the bear there was a sporting chance of our being able to accomplish our task without serious mishap. We accordingly set off, I leading the way, followed by three men, the rear being brought up by two men each with a ghooral strapped to his back. Arrived at the spot where I had fired my last shot, additional blood on the track greatly encouraged us. Two hundred yards further on the blood trail led down into a deep ravine. Here we divided up our force, two men crossing to the far side, the owner of the axe and I remaining on the near side, with the men carrying the ghooral following in our rear. On the word being given we started to advance down the hill. In the bed of the ravine, and fifty feet below us, was a dense patch of stunted bamboo, and when a stone was thrown into this thicket, the bear got up with a scream of rage; and six men, putting their best foot foremost, went straight up the hill. I was not trained to this form of exercise, and on looking back to see if the bear was gaining on us, I saw, much to my relief, that he was going as hard downhill as we were going uphill. A shout to my companions, a rapid change of direction, and we were off in full cry and rapidly gaining on our quarry. A few well-aimed shots had been registered, followed by delighted shouts from the marksmen, and angry grunts from the bear, when, at a sharp bend in the ravine, which necessitated a cautious advance, we lost touch with the bear. To have followed the blood trail would have been easy, but here the ravine was full of big rocks, behind any of which the bear might have been lurking, so while the encumbered men sat down for a rest a cast was made on either side of the ravine. While my companion went forward to look down into the ravine, I went to the right to prospect a rocky cliff that went sheer down for some two hundred feet. Holding to a tree for support, I leaned over and saw the bear lying on a narrow ledge forty feet immediately below me. I picked up a stone, about thirty pounds in weight, and, again advancing to the edge and in imminent danger of going over myself, I raised the stone above my head with both hands and hurled it.

The stone struck the ledge a few inches from the bear's head, and scrambling to his feet he disappeared from sight, to reappear a minute later on the side of the hill. Once again the hunt was on. The ground was here more open and less encumbered with rocks, and the four of us who were running light had no difficulty in keeping up with him. For a mile or more we ran him at top speed, until we eventually cleared the forest and emerged on to the terraced fields. Rain-water had cut several deep and narrow channels across the fields, and in one of these channels the bear took cover.

The man with the distorted face was the only armed member of the party and he was unanimously elected executioner. Nothing loth, he cautiously approached the bear, and, swinging his beautifully polished axe aloft, brought the square head down on the bear's skull. The result was as alarming as it was unexpected. The axe-head rebounded off the bear's skull as though it had been struck on a block of rubber, and with a scream of rage the animal reared up on his hind legs. Fortunately, he did not follow up his advantage, for we were bunched together and in trying to run got in each other's way.

The bear did not appear to like this open ground, and after going a short way down the channel again took cover. It was now my turn for the axe. The bear, however, having once been struck, resented my approach, and it was only after a great deal of manœuvring that I eventually got within striking distance. It had been my ambition when a boy to be a lumberman in Canada, and I had attained sufficient proficiency with an axe to split a matchstick. I had no fear, therefore, as the owner had, of the axe glancing off and getting damaged on the stones, and the moment I got within reach I buried the entire blade in the bear's skull.

Himalayan bearskins are very greatly prized by our hill folk, and the owner of the axe was a very proud and envied man when I told him he could have the skin in addition to a double share of the ghooral meat. Leaving the men, whose numbers were being rapidly augmented by new arrivals from the village, to skin and divide up the bag, I climbed up to the village and paid, as already related, a last visit to the injured girl. The day had been a strenuous one, and if the man-eater had paid me a visit that night she would have caught me napping.

On the road I had taken when coming to Dalkania there were several long, stiff climbs up treeless hills, and when I mentioned the discomforts of this road to the villagers they had suggested that I should go back via Haira Khan. This route would necessitate only one climb to the ridge above the village, from where it was downhill all the way to Ranibagh, whence I could complete the journey to Naini Tal by car.

I had warned my men overnight to prepare for an early start, and a little before sunrise, leaving them to pack up and follow me, I said goodbye to my friends at Dalkania and started on the two-mile climb to the forest road on the ridge above. The footpath I took was not the one by which my men, and later I, had arrived at Dalkania, but was the one the villagers used when going to, and returning from, the bazaars in the foothills.

The path wound in and out of deep ravines, through thick oak and pine forests and dense undergrowth. There had been no news of the tigress for a week. This absence of news made me all the more careful, and an hour after leaving camp I arrived without mishap at an open glade near the top of the hill, within a hundred yards of the forest road.

The glade was pear-shaped, roughly a hundred yards long and fifty yards wide, with a stagnant pool of rain-water in the centre of it. Sambur and other game used this pool as a drinking place and wallow, and, curious to see the tracks round it, I left the path, which skirted the left-hand side of the glade and passed close under a cliff of rock which extended up to the road. As I approached the pool I saw the pug marks of the tigress in the soft earth at the edge of the water. She had approached the pool from the same direction as I had, and, evidently disturbed by me, had crossed the water and gone into the dense tree and scrub jungle on the right-hand side of the glade. A great chance lost, for had I kept as careful a look-out in front as I had behind I should have seen her before she saw me. However, though I had missed a chance, the advantages were now all on my side and distinctly in my favour.

The tigress had seen me, or she would not have crossed the pool and hurried for shelter, as her tracks showed she had done. Having seen me, she had also seen that I was alone, and, watching me from cover, as she undoubtedly was, she would assume I was going to the pool to drink as she had done. My movements up to this had been quite natural, and if I could continue to make her think I was unaware of her presence, she would possibly give me a second chance. Stooping down and keeping a very sharp look-out from under my hat, I coughed several times, splashed the water about, and then, moving very slowly and gathering dry sticks on the way, I went to the foot of the steep rock. Here I built a small fire, and putting my back to the rock lit a cigarette. By the time the cigarette had been smoked the fire had burnt out. I then lay down, and pillowing my head on my left arm placed the rifle on the ground with my finger on the trigger.

The rock above me was too steep for any animal to find foothold on. I had therefore only my front to guard, and as the heavy cover no-where approached to within less than twenty yards of my position I was quite safe. I had all this time neither seen nor heard anything; never-theless, I was convinced that the tigress was watching me. The rim of my hat, while effectually shading my eyes, did not obstruct my vision, and inch by inch I scanned every bit of the jungle within my range of view. There was not a breath of wind blowing, and not a leaf or blade of grass stirred. My men, whom I had instructed to keep close together and sing from the time they left camp until they joined me on the forest road, were not due for an hour and a half, and during this time it was more than likely that the tigress would break cover and try to stalk or rush me.

There are occasions when time drags, and others when it flies. My left arm, on which my head was pillowed, had long since ceased to prick and had gone dead, but even so the singing of the men in the valley below reached me all too soon. The voices grew louder, and presently I caught sight of the men as they rounded a sharp bend. It was possibly at this bend that the tigress had seen me as she turned round to retrace her steps after having her drink. Another failure, and the last chance on this trip gone.

After my men had rested we climbed up to the road, and set off on what proved to be a very long twenty-mile march to the Forest Rest House at Haira Khan. After going a couple of hundred yards over open ground, the road entered very thick forest, and here I made the men walk in front while I brought up the rear. We had gone about two miles in this order when, on turning a corner, I saw a man sitting on the road, herding buffaloes. It was now time to call a halt for breakfast, so I asked the man where we could get water. He pointed down the hill straight in front of him, and said there was a spring down there from which his village, which was just round the shoulder of the hill, drew its water supply. There was, however, no necessity for us to go down the hill for water, for if we continued a little further we should find a good spring on the road.

His village was at the upper end of the valley in which the woman of Lohali had been killed the previous week, and he told me that nothing had been heard of the man-eater since, and added that the animal was possibly now at the other end of the district. I disabused his mind on this point by telling him about the fresh pug marks I had seen at the pool, and advised him very strongly to collect his buffaloes and return to the village. His buffaloes, some ten in number, were straggling up towards the road and he said he would leave as soon as they had grazed up to where he was sitting. Handing him a cigarette, I left him with a final warning. What occurred after I left was related to me by the men of the village when I paid the district a second visit some months later.

When the man eventually got home that day he told the assembled villagers of our meeting, and my warning, and said that after he had watched me go round a bend in the road a hundred yards away he started to light the cigarette I had given him. A wind was blowing, and to protect the flame of the match he bent forward, and while in this position he was seized from behind by the right shoulder and pulled backwards. His first thought was of the party who had just left him, but unfortunately his cry for help was not heard by them. Help, however, was near at hand, for as soon as the buffaloes heard his cry, mingled with the growl of the tigress, they charged on to the road and drove the tigress off. His shoulder and arm were broken, and with great difficulty he managed to climb on the back of one of his brave rescuers, and, followed by the rest of the herd, reached his home. The villagers tied up his wounds as best they could and carried him thirty miles, nonstop, to the Haldwani hospital, where he died shortly after admission.

When Atropos, who snips the threads of life, misses one thread she cuts another, and we who do not know why one thread is missed and another cut call it Fate, Kismet, or what we will.

For a month I had lived in an open tent, a hundred yards from the nearest human being, and from dawn to dusk had wandered through the jungles, and on several occasions had disguised myself as a woman and cut grass in places where no local inhabitant dared to go. During this period the man-eater had, quite possibly, missed many opportunities of adding me to her bag, and now, when making a final effort, she had quite by chance encountered this unfortunate man and claimed him as a victim.

2

The following February I returned to Dalkania. A number of human beings had been killed, and many more wounded, over a wide area since my departure from the district the previous summer, and as the whereabouts of the tigress was not known and the chances in one place were as good as in another, I decided to return and camp on the ground with which I was now familiar.

On my arrival at Dalkania I was told that a cow had been killed the previous evening, on the hill on which the bear hunt had taken place. The men who had been herding the cattle at the time were positive that the animal they had seen killing the cow was a tiger. The kill was lying near some bushes at the edge of a deserted field, and was clearly visible from the spot where my tent was being put up. Vultures were circling over the hill and, looking through my field-glasses, I saw several of these birds perched on a tree to the left of the kill. From the fact that the kill was lying out in the open, and the vultures had not descended on it, I concluded (*a*) that the cow had been killed by a leopard and (*b*) that the leopard was lying up close to the kill.

The ground below the field on which the cow was lying was very steep and overgrown with dense brushwood. The man-eater was still at large, and an approach over this ground was therefore inadvisable.

To the right was a grassy slope, but the ground here was too open to admit of my approaching the kill without being seen. A deep heavily-wooded ravine, starting from near the crest of the hill, ran right down to the Nandhour river, passing within a short distance of the kill. The tree on which the vultures were perched was growing on the edge of this ravine. I decided on this ravine as my line of approach. While I had been planning out the stalk with the assistance of the villagers, who knew every foot of the ground, my men had prepared tea for me. The day was now on the decline, but by going hard I should just have time to visit the kill and return to camp before nightfall.

Before setting off I instructed my men to be on the look-out. If, after hearing a shot, they saw me on the open ground near the kill, three or four of them were immediately to leave camp and, keeping to the open ground, to join me. On the other hand, if I did not fire and failed to return by morning, a search-party was to be organized.

The ravine was overgrown with raspberry bushes and strewn with great rocks, and as the wind was blowing downhill my progress was slow. After a stiff climb I eventually reached the tree on which the vultures were perched, only to find that the kill was not visible from this spot. The deserted field, which through my field-glasses had appeared to be quite straight, I found to be crescent-shaped, ten yards across at its widest part and tapering to a point at both ends. The outer edge was bordered with dense undergrowth, and the hill fell steeply away from the inner edge. Only two-thirds of the field was visible from where I was standing, and in order to see the remaining one-third, on which the kill was lying, it would be necessary either to make a wide detour and approach from the far side or climb the tree on which the vultures were perched.

I decided on the latter course. The cow, as far as I could judge, was about twenty yards from the tree, and it was quite possible that the animal that had killed her was even less than that distance from me. To climb the tree without disturbing the killer would have been an impossible feat, and would not have been attempted had it not been for the vultures. There were by now some twenty of these birds on the tree and their number was being added to by new arrivals, and as the accommodation on the upper branches was limited there was much flapping of wings and quarrelling. The tree was leaning outwards away from the hill, and about ten feet from the ground a great limb projected out over the steep hillside. Hampered with the rifle I had great difficulty in reaching this limb. Waiting until a fresh quarrel had broken out among the vultures, I stepped out along the branch – a difficult balancing feat, where a slip or false step would have resulted in a fall of a hundred or more feet on to the rocks below – reached a fork and sat down.

The kill, from which only a few pounds of flesh had been eaten, was now in full view. I had been in position about ten minutes, and was finding my perch none too comfortable, when two vultures, who had been circling round and were uncertain of their reception on the tree, alighted on the field a short distance from the cow. They had hardly come to rest when they were on the wing again, and at the same moment the bushes on my side of the kill were gently agitated and out into the open stepped a fine male leopard.

Those who have never seen a leopard under favourable conditions in his natural surroundings can have no conception of the grace of movement and beauty of colouring of this the most graceful and the most beautiful of all animals in our Indian jungles. Nor are his attractions limited to outward appearances, for, pound for pound, his strength is second to none, and in courage he lacks nothing. To class such an animal as 'vermin', as is done in some parts of India, is a crime which only those could perpetrate whose knowledge of the leopard is limited to the miserable, underfed, and mangy specimens seen in captivity.

But, beautiful as the specimen was that stood before me, his life was forfeit, for he had taken to cattle-killing, and I had promised the people of Dalkania and other villages, on my last visit, that I would rid them of their minor enemy if opportunity offered. The opportunity had now come, and I do not think the leopard heard the shot that killed him.

Of the many incomprehensible things one meets with in life, the hardest to assign any reason for is the way in which misfortune dogs an individual, or a family. Take as an example the case of the owner of the cow over which I had shot the leopard. He was a boy, eight years of age, and an only child. Two years previously his mother, while out cutting grass for the cow, had been killed and eaten by the man-eater, and twelve months later his father had suffered a like fate. The few pots and pans the family possessed had been sold to pay off the small debt left by the father, and the son started life as the owner of one cow; and this particular cow the leopard had selected, out of a herd of two or three hundred head of village cattle, and killed. (I am afraid my attempt to repair a heartbreak was not very successful in this case, for though the new cow, a red one, was an animal of parts, it did not make up to the boy for the loss of his lifelong white companion.)

My young buffaloes had been well cared for by the man in whose charge I had left them, and the day after my arrival I started tying them out, though I had little hope of the tigress accepting them as bait.

Five miles down the Nandhour valley nestles a little village at the foot of a great cliff of rock, some thousand or more feet high. The man-eater had, during the past few months, killed four people on the outskirts of this village. Shortly after I shot the leopard a deputation came from this village to request me to move my camp from Dalkania to a site that had been selected for me near their village. I was told that the tiger had frequently been seen on the cliff above the village and that it appeared to have its home in one of the many caves in the cliff face. That very morning, I was informed, some women out cutting grass had seen the tiger, and the villagers were now in a state of terror and too frightened to leave their homes. Promising the deputation I would do all I could to help them, I made a very early start next morning, climbed the hill opposite the village, and scanned the cliff for an hour or more through my field-glasses. I then crossed the valley, and by way of a very deep ravine climbed the cliff above the village. Here the going was very difficult and not at all to my liking, for, added to the danger of a fall, which would have resulted in a broken neck, was the danger of an attack on ground on which it would be impossible to defend oneself.

By 2 p.m. I had seen as much of the rock cliff as I shall ever want to see again, and was making my way up the valley towards my camp and breakfast when, on looking back before starting the stiff climb to Dalkania, I saw two men running towards me from the direction in which I had just come. On joining me the men informed me that a tiger had just killed a bullock in the deep ravine up which I had gone earlier in the day. Telling one of the men to go on up to my camp and instruct my servant to send tea and some food, I turned round and, accompanied by the other man, retraced my steps down the valley.

The ravine where the bullock had been killed was about two hundred feet deep and one hundred feet wide. As we approached it I saw a number of vultures rising, and when we arrived at the kill I found the vultures had cleaned it out, leaving only the skin and bones. The spot where the remains of the bullock were lying was only a hundred yards from the village, but there was no way up the steep bank, so my guide took me a quarter of a mile down the ravine, to where a cattle-track crossed it. This track, after gaining the high ground, wound in and out through dense scrub jungle before it finally fetched up at the village. On arrival at the village I told the Headman that the vultures had ruined the kill, and asked him to provide me with a young buffalo and a short length of stout rope; while these were being procured, two of my men arrived from Dalkania with the food I had sent for.

The sun was near setting when I re-entered the ravine, followed by several men leading a vigorous young male buffalo which the Headman had purchased for me from an adjoining village. Fifty yards from where the bullock had been killed, one end of a pine-tree, washed down from the hill above, had been buried deep in the bed of the ravine. After tying the buffalo very securely to the exposed end of the pine, the men returned to the village. There were no trees in the vicinity, and the only possible place for a sit-up was a narrow ledge on the village side of the ravine. With great difficulty I climbed to this ledge, which was about two feet wide by five feet long, and twenty feet above the bed of the ravine. From a little below the ledge the rock shelved inwards, forming a deep recess that was not visible from the ledge. The ledge canted downwards at an uncomfortable angle, and when I had taken my seat on it I had my back towards the direction from which I expected the tiger to come, while the tethered buffalo was to my left front and distant about thirty yards from me.

The sun had set when the buffalo, who had been lying down, scrambled to his feet and faced up the ravine, and a moment later a stone came rolling down. It would not have been possible for me to have fired in the direction from which the sound had come, so to avoid detection I sat perfectly still. After some time the buffalo gradually turned to the left until he was facing in my direction. This showed that whatever he was frightened of – and I could see he was frightened – was in the recess below me. Presently the head of a tiger appeared directly under me. A head-shot at a tiger is only justified in an emergency, and any movement on my part might have betrayed my presence. For a long minute or two the head remained perfectly still, and then, with a quick dash forward, and one great bound, the tiger was on the buffalo. The buffalo, as I have stated, was facing the tiger, and to avoid a frontal attack with the possibility of injury from the buffalo's horns the tiger's dash carried him to the left of the buffalo, and he made his attack at right angles. There was no fumbling for tooth-hold, no struggle, and no sound beyond the impact of the two heavy bodies, after which the buffalo lay quite still with the tiger lying partly over it and holding it by the throat. It is generally believed that tigers kill by delivering a smashing blow on the neck. This is incorrect. Tigers kill with their teeth.

The right side of the tiger was towards me and, taking careful aim with the ·275 I had armed myself with when leaving the camp that morning, I fired. Relinquishing its hold on the buffalo, the tiger, without making a sound, turned and bounded off up the ravine and out of sight. Clearly a miss, for which I was unable to assign any reason. If the tiger had not seen me or the flash of the rifle there was a possibility that it would return; so recharging the rifle I sat on.

The buffalo, after the tiger left him, lay without movement, and the conviction grew on me that I had shot him instead of the tiger. Ten, fifteen minutes had dragged by, when the tiger's head for a second time appeared from the recess below me. Again there was a long pause, and then, very slowly, the tiger emerged, walked up to the buffalo and stood looking at it. With the whole length of the back as a target I was going to make no mistake the second time. Very carefully the sights were aligned and the trigger slowly pressed; but instead of the tiger falling dead as I expected it to, it sprang to the left and went tearing up a little side ravine, dislodging stones as it went up the steep hillside.

Two shots fired in comparatively good light at a range of thirty yards, and heard by anxious villagers for miles round: and all I should have to show for them would be, certainly one, and quite possibly two, bullet holes in a dead buffalo. Clearly my eyesight was failing, or in climbing the rock I had knocked the foresight out of alignment. But on focussing my eyes on small objects I found there was nothing wrong with my eyesight, and a glance along the barrel showed that the sights were all right, so the only reason I could assign for having missed the tiger twice was bad shooting.

There was no chance of the tiger returning a third time; and even if it did return, there was nothing to be gained by risking the possibility of only wounding it in bad light when I had not been able to kill it while the light had been comparatively good. Under these circumstances there was no object in my remaining any longer on the ledge.

My clothes were still damp from my exertions earlier in the day, a cold wind was blowing and promised to get colder, my shorts were of thin khaki and the rock was hard and cold, and a hot cup of tea awaited me in the village. Good as these reasons were, there was a better and more convincing reason for my remaining where I was – the man-eater. It was now quite dark. A quarter-of-a-mile walk, along a boulder-strewn ravine and a winding path through dense undergrowth, lay between me and the village. Beyond the suspicions of the villagers that the tiger they had seen the previous day – and that I had quite evidently just fired at – was the man-eater, I had no definite knowledge of the man-eater's whereabouts; and though at that moment she might have been fifty miles away, she might also have been watching me from a distance of fifty yards, so, uncomfortable as my perch was, prudence dictated that I should remain where I was. As the long hours dragged by, the conviction grew on me that man-eater shooting by night was not a pastime that appealed to me, and that if this animal could not be shot during daylight hours she would have to be left to die of old age. This conviction was strengthened when, cold and stiff, I started to climb down as soon as there was sufficient light to shoot by, and slipping on the dew-drenched rock completed the descent with my feet in the air. Fortunately I landed on a bed of sand without doing myself or the rifle any injury.

Early as it was I found the village astir, and I was quickly the middle of a small crowd. In reply to the eager questions from all sides, I was only able to say that I had been firing at an imaginary tiger with blank ammunition.

A pot of tea drunk while sitting near a roaring fire did much to restore warmth to my inner and outer man, and then, accompanied by most of the men and all the boys of the village, I went to where a rock jutted out over the ravine and directly above my overnight exploit. To the assembled throng I explained how the tiger had appeared from the recess under me and had bounded on to the buffalo, and how after I had fired it had dashed off in *that* direction; and as I pointed up the ravine there was an excited shout of 'Look, sahib, there's the tiger lying dead!' My eyes were strained with an all-night vigil, but even after looking away and back again there was no denying the fact that the tiger was lying there, dead. To the very natural question of why I had fired a second shot after a period of twenty or thirty minutes, I said that the tiger had appeared a second time from exactly the same place, and that I had fired at it while it was standing near the buffalo, and that it had gone up *that* side ravine – and there were renewed shouts, in which the women and girls who had now come up joined, of 'Look, sahib, there is another tiger lying dead!' Both tigers appeared to be about the same size, and both were lying sixty yards from where I had fired.

Questioned on the subject of this second tiger, the villagers said that when the four human beings had been killed, and also on the previous day when the bullock had been killed, only one tiger had been seen.

The mating season for tigers is an elastic one extending from November to April, and the man-eater – if either of the two tigers lying within view was the man-eater – had evidently provided herself with a mate.

A way into the ravine, down the steep rock face, was found some two hundred yards below where I had sat up, and, followed by the entire population of the village, I went past the dead buffalo to where the first tiger was lying. As I approached it hopes ran high, for she was an old tigress. Handing the rifle to the nearest man I got down on my knees to examine her feet. On that day when the tigress had tried to stalk the women cutting wheat she had left some beautiful pug marks on the edge of the field. They were the first pug marks I had seen of the man-eater, and I had examined them very carefully. They showed the tigress to be a very old animal, whose feet had splayed out with age. The pads of the forefeet were heavily rutted, one deep rut running right across the pad of the right forefoot, and the toes were elongated to a length I had never before seen in a tiger. With these distinctive feet it would have been easy to pick the man-eater out of a hundred dead tigers. The animal before me was, I found to my great regret, not the man-eater. When I conveyed this information to the assembled throng of people there was a murmur of dissent from all sides. It was asserted that I myself, on my previous visit, had declared the man-eater to be an old tigress, and such an animal I had now shot a few yards from where, only a short time previously, four of their number had been killed. Against this convincing evidence, of what value was the evidence of the feet, for the feet of all tigers were alike!

The second tiger could, under the circumstances, only be a male, and while I made preparations to skin the tigress I sent a party of men to fetch him. The side ravine was steep and narrow, and after a great deal of shouting and laughter the second tiger – a fine male – was laid down alongside the tigress.

The skinning of those two tigers, that had been dead fourteen hours, with the sun beating down on my back and an ever-growing crowd pressing round, was one of the most unpleasant tasks I have ever undertaken. By early afternoon the job was completed, and with the skins neatly tied up for my men to carry I was ready to start on my five-mile walk back to camp.

During the morning Headmen and others had come in from adjoining villages, and before leaving I assured them that the Chowgarh man-eater was not dead and warned them that the slackening of precautions would give the tigress the opportunity she was waiting for. Had my warning been heeded, the man-eater would not have claimed as many victims as she did during the succeeding months.

There was no further news of the man-eater, and after a stay of a few weeks at Dalkania, I left to keep an appointment with the district officials in the terai.

### 3

In March 1930, Vivian, our District Commissioner, was touring through the man-eater's domain, and on the 22nd of the month I received an urgent request from him to go to Kala Agar, where he said he would await my arrival. It is roughly fifty miles from Naini Tal to Kala Agar, and two days after receipt of Vivian's letter I arrived in time for breakfast at the Kala Agar Forest Bungalow, where he and Mrs Vivian were staying.

Over breakfast the Vivians told me they had arrived at the bungalow on the afternoon of the 21st, and while they were having tea in the veranda, one of six women who were cutting grass in the compound of the bungalow had been killed and carried off by the man-eater. Rifles were hurriedly seized and, accompanied by some of his staff, Vivian followed up the drag and found the dead woman tucked away under a bush at the foot of an oak tree. On examining the ground later, I found that on the approach of Vivian's party the tigress had gone off down the hill, and throughout the subsequent proceedings had remained in a thicket of raspberry bushes, fifty yards from the kill. A machan was put up in the oak tree for Vivian, and two others in trees near the forest road which passed thirty yards above the kill, for members of his staff. The machans were occupied as soon as they were ready and the party sat up the whole night without, however, seeing anything of the tigress.

Next morning the body of the woman was removed for cremation, and a young buffalo was tied up on the forest road about half a mile from the bungalow, and killed by the tigress the same night. The following evening the Vivians sat up over the buffalo. There was no moon, and just as daylight was fading out and nearby objects becoming indistinct, they first heard, and then saw, an animal coming up to the kill which, in the uncertain light, they mistook for a bear; but for this unfortunate mistake their very sporting effort would have resulted in their bagging the man-eater, for both the Vivians are good rifle shots.

On the 25th the Vivians left Kala Agar, and during the course of the day my four buffaloes arrived from Dalkania. As the tigress now appeared to be inclined to accept this form of bait I tied them up at intervals of a few hundred yards along the forest road. For three nights in succession the tigress passed within a few feet of the buffaloes without touching them, but on the fourth night the buffalo nearest the bungalow was killed. On examining the kill in the morning I was disappointed to find that the buffalo had been killed by a pair of leopards I had heard calling the previous night above the bungalow. I did not like the idea of firing in this locality, for fear of driving away the tigress, but it was quite evident that if I did not shoot the leopards they would kill my three remaining buffaloes, so I stalked them while they were sunning themselves on some big rocks above the kill, and shot both of them.

The forest road from the Kala Agar bungalow runs for several miles due west through very beautiful forests of pine, oak, and rhododendron, and in these forests there is, compared with the rest of Kumaon, quite a lot of game in the way of sambur, karker, and pig, in addition to a great wealth of bird life. On two occasions I suspected the tigress of having killed sambur in this forest, and though on both occasions I found the blood-stained spot where the animals had been killed, I failed to find either of the kills.

For the next fourteen days I spent all the daylight hours either on the forest road, on which no one but myself ever set foot, or in the jungle, and only twice during that period did I get near the tigress. On the first occasion I had been down to visit an isolated village, on the south face of Kala Agar ridge, that had been abandoned the previous year owing to the depredations of the man-eater, and on the way back had taken a cattle-track that went over the ridge and down the far side of the forest road, when, approaching a pile of rocks, I suddenly felt there was danger ahead. The distance from the ridge to the forest road was roughly three hundred yards. The track, after leaving the ridge, went steeply down for a few yards and then turned to the right and ran diagonally across the hill for a hundred yards; the pile of rocks was about midway on the right-hand side of this length of the track. Beyond the rocks a hairpin bend carried the track to the left, and a hundred yards further on, another sharp bend took it down to its junction with the forest road.

I had been along this track many times, and this was the first occasion on which I hesitated to pass the rocks. To avoid them I should either have had to go several hundred yards through dense undergrowth or make a wide detour round and above them; the former would have subjected me to very great danger, and there was no time for the latter, for the sun was near setting and I had still two miles to go. So, whether I liked it or not, there was nothing for it but to face the rocks. The wind was blowing up the hill so I was able to ignore the thick cover on the left of the track, and concentrate all my attention on the rocks to my right. A hundred feet would see me clear of the danger zone, and this distance I covered foot by foot, walking sideways with my face to the rocks and the rifle to my shoulder: a strange mode of progression, had there been any to see it.

Thirty yards beyond the rocks was an open glade, starting from the right-hand side of the track and extending up the hill for fifty or sixty yards, and screened from the rocks by a fringe of bushes. In this glade a karker was grazing. I saw her before she saw me, and watched her out of the corner of my eye. On catching sight of me she threw up her head, and as I was not looking in her direction and was moving slowly she stood stock still, as these animals have a habit of doing when they are under the impression that they have not been seen. On arrival at the hairpin bend I looked over my shoulder and saw that the karker had lowered her head, and was once more cropping the grass.

I had walked a short distance along the track after passing the bend when the karker went dashing up the hill, barking hysterically. In a few quick strides I was back at the bend, and was just in time to see a movement in the bushes on the lower side of the track. That the karker had seen the tigress was quite evident, and the only place where she could have seen her was on the track. The movement I had seen might have been caused by the passage of a bird, on the other hand it might have been caused by the tigress; anyway, a little investigation was necessary before proceeding further on my way.

A trickle of water seeping out from under the rocks had damped the red clay of which the track was composed, making an ideal surface for the impression of tracks. In this damp clay I had left footprints, and over these footprints I now found the splayed-out pug marks of the tigress where she had jumped down from the rocks and followed me, until the karker had seen her and given its alarm-call, whereupon the tigress had left the track and entered the bushes where I had seen the movement. The tigress was undoubtedly familiar with every foot of the ground and, not having had an opportunity of killing me at the rocks – and her chance of bagging me at the first hairpin bend having been spoilt by the karker – she was probably now making her way through the dense undergrowth to try to intercept me at the second bend.

Further progress along the track was not now advisable, so I followed the karker up the glade, and turning to the left worked my way down, over open ground, to the forest road below. Had there been sufficient daylight I believe I could, that evening, have turned the tables on the tigress, for the conditions, after she left the shelter of the rocks, were all in my favour. I knew the ground as well as she did, and while she had no reason to suspect my intentions towards her, I had the advantage of knowing, very clearly, her intentions towards me. However, though the conditions were in my favour, I was unable to take advantage of them owing to the lateness of the evening.

I have made mention elsewhere of the sense that warns us of impending danger, and will not labour the subject further beyond stating that this sense is a very real one and that I do not know, and therefore cannot explain, what brings it into operation. On this occasion I had neither heard nor seen the tigress, nor had I received any indication from bird or beast of her presence, and yet I knew, without any shadow of doubt, that she was lying up for me among the rocks. I had been out for many hours that day and had covered many miles of jungle with unflagging caution, but without one moment's unease, and then, on cresting the ridge, and coming in sight of the rocks, I knew they held danger for me, and this knowledge was confirmed a few minutes later by the karker's warning call to the jungle folk, and by my finding the man-eater's pug marks superimposed on my footprints.

4

To those of my readers who have had the patience to accompany me so far in my narrative, I should like to give a clear and a detailed account of my first – and last – meeting with the tigress.

The meeting took place in the early afternoon of 11 April 1930, nineteen days after my arrival at Kala Agar.

I had gone out that day at 2 p.m. with the intention of tying up my three buffaloes at selected places along the forest road, when at a point a mile from the bungalow, where the road crosses a ridge and goes from the north to the west face of the Kala Agar range, I came on a large party of men who had been out collecting firewood. In the party was an old man who, pointing down the hill to a thicket of young oak trees some five hundred yards from where we were standing, said it was in that thicket where the man-eater, a month previously, had killed his only son, a lad eighteen years of age. I had not heard the father's version of the killing of his son, so, while we sat on the edge of the road smoking, he told his story, pointing out the spot where the lad had been killed, and where all that was left of him had been found the following day. The old man blamed the twenty-five men who had been out collecting firewood on that day for the death of his son, saying, very bitterly, that they had run away and left him to be killed by the tiger. Some of the men sitting near me had been in that party of twenty-five and they hotly repudiated responsibility for the lad's death, accusing him of having been responsible for the stampede by screaming out that he had heard the tiger growling and telling everyone to run for his life. This did not satisfy the old man. He shook his head and said, 'You are grown men and he was only a boy, and you ran away and left him to be killed.' I was sorry for having asked the questions that had led to this heated discussion, and more to placate the old man than for any good it would do I said I would tie up one of my buffaloes near the spot where he said his son had been killed. So, handing two of the buffaloes over to the party to take back to the bungalow, I set off, followed by two of my men leading the remaining buffalo.

A footpath, taking off close to where we had been sitting, went down the hill to the valley below and zigzagged up the opposite pine-clad slope to join the forest road two miles further on. The path passed close to an open patch of ground which bordered the oak thicket in which the lad had been killed. On this patch of ground, which was about thirty yards square, there was a solitary pine sapling. This I cut down. I tied the buffalo to the stump, set one man to cutting a supply of grass for it, and sent the other man, Madho Singh, who served in the Garhwalis during the Great War and is now serving in the United Provinces Civil Pioneer Force, up an oak tree with instructions to strike a dry branch with the head of his axe and call at the top of his voice as hill people do when cutting leaves for their cattle. I then took up a position on a rock, about four feet high, on the lower edge of the open ground. Beyond the rock the hill fell steeply away to the valley below and was densely clothed with tree and scrub jungle.

The man on the ground had made several trips with the grass he had cut, and Madho Singh on the tree was alternately shouting and singing lustily, while I stood on the rock smoking, with the rifle in the hollow of my left arm, when, all at once, I became aware that the man-eater had arrived. Beckoning urgently to the man on the ground to come to me, I whistled to attract Madho Singh's attention and signalled to him to remain quiet. Madho Singh on the tree was to my left front, the man cutting grass had been in front of me, while the buffalo – now showing signs of uneasiness – was to my right front. In this area the tigress could not have approached without my seeing her; and as she *had* approached, there was only one place where she could now be, and that was behind and immediately below me.

When taking up my position I had noticed that the further side of the rock was steep and smooth, that it extended down the hill for eight or ten feet, and that the lower portion of it was masked by thick undergrowth and young pine saplings. It would have been a little difficult, but quite possible, for the tigress to have climbed the rock, and I relied for my safety on hearing her in the undergrowth should she make the attempt.

I have no doubt that the tigress, attracted, as I had intended she should be, by the noise Madho Singh was making, had come to the rock, and that it was while she was looking up at me and planning her next move that I had become aware of her presence. My change of front, coupled with the silence of the men, may have made her suspicious; anyway, after a lapse of a few minutes, I heard a dry twig snap a little way down the hill; thereafter the feeling of unease left me, and the tension relaxed. An opportunity lost; but there was still a very good chance of my getting a shot, for she would undoubtedly return before long, and when she found us gone would probably content herself with killing the buffalo. There were still four or five hours of daylight, and by crossing the valley and going up the opposite slope I should be able to overlook the whole of the hillside on which the buffalo was tethered. The shot, if I did get one, would be a long one from two to three hundred yards, but the ·275 rifle I was carrying was accurate, and even if I only wounded the tigress I should have a blood trail to follow, which would be better than feeling about for her in hundreds of square miles of jungle, as I had been doing these many months.

The men were a difficulty. To have sent them back to the bungalow alone would have been nothing short of murder, so, of necessity, I kept them with me.

Tying the buffalo to the stump in such a manner as to make it impossible for the tigress to carry it away, I left the open ground and rejoined the path to carry out the plan I have outlined, of trying to get a shot from the opposite hill.

About a hundred yards along the path I came to a ravine. On the far side of this the path entered very heavy undergrowth, and as it was inadvisable to go into thick cover with two men following me, I decided to take to the ravine, follow it down to its junction with the valley, work up the valley and pick up the path on the far side of the undergrowth.

The ravine was about ten yards wide and four or five feet deep, and as I stepped down into it a nightjar fluttered off a rock on which I had put my hand. On looking at the spot from which the bird had risen, I saw two eggs. These eggs, straw-coloured, with rich brown markings, were of a most unusual shape, one being long and very pointed, while the other was as round as a marble; and as my collection lacked nightjar eggs I decided to add this odd clutch to it. I had no receptacle of any kind in which to carry the eggs, so cupping my left hand I placed the eggs in it and packed them round with a little moss.

As I went down the ravine the banks became higher, and sixty yards from where I had entered it I came on a deep drop of some twelve to fourteen feet. The water that rushes down all these hill ravines in the rains had worn the rock as smooth as glass, and as it was too steep to offer a foothold I handed the rifle to the men and, sitting on the edge, proceeded to slide down. My feet had hardly touched the sandy bottom when the two men, with a flying leap, landed one on either side of me, and thrusting the rifle into my hand asked in a very agitated manner if I had heard the tiger. As a matter of fact I had heard nothing, possibly due to the scraping of my clothes on the rocks, and when questioned, the men said that what they had heard was a deep-throated growl from somewhere close at hand, but exactly from which direction the sound had come, they were unable to say. Tigers do not betray their presence by growling when looking for their dinner, and the only, and very unsatisfactory, explanation I can offer is that the tigress followed us after we left the open ground, and on seeing that we were going down the ravine had gone ahead and taken up a position where the ravine narrowed to half its width; and that when she was on the point of springing out on me, I had disappeared out of sight down the slide and she had involuntarily given vent to her disappointment with a low growl. Not a satisfactory reason, unless one assumes – without any reason – that she had selected me for her dinner, and therefore had no interest in the two men.

Where the three of us now stood in a bunch we had the smooth, steep rock behind us, to our right a wall of rock slightly leaning over the ravine and fifteen feet high, and to our left a tumbled bank of big rocks thirty or forty feet high. The sandy bed of the ravine, on which we were standing, was roughly forty feet long and ten feet wide. At the lower end of this sandy bed a great pine-tree had fallen across, damming the ravine, and the collection of sand was due to this dam. The wall of overhanging rock came to an end twelve or fifteen feet from the fallen tree, and as I approached the end of the rock, my feet making no sound on the sand, I very fortunately noticed that the sandy bed continued round to the back of the rock.

This rock about which I have said so much I can best describe as a giant school slate, two feet thick at its lower end, and standing up – not quite perpendicularly – on one of its long sides.

As I stepped clear of this giant slate, I looked behind me over my right shoulder and – looked straight into the tigress's face.

I would like you to have a clear picture of the situation.

The sandy bed behind the rock was quite flat. To the right of it was the smooth slate fifteen feet high and leaning slightly outwards, to the left of it was a scoured-out steep bank also some fifteen feet high overhung by a dense tangle of thorn-bushes, while at the far end was a slide similar to, but a little higher than, the one I had glissaded down. The sandy bed, enclosed by these three natural walls, was about twenty feet long and half as wide, and lying on it, with her fore-paws stretched out and her hind legs well tucked under her, was the tigress. Her head, which was raised a few inches off her paws, was eight feet (measured later) from me, and on her face was a smile similar to that one sees on the face of a dog welcoming his master home after a long absence.

Two thoughts flashed through my mind: one, that it was up to me to make the first move, and the other, that the move would have to be made in such a manner as not to alarm the tigress or make her nervous.

The rifle was in my right hand held diagonally across my chest, with the safety-catch off, and in order to get it to bear on the tigress the muzzle would have to be swung round three-quarters of a circle.

The movement of swinging round the rifle, with one hand, was begun very slowly, and hardly perceptibly, and when a quarter of a circle had been made, the stock came in contact with my right side. It was now necessary to extend my arm, and as the stock cleared my side, the swing was very slowly continued. My arm was now at full stretch and the weight of the rifle was beginning to tell. Only a little further now for the muzzle to go, and the tigress – who had not once taken her eyes off mine – was still looking up at me, with the pleased expression still on her face.

How long it took the rifle to make the three-quarter circle I am not in a position to say. To me, looking into the tigress's eyes and unable to follow the movement of the barrel, it appeared that my arm was paralysed, and that the swing would never be completed. However, the movement was completed at last, and as soon as the rifle was pointing at the tigress's body, I pressed the trigger.

I heard the report, exaggerated in that restricted space, and felt the jar of the recoil, and but for these tangible proofs that the rifle had gone off I might, for all the immediate result the shot produced, have been in the grip of one of those awful nightmares in which triggers are vainly pulled of rifles that refuse to be discharged at the critical moment.

For a perceptible fraction of time the tigress remained perfectly still, and then, very slowly, her head sank on to her outstretched paws, while at the same time a jet of blood issued from the bullet-hole. The bullet had injured her spine and shattered the upper portion of her heart.

The two men who were following a few yards behind me, and who were separated from the tigress by the thickness of the rock, came to a halt when they saw me stop and turn my head. They knew instinctively that I had seen the tigress and judged from my behaviour that she was close at hand, and Madho Singh said afterwards that he wanted to call out and tell me to drop the eggs and get both hands on the rifle. When I had fired my shot and lowered the point of the rifle on to my toes, Madho Singh, at a sign, came forward to relieve me of it, for very suddenly my legs appeared to be unable to support me, so I made for the fallen tree and sat down. Even before looking at the pads of her feet I knew it was the Chowgarh tigress I had sent to the Happy Hunting Grounds, and that the shears that had assisted her to cut the threads of sixty-four human lives – the people of the district put the number at twice that figure – had, while the game was in her hands, turned, and cut the thread of her own life.

Three things, each of which would appear to you to have been to my disadvantage, were actually in my favour. These were (*a*) the eggs in my left hand, (*b*) the light rifle I was carrying, and (*c*) the tiger being a man-eater. If I had not had the eggs in my hand I should have had both hands on the rifle, and when I looked back and saw the tiger at such close quarters I should instinctively have tried to swing round to face her, and the spring that was arrested by my lack of movement would inevitably have been launched. Again, if the rifle had not been a light one it would not have been possible for me to have moved it in the way it was imperative I should move it, and then discharge it at the full extent of my arm. And lastly, if the tiger had been just an ordinary tiger, and not a man-eater, it would, on finding itself cornered, have made for the opening and wiped me out of the way; and to be wiped out of the way by a tiger usually has fatal results.

While the men made a detour and went up the hill to free the buffalo and secure the rope, which was needed for another and more pleasant purpose, I climbed over the rocks and went up the ravine to restore the eggs to their rightful owner. I plead guilty of being as superstitious as my brother sportsmen. For three long periods, extending over a whole year, I had tried – and tried hard – to get a shot at the tigress, and had failed; and now within a few minutes of having picked up the eggs my luck had changed.

The eggs, which all this time had remained safely in the hollow of my left hand, were still warm when I replaced them in the little depression in the rock that did duty as a nest, and when I again passed that way half an hour later, they had vanished under the brooding mother whose colouring so exactly matched the mottled rock that it was difficult for me, who knew the exact spot where the nest was situated, to distinguish her from her surroundings.

The buffalo, who after months of care was now so tame that it followed like a dog, came scrambling down the hill in the wake of the men, nosed the tigress and lay down on the sand to chew the cud of contentment, while we lashed the tigress to the stout pole the men had cut.

I had tried to get Madho Singh to return to the bungalow for help, but this he would not hear of doing. With no one would he and his companion share the honour of carrying in the man-eater, and if I would lend a hand, the task, he said, with frequent halts for rest, would not be too difficult. We were three hefty men – two accustomed from childhood to carrying heavy loads – and all three hardened by a life of exposure; but even so, the task we set ourselves was a herculean one.

The path down which we had come was too narrow and too winding for the long pole to which the tigress was lashed, so, with frequent halts to regain breath and readjust pads to prevent the pole biting too deep into shoulder muscles, we went straight up the hill through a tangle of raspberry and briar bushes, on the thorns of which we left a portion of our clothing and an amount of skin which made bathing for many days a painful operation.

The sun was still shining on the surrounding hills when three dishevelled and very happy men, followed by a buffalo, carried the tigress to the Kala Agar Forest Bungalow, and from that evening to this day no human being has been killed – or wounded – over the hundreds of square miles of mountain and vale over which the Chowgarh tigress, for a period of five years, held sway.

I have added one more cross and date to the map of Eastern Kumaon that hangs on the wall before me – the cross and the date the man-eater earned. The cross is two miles west of Kala Agar, and the date under it is 11 April 1930.

The tigress's claws were broken and bushed out, and one of her canine teeth was broken, and her front teeth were worn down to the bone. It was these defects that had made her a man-eater and were the cause of her not being able to kill outright – and by her own efforts – a large proportion of the human beings she had attacked since the day she had been deprived of the assistance of the cub I had, on my first visit, shot by mistake.

## 15

# The Bachelor of Powalgarh

I

Three miles from our winter home, and in the heart of the forest, there is an open glade some four hundred yards long and half as wide, grassed with emerald green and surrounded with big trees interlaced with cane creepers. It was in this glade, which for beauty has no equal, that I first saw the tiger who was known throughout the United Provinces as 'The Bachelor of Powalgarh', who from 1920 to 1930 was the most-sought-after big-game trophy in the province.

The sun had just risen, one winter's morning, when I crested the high ground overlooking the glade. On the far side, a score of red junglefowl were scratching among the dead leaves bordering a crystal-clear stream, and scattered over the emerald-green grass, now sparkling with dew, fifty or more chital were feeding. Sitting on a tree stump and smoking, I had been looking at this scene for some time when the hind nearest to me raised her head, turned in my direction and called; and a moment later the Bachelor stepped into the open from the thick bushes below me. For a long minute he stood with head held high surveying the scene, and then with slow, unhurried steps started to cross the glade. In his rich winter coat, which the newly risen sun was lighting up, he was a magnificent sight as, with head turning now to the right and now to the left, he walked down the wide lane the deer had made for him. At the stream he lay down and quenched his thirst, then sprang across and, as he entered the dense tree jungle beyond, called three times in acknowledgement of the homage the jungle folk had paid him, for from the time he had entered the glade every chital had called, every junglefowl had cackled, and every one of a troop of monkeys on the trees had chattered.

The Bachelor was far afield that morning, for his home was in a ravine six miles away. Living in an area in which the majority of tigers are bagged with the aid of elephants, he had chosen his home wisely. The ravine, running into the foothills, was half a mile long, with steep hills on either side rising to a height of a thousand feet. At the upper end of the ravine there was a waterfall some twenty feet high, and at the lower end, where the water had cut through red clay, it narrowed to four feet. Any sportsman, therefore, who wished to try conclusions with the Bachelor, while he was at home, would of necessity have to do so on foot. It was this secure retreat, and the Government rules prohibiting night shooting, that had enabled the Bachelor to retain possession of his much-sought-after skin.

In spite of the many and repeated attempts that had been made to bag him with the aid of buffalo bait, the Bachelor had never been fired at, though on two occasions, to my knowledge, he had only escaped death by the skin of his teeth. On the first occasion, after a perfect beat, a guy-rope by which the machan was suspended interfered with the movement of Fred Anderson's rifle at the critical moment, and on the second occasion the Bachelor arrived at the machan before the beat started and found Huish Edye filling his pipe. On both these occasions he had been viewed at a range of only a few feet, and while Anderson described him as being as big as a Shetland pony, Edye said he was as big as a donkey.

The winter following these and other unsuccessful attempts I took Wyndham, our Commissioner, who knows more about tigers than any other man in India, to a fire-track skirting the upper end of the ravine in which the Bachelor lived, to show him the fresh pug marks of the tiger which I had found on the fire-track that morning. Wyndham was accompanied by two of his most experienced shikaris, and after the three of them had carefully measured and examined the pug marks, Wyndham said that in his opinion the tiger was ten feet between pegs, and while one shikari said he was ten feet five inches over curves, the other said he was ten feet six inches or a little more. All three agreed that they had never seen the pug marks of a bigger tiger.

In 1930 the Forest Department started extensive fellings in the area surrounding the Bachelor's home and, annoyed at the disturbance, he changed his quarters; this I learnt from two sportsmen who had taken out a shooting pass with the object of hunting down the tiger. Shooting passes are only issued for fifteen days of each month, and throughout that winter, shooting party after shooting party failed to make contact with the tiger.

Towards the end of the winter an old dak runner, who passes our gate every morning and evening on his seven-mile run through the forest to a hill village, came to me one evening and reported that on his way out that morning he had seen the biggest pug marks of a tiger that he had seen during the thirty years of his service. The tiger, he said, had come from the west and after proceeding along the road for two hundred yards had gone east, taking a path that started from near an almond tree. This tree was about two miles from our home, and was a well-known landmark. The path the tiger had taken then runs through a very heavy jungle for half a mile before crossing a wide watercourse, and then joins a cattle-track which skirts the foot of the hills before entering a deep and well-wooded valley; a favourite haunt of tigers.

Early next morning, with Robin at my heels, I set out to prospect, my objective being the point where the cattle-track entered the valley, for at this point the tracks of all the animals entering or leaving the valley are to be found. From the time we started Robin appeared to know that we had a special job in hand and he paid not the least attention to the junglefowl we disturbed, the karker that let us get quite close to it, and the two sambur that stood and belled at us. Where the cattle-track entered the valley the ground was hard and stony, and when we reached this spot Robin put down his head and very carefully smelt the stones, and on receiving a signal from me to carry on he turned and started down the track, keeping a yard ahead of me; I could tell from his behaviour that he was on the scent of a tiger, and that the scent was hot. A hundred yards further down, where the track flattens out and runs along the foot of the hill, the ground is soft; here I saw the pug marks of a tiger, and a glance at them satisfied me we were on the heels of the Bachelor and that he was only a minute or two ahead of us.

Beyond the soft ground the track runs for three hundred yards over stones, before going steeply down on to an open plain. If the tiger kept to the track we should probably see him on this open ground. We had gone another fifty yards when Robin stopped and, after running his nose up and down a blade of grass on the left of the track, turned and entered the grass which was here about two feet high. On the far side of the grass there was a patch of clerodendron, about forty yards wide. This plant grows in dense patches to a height of five feet, and has widely spread leaves and a big head of flowers not unlike horse-chestnut. It is greatly fancied by tiger, sambur, and pig because of the shade it gives. When Robin reached the clerodendron he stopped and backed towards me, thus telling me that he could not see into the bushes ahead and wished to be carried. Lifting him up, I put his hind legs into my left-hand pocket, and when he had hooked his forefeet over my left arm, he was safe and secure, and I had both hands free for the rifle. On these occasions Robin was always in deadly earnest, and no matter what he saw, or how our quarry behaved before or after being fired at, he never moved, spoilt my shot or impeded my view. Proceeding very slowly, we had gone half-way through the clerodendron when I saw the bushes directly in front of us swaying. Waiting until the tiger had cleared the bushes, I went forward expecting to see him in the more or less open jungle, but he was nowhere in sight, and when I put Robin down he turned to the left and indicated that the tiger had gone into a deep and narrow ravine nearby. This ravine ran to the foot of an isolated hill on which there were caves frequented by tigers, and as I was not armed to deal with a tiger at close quarters, and, further, as it was time for breakfast, Robin and I turned and made for home.

After breakfast I returned alone, armed with a heavy ·450 rifle, and as I approached the hill, which in the days of long ago had been used by the local inhabitants as a rallying-point against the Gurkha invaders, I heard the boom of a big buffalo bell and a man shouting. These sounds were coming from the top of the hill, which is flat, and about half an acre in extent, so I climbed up and saw a man on a tree, striking a dead branch with the head of his axe and shouting, while at the foot of the tree a number of buffaloes were collected. When he saw me the man called out, saying I had just arrived in time to save him and his buffaloes from a *shaitan* of a tiger, the size of a camel, that had been threatening them for hours. From this story I gathered that he had arrived on the hill shortly after Robin and I had left for home, and that as he started to cut bamboo leaves for his buffaloes he saw a tiger coming towards him. He shouted to drive the tiger away, as he had done on many previous occasions with other tigers, but instead of going away this one had started to growl. He took to his heels, followed by his buffaloes, and climbed up the nearest tree. The tiger, paying no heed to his shouts, had then set to pacing round and round, while the buffaloes kept their heads towards it. Probably the tiger had heard me coming, for it had left only a moment before I had arrived. The man was an old friend who, before his quarrel with the Headman of his village, had done a considerable amount of poaching in these jungles with the Headman's gun. He now begged me to conduct both himself and his cattle safely out of the jungle; so telling him to lead on, I followed behind to see that there were no stragglers. At first the buffaloes were disinclined to break up their close formation, but after a little persuasion we got them to start, and we had gone half-way across the open plain I have alluded to when the tiger called in the jungle to our right. The man quickened his pace, and I urged on the buffaloes, for a mile of very thick jungle lay between us and the wide, open watercourse beyond which lay my friend's village and safety for his buffaloes.

I have earned the reputation of being keener on photographing animals than on killing them, and before I left my friend he begged me to put aside photography for this once and kill the tiger, which he said was big enough to eat a buffalo a day, and ruin him in twenty-five days. I promised to do my best and turned to retrace my steps to the open plain, to meet with an experience every detail of which has burnt itself deep into my memory.

On reaching the plain I sat down to wait for the tiger to disclose his whereabouts or for the jungle folk to tell me where he was. It was then about 3 p.m., and as the sun was warm and comforting, I put my head down on my drawn-up knees and had been dozing a few minutes when I was awakened by the tiger calling; thereafter he continued to call at short intervals.

Between the plain and the hills there is a belt, some half-mile wide, of the densest scrub jungle for a hundred miles round, and I located the tiger as being on the hills on the far side of the scrub – about three-quarters of a mile from me – and from the way he was calling it was evident he was in search of a mate.

Starting from the upper left-hand corner of the plain, and close to where I was sitting, an old cart-track, used some years previously for extracting timber, ran in an almost direct line to where the tiger was calling. This track would take me in the direction of the calling animal, but on the hills was high grass, and without Robin to help me there would be little chance of my seeing him. So instead of my going to look for the tiger, I decided he should come and look for me. I was too far away for him to hear me, so I sprinted up the cart-track for a few hundred yards, laid down my rifle, climbed to the top of a high tree and called three times. I was immediately answered by the tiger. After climbing down, I ran back, calling as I went, and arrived on the plain without having found a suitable place in which to sit and await the tiger. Something would have to be done and done in a hurry, for the tiger was rapidly coming nearer, so, after rejecting a little hollow which I found to be full of black, stinking water, I lay down flat in the open, twenty yards from where the track entered the scrub. From this point I had a clear view up the track for fifty yards, to where a bush, leaning over it, impeded my further view. If the tiger came down the track, as I expected him to, I decided to fire at him as soon as he cleared the obstruction.

After opening the rifle to make quite sure it was loaded, I threw off the safety-catch and, with elbows comfortably resting on the soft ground, waited for the tiger to appear. I had not called since I came out on the plain, so to give him direction I now gave a low call, which he immediately answered from a distance of a hundred yards. If he came on at his usual pace, I judged he would clear the obstruction in thirty seconds. I counted this number very slowly, and went on counting up to eighty, when out of the corner of my eye I saw a movement to my right front, where the bushes approached to within ten yards of me. Turning my eyes in that direction I saw a great head projecting above the bushes, which here were four feet high. The tiger was only a foot or two inside the bushes, but all I could see of him was his head. As I very slowly swung the point of the rifle round and ran my eyes along the sights I noticed that his head was not quite square on to me, and as I was firing up and he was looking down, I aimed an inch below his right eye, pressed the trigger, and for the next half-hour nearly died of fright.

Instead of dropping dead, as I expected him to, the tiger went straight up into the air above the bushes for his full length, falling backwards on to a tree a foot thick which had been blown down in a storm and was still green. With unbelievable fury he attacked this tree and tore it to bits, emitting as he did so roar upon roar, and, what was even worse, a dreadful blood-curdling sound as though he was savaging his worst enemy. The branches of the tree tossed about as though struck by a tornado, while the bushes on my side shook and bulged out, and every moment I expected to have him on top of me, for he had been looking at me when I fired and knew where I was.

Too frightened even to recharge the rifle for fear the slight movement and sound should attract the attention of the tiger, I lay and sweated for half an hour with my finger on the left trigger. At last the branches of the tree and the bushes ceased waving about, and the roaring became less frequent, and eventually, to my great relief, ceased. For another half-hour I lay perfectly still, with arms cramped by the weight of the heavy rifle, and then started to pull myself backwards with my toes. After progressing for thirty yards in this manner I got to my feet, and, crouching low, made for the welcome shelter of the nearest tree. Here I remained for some minutes, and as all was now silent I turned and made for home.

2

Next morning I returned accompanied by one of my men, an expert tree-climber. I had noticed the previous evening that there was a tree growing on the edge of the open ground and about forty yards from where the tiger had fallen. We approached this tree very cautiously, and I stood behind it while the man climbed to the top. After a long and a careful scrutiny he looked down and shook his head, and when he rejoined me on the ground he told me that the bushes over a big area had been flattened down, but that the tiger was not in sight.

I sent him back to his perch on the tree with instructions to keep a sharp look-out and warn me if he saw any movement in the bushes, and went forward to have a look at the spot where the tiger had raged. He had raged to some purpose, for, in addition to tearing branches and great strips of wood off the tree, he had torn up several bushes by the roots and bitten down others. Blood in profusion was sprinkled everywhere, and on the ground were two congealed pools, near one of which was lying a bit of bone two inches square, which I found on examination to be part of the tiger's skull.

No blood trail led away from this spot and this, combined with the two pools of blood, was proof that the tiger was still here when I left and that the precautions I had taken the previous evening had been very necessary, for when I started on my 'get-away' I was only ten yards from the most dangerous animal in the world – a freshly wounded tiger. On circling round the spot I found a small smear of blood here and there on leaves that had brushed against his face. Noting that these indications of the tiger's passage led in a direct line to a giant semul tree[1] two hundred yards away, I went back and climbed the tree my man was on in order to get a bird's-eye view of the ground I should have to go over, for I had a very uneasy feeling that I should find him alive: a tiger shot in the head can live for days and can even recover from the wound. True, this tiger had a bit of his skull missing, and as I had never dealt with an animal in his condition before, I did not know whether he was likely to live for a few hours or days, or live on to die of old age. For this reason I decided to treat him as an

---

[1] *Bombax malabaricum*, the silk-cotton tree.

ordinary wounded tiger, and not to take any avoidable risks when following him up.

From my elevated position on the tree I saw that, a little to the left of the line to the semul tree, there were two trees, the nearer one thirty yards from where the blood was and the other fifty yards further on. Leaving my man on the tree, I climbed down, picked up my rifle and a shot-gun and bag of a hundred cartridges, and very cautiously approached the nearer tree and climbed up it to a height of thirty feet, pulling the rifle and gun, which I had tied to one end of a strong cord, up after me. After fixing the rifle in a fork of the tree where it would be handy if needed, I started to spray the bushes with small shot, yard by yard up to the foot of the second tree. I did this with the object of locating the tiger, assuming he was alive and in that area, for a wounded tiger, on hearing a shot fired close to him, or on being struck by a pellet, will either growl or charge. Receiving no indication of the tiger's presence I went to the second tree and sprayed the bushes to within a few yards of the semul tree, firing the last shot at the tree itself. After this last shot I thought I heard a low growl, but it was not repeated and I put it down to my imagination. My bag of cartridges was now empty, so after recovering my man I called it a day and went home.

When I returned next morning I found my friend the buffalo man feeding his buffaloes on the plain. He appeared to be very much relieved to see me, and the reason for this I learnt later. The grass was still wet with dew, but we found a dry spot and there sat down to have a smoke and relate our experiences. My friend, as I have already told you, had done a lot of poaching, and having spent all his life in tiger-infested jungles tending his buffaloes, or shooting, his jungle knowledge was considerable.

After I had left him that day at the wide, open watercourse, he had crossed to the far side and had sat down to listen for sounds coming from the direction in which I had gone. He had heard two tigers calling; he had heard my shot, followed by the continuous roaring of a tiger, and very naturally concluded I had wounded one of the tigers and that it had killed me. On his return next morning to the same spot he had been greatly mystified by hearing a hundred shots fired, and this morning, not being able to contain his curiosity any longer, he had come to see what had happened. Attracted by the smell of blood, his buffaloes had shown him where the tiger had fallen, and he had seen the patches of dry blood and had found the bit of bone. No animal, in his opinion, could possibly live for more than a few hours after having a bit of its skull blown away, and so sure was he that the tiger was dead that he offered to take his buffaloes into the jungle and find it for me. I had heard of this method of recovering tigers with the help of buffaloes but had never tried it myself, and after my friend had agreed to accepting compensation for any damage to his cattle I accepted his offer.

Rounding up the buffaloes, twenty-five in number, and keeping to the line I had sprinkled with shot the previous day, we made for the semul tree, followed by the buffaloes. Our progress was slow, for not only had we to move the chin-high bushes with our hands to see where to put our feet, but we also had frequently to check a very natural tendency on the part of the buffaloes to stray. As we approached the semul tree, where the bushes were lighter, I saw a little hollow filled with dead leaves that had been pressed flat and on which were several patches of blood, some dry, others in process of congealing, and one quite fresh; and when I put my hand to the ground I found it was warm. Incredible as it may appear, the tiger had lain in this hollow the previous day while I had expended a hundred cartridges, and had only moved off when he saw us and the buffaloes approaching. The buffaloes had now found the blood and were pawing up the ground and snorting, and as the prospect of being caught between a charging tiger and angry buffaloes did not appeal to me, I took hold of my friend's arm, turned him round and made for the open plain, followed by the buffaloes. When we were back on safe ground I told the man to go home, and said I would return next day and deal with the tiger alone.

The path through the jungles that I had taken each day when coming from and going home ran for some distance over soft ground, and on this soft ground, on this fourth day, I found the pug marks of a big male tiger. By following these pug marks I found the tiger had entered the dense brushwood a hundred yards to the right of the semul tree. Here was an unexpected complication, for if I now saw a tiger in this jungle I should not know – unless I got a very close look at it – whether it was the wounded or the unwounded one. However, this contingency would have to be dealt with when met, and in the meantime worrying would not help, so I entered the bushes and made for the hollow at the foot of the semul tree.

There was no blood trail to follow, so I zigzagged through the bushes, into which it was impossible to see further than a few inches, for an hour or more, until I came to a ten-foot-wide dry watercourse. Before stepping down into this watercourse I looked up it, and saw the left hind leg and tail of a tiger. The tiger was standing perfectly still with its body and head hidden by a tree, and only this one leg visible. I raised the rifle to my shoulder, and then lowered it. To have broken the leg would have been easy, for the tiger was only ten yards away, and it would have been the right thing to do if its owner was the wounded animal; but there were two tigers in this area, and to have broken the leg of the wrong one would have doubled my difficulties, which were already considerable. Presently the leg was withdrawn and I heard the tiger moving away, and, going to the spot where he had been standing, I found a few drops of blood – too late now to regret not having broken that leg.

A quarter of a mile further on there was a little stream and it was possible that the tiger, now recovering from his wound, was making for this stream. With the object of intercepting him or, failing that, waiting for him at the water, I took a game-path which I knew went to the stream and proceeded along it for some distance when a sambur belled to my left, and went dashing off through the jungle. It was evident now that I was abreast of the tiger, and I had only taken a few more steps when I heard the loud crack of a dry stick breaking as though some heavy animal had fallen on it; the sound had come from a distance of fifty yards and from the exact spot where the sambur had belled. The sambur had in unmistakable tones warned the jungle folk of the presence of a tiger, and the stick therefore could only have been broken by the same animal; so, getting down on my hands and knees, I started to crawl in the direction from which the sound had come.

The bushes here were from six to eight feet high, with dense foliage on the upper branches and very few leaves on the stems, so that I could see through them for a distance of ten to fifteen feet. I had covered thirty yards, hoping fervently that if the tiger charged he would come from in front (for in no other direction could I have fired), when I caught sight of something red on which the sun, drifting through the upper leaves, was shining; it might only be a bunch of dead leaves; on the other hand, it might be the tiger. I could get a better view of this object from two yards to the right, so, lowering my head until my chin touched the ground, I crawled this distance with belly to ground, and on raising my head saw the tiger in front of me. He was crouching down looking at me, with the sun shining on his left shoulder, and on receiving my two bullets he rolled over on his side without making a sound.

As I stood over him and ran my eyes over his magnificent proportions it was not necessary to examine the pads of his feet to know that before me lay the Bachelor of Powalgarh.

The entry of the bullet fired four days previously was hidden by a wrinkle of skin, and at the back of his head was a big hole which, surprisingly, was perfectly clean and healthy.

The report of my rifle was, I knew, being listened for, so I hurried home to relieve anxiety, and while I related the last chapter of the hunt and drank a pot of tea my men were collecting.

Accompanied by my sister and Robin and a carrying party of twenty men, I returned to where the tiger was lying, and before he was roped to a pole my sister and I measured him from nose to tip of tail, and from tip of tail to nose. At home we again measured him to make quite sure we had made no mistake the first time. These measurements are valueless, for there were no independent witnesses present to certify them; they are, however, interesting as showing the accuracy with which experienced woodsmen can judge the length of a tiger from his pug marks. Wyndham, you will remember, said the tiger was ten feet between pegs, which would give roughly ten feet six inches over curves; and while one shikari said he was ten feet five inches over curves, the other said he was ten feet six inches, or a little more. Shot seven years after these estimates were made, my sister and I measured the tiger as being ten feet seven inches over curves.

I have told the story at some length, as I feel sure that those who hunted the tiger between 1920 and 1930 will be interested to know how the Bachelor of Powalgarh met his end.

## 16

## The Fish of my Dreams

Fishing for mahseer in a well-stocked submontane river is, in my opinion, the most fascinating of all field sports. Our environments, even though we may not be continuously conscious of them, nevertheless play a very important part in the sum total of our enjoyment of any form of outdoor sport. I am convinced that the killing of the fish of one's dreams in uncongenial surroundings would afford an angler as little pleasure as the winning of the Davis Cup would to a tennis player if the contest were staged in the Sahara.

The river I have recently been fishing in flows, for some forty miles of its length, through a beautifully wooded valley well stocked with game and teeming with bird life. I had the curiosity to count the various kinds of animals and birds seen in one day, and by the evening of that day my count showed, among animals, sambur, chital, karker, ghooral, pig, langur, and red monkeys; and among birds, seventy-five varieties, including peafowl, red junglefowl, kaleege pheasants, black partridge, and bush quail.

In addition to these I saw a school of five otter in the river, several small mugger, and a python. The python was lying on the surface of a big still pool, with only the top of its flat head and eyes projecting above the gin-clear water. The subject was one I had long wished to photograph, and in order to do this it was necessary to cross the river above the pool and climb the opposite hillside; but unfortunately I had been seen by those projecting eyes, and as I cautiously stepped backwards, the reptile, which appeared to be about eighteen feet long, submerged, to retire to its subterranean home among the piled-up boulders at the head of the pool.

In some places the valley through which the river flows is so narrow that a stone can be tossed with ease from one side to the other, and in other places it widens out to a mile or more. In these open spaces grow amaltas with their two-feet-long sprays of golden bloom, karaunda and box bushes with their white star-shaped flowers. The combined scent from these flowers fills the air, throbbing with the spring songs of a multitude of birds, with the most delicate and pleasing of perfumes. In these surroundings angling for mahseer might well be described as sport fit for kings. My object in visiting this sportsman's paradise was not, however, to kill mahseer, but to try to secure a daylight picture of a tiger, and it was only when light conditions were unfavourable that I laid aside my movie camera for a rod.

I had been out from dawn one day trying, hour after hour, to get a picture of a tigress and her two cubs. The tigress was a young animal, nervous as all young mothers are, and as often as I stalked her she retired with the cubs into heavy cover. There is a limit to the disturbance a tigress, be she young or old, will suffer when accompanied by cubs, and when the limit on this occasion had been reached I altered my tactics and tried sitting up in trees over open glades, and lying in high grass near a stagnant pool in which she and her family were accustomed to drink, but with no better success.

When the declining sun was beginning to cast shadows over the open places I was watching, I gave up the attempt, and added the day to the several hundred days I had already spent in trying to get a picture of a tiger in its natural surroundings. The two men I had brought from camp had passed the day in the shade of a tree on the far side of the river. I instructed them to return to camp by way of the forest track, and, exchanging my camera for a rod, set off alone along the river, intent on catching a fish for my dinner.

The fashion in rods and tackle has altered in recent years as much as the fashion in ladies' dress. Gone, one often wonders where, are the 18-foot greenheart rods with their unbreakable accompaniments, and gone the muscles to wield them, and their place has been taken by light one-handed fly rods.

I was armed with an 11-foot tournament trout rod, a reel containing 50 yards of casting line, and 200 yards of fine silk backing, a medium gut cast, and a one-inch home-made brass spoon.

When one has unlimited undisturbed water to fish one is apt to be over-critical. A pool is discarded because the approach to it is over rough ground, or a run is rejected because of a suspected snag. On this occasion, half a mile had been traversed before a final selection was made: a welter of white water cascading over rocks at the head of a deep oily run 80 yards long, and at the end of the run a deep still pool 200 yards long and 70 yards wide. Here was the place to catch the fish for my dinner.

Standing just clear of the white water I flicked the spoon into the run, pulling a few yards of the line off the reel as I did so, and as I raised the rod to allow the line to run through the rings the spoon was taken by a fish, near the bank and close to where I was standing. By great good luck the remaining portion of the slack line tightened on the drum of the reel and did not foul the butt of the rod or handle of the reel, as so often happens.

In a flash the fish was off downstream, the good well-oiled reel singing a paean of joy as the line was stripped off it. The 50 yards of casting line followed by 100 yards of backing were gone, leaving in their passage burned furrows in the fingers of my left hand, when all at once the mad rush ceased as abruptly as it had begun, and the line went dead.

The speculations one makes on these occasions chased each other through my mind, accompanied by a little strong language to ease my feelings. The hold had been good without question. The cast, made up a few days previously from short lengths of gut procured from the Pilot Gut Coy., had been carefully tied and tested. Suspicion centred on the split ring: possibly, cracked on a stone on some previous occasion, it had now given way.

Sixty yards of the line are back on the reel, when the slack line is seen to curve to the left, and a moment later is cutting a strong furrow upstream – the fish is still on, and is heading for the white water. Established here, pulling alternately from upstream, at right angles, and downstream fails to dislodge him. Time drags on, and the conviction grows that the fish has gone, leaving the line hung up on a snag. Once again, and just as hope is being abandoned, the line goes slack, and then tightens a moment later as the fish for the second time goes madly downstream.

And now he appears to have made up his mind to leave this reach of the river for the rapids below the pool. In one strong steady run he reaches the tail of the pool. Here, where the water fans out and shallows, he hesitates, and finally returns to the pool. A little later he shows on the surface for the first time, and but for the fact that the taut line runs direct from the point of the rod to the indistinctly seen object on the far side of the pool, it would be impossible to believe that the owner of that great triangular fin, projecting five inches out of the water, had taken a fly spoon a yard or two from my feet.

Back in the depths of the pool, he was drawn inch by inch into slack water. To land a big fish single-handed on a trout rod is not an easy accomplishment. Four times he was stranded with a portion of his great shoulders out of water, and four times at my very cautious approach he lashed out, and, returning to the pool, had to be fought back inch by inch. At the fifth attempt, with the butt of the rod held in the crook of my thumb and reversed, rings upwards to avoid the handle of the reel coming into contact with him, he permits me to place one hand and then the other against his sides and very gently propel him through the shallow water up on to dry land.

A fish I had set out to catch, and a fish I had caught, but he would take no part in my dinner that night, for between me and camp lay three and a half miles of rough ground, half of which would have to be covered in the dark.

When sending away my eleven-pound camera I had retained the cotton cord I use for drawing it up after me when I sit in trees. One end of this cord was passed through the gills of the fish and out at his mouth, and securely tied in a loop. The other end was made fast to the branch of a tree. When the cord was paid out the fish lay snugly against a great slab of rock, in comparatively still water. Otter were the only danger, and to scare them off I made a flag of my handkerchief, and fixed the end of the improvised flagstaff in the bed of the river a little below the fish.

The sun was gilding the mountain tops next morning when I was back at the pool, and found the fish lying just where I had left it the previous evening. Having unfastened the cord from the branch, I wound it round my hand as I descended the slab of rock towards the fish. Alarmed at my approach, or feeling the vibration of the cord, the fish suddenly galvanized into life, and with a mighty splash dashed upstream. Caught at a disadvantage, I had no time to brace my feet on the sloping and slippery rock, but was jerked headlong into the pool.

I have a great distaste for going over my depth in these submontane rivers, for the thought of being encircled by a hungry python is very repugnant to me, and I am glad there were no witnesses to the manner in which I floundered out of that pool. I had just scrambled out on the far side, with the fish still attached to my right hand, when the men I had instructed to follow me arrived. Handing the fish over to them to take down to our camp on the bank of the river, I went on ahead to change and get my camera ready.

I had no means of weighing the fish and at a rough guess both the men and I put it at fifty pounds.

The weight of the fish is immaterial, for weights are soon forgotten. Not so forgotten are the surroundings in which the sport is indulged in. The steel blue of the fern-fringed pool where the water rests a little before cascading over rock and shingle to draw breath again in another pool more beautiful than the one just left – the flash of the gaily-coloured kingfisher as he breaks the surface of the water, shedding a shower of diamonds from his wings as he rises with a chirp of delight, a silver minnow held firmly in his vermilion bill – the belling of the sambur and the clear tuneful call of the chital apprising the jungle folk that the tiger, whose pug marks show wet on the sand where a few minutes before he crossed the river, is out in search of his dinner. These are things that will not be forgotten and will live in my memory, the lodestone to draw me back to that beautiful valley, as yet unspoiled by the hand of man.

## 17

## *Robin*

I never saw either of his parents. The Knight of the Broom I purchased him from said he was a spaniel, that his name was Pincha, and that his father was a 'keen gun dog'. This is all I can tell you about his pedigree.

I did not want a pup, and it was quite by accident that I happened to be with a friend when the litter of seven was decanted from a very filthy basket for her inspection. Pincha was the smallest and the thinnest of the litter, and it was quite evident he had reached the last ditch in his fight for survival. Leaving his little less miserable brothers and sisters, he walked once round me, and then curled himself up between my big feet. When I picked him up and put him inside my coat – it was a bitterly cold morning – he tried to show his gratitude by licking my face, and I tried to show him I was not aware of his appalling stench.

He was rising three months then, and I bought him for fifteen rupees. He is rising thirteen years now, and all the gold in India would not buy him.

When I got him home, and he had made his first acquaintance with a square meal, warm water, and soap, we scrapped his kennel name of Pincha and rechristened him Robin, in memory of a faithful old collie who had saved my young brother, aged four, and myself, aged six, from the attack of an infuriated she-bear.

Robin responded to regular meals as parched land does to rain, and after he had been with us for a few weeks, acting on the principle that a boy's and a pup's training cannot be started too early, I took him out one morning, intending to get a little away from him and fire a shot or two to get him used to the sound of gunfire.

At the lower end of our estate there are some dense thorn-bushes, and while I was skirting round them a peafowl got up and, forgetting all about Robin who was following at heel, I brought the bird fluttering down. It landed in the thorn-bushes and Robin dashed in after it. The bushes were too thick and thorny for me to enter them, so I ran round to the far side where beyond the bushes was open ground, and beyond that again heavy tree and grass jungle which I knew the wounded bird would make for. The open ground was flooded with morning sunlight, and if I had been armed with a movie camera I should have had an opportunity of securing a unique picture. The peafowl, an old hen, with neck feathers stuck out at right angles and one wing broken, was making for the tree jungle, while Robin, with stern to the ground, was hanging on to her tail and being dragged along. Running forward I very foolishly caught the bird by the neck and lifted it clear of the ground, whereon it promptly lashed out with both legs and sent Robin heels-over-head. In a second he was up and on his feet again, and when I laid the dead bird down he danced round it making little dabs alternately at its head and tail. The lesson was over for that morning, and as we returned home it would have been difficult to say which of us was the more proud – Robin, at bringing home his first bird, or I, at having picked a winner out of a filthy basket. The shooting season was now drawing to a close, and for the next few days Robin was not given anything larger than a quail, doves, and an occasional partridge to retrieve.

We spent the summer on the hills, and on our annual migration to the foothills in November, at the end of a long fifteen-mile march, as we turned a sharp corner, one of a big troop of langurs jumped off the hillside and crossed the road a few inches in front of Robin's nose. Disregarding my whistle, Robin dashed down the khudside after the langur, which promptly sought safety in a tree. The ground was open, with a few trees here and there, and after going steeply down for thirty or forty yards flattened out for a few yards before going sharply down into the valley below. On the right-hand side of this flat ground there were a few bushes, with a deep channel scoured out by rain-water running through them. Robin had hardly entered these bushes when he was out again, and with ears laid back and tail tucked in was running for dear life, with an enormous leopard bounding after him and gaining on him at every bound. I was unarmed, and all the assistance I could render was to 'Ho' and 'Har' at the full extent of my lungs. The men carrying M.'s dandy joined in lustily, the pandemonium reaching its climax when the hundred or more langurs added their alarm-calls, in varying keys. For twenty-five or thirty yards the desperate and unequal race continued, and just as the leopard was within reach of Robin, it unaccountably swerved and disappeared into the valley, while Robin circled round a shoulder of the hill and rejoined us on the road. Two very useful lessons Robin learned from his hair-breadth escape, which he never in after-life forgot. First, that it was dangerous to chase langurs, and, second, that the alarm-call of a langur denoted the presence of a leopard.

Robin resumed his training where it had been interrupted in spring, but it soon became apparent that his early neglect and starvation had affected his heart, for he fainted now after the least exertion.

There is nothing more disappointing for a gun dog than to be left at home when his master goes out, and as bird-shooting was now taboo for Robin I started taking him with me when I went out after big game. He took to this new form of sport as readily as a duck takes to water, and from then on has accompanied me whenever I have been out with a rifle.

The method we employ is to go out early in the morning, pick up the tracks of a leopard or a tiger, and follow them. When the pug marks can be seen I do the tracking, and when the animal we are after takes to the jungle Robin does the tracking. In this way we have on occasions followed an animal for miles before coming up with it.

When shooting on foot it is very much easier to kill an animal outright than when shooting down on it from a machan, or from the back of an elephant. For one thing, when wounded animals have to be followed up on foot, chance shots are not indulged in, and, for another, the vital parts are more accessible when shooting on the same level as the animal than when shooting down on it. However, even after exercising the greatest care over the shot, I have sometimes only wounded leopards and tigers, who have rampaged round before being quietened by a second or third shot, and only once during all the years that we have shot together has Robin left me in a tight corner. When he rejoined me after this brief absence that day we decided that the incident was closed and would never be referred to again, but we are older now and possibly less sensitive; anyway, Robin – who has exceeded the canine equivalent of three-score years and ten, and who lies at my feet as I write, on a bed he will never again leave – has with a smile from his wise brown eyes and a wag of his small stump of a tail given me permission to go ahead and tell you the story.

We did not see the leopard until it stepped clear of the thick under-growth and, coming to a stand, looked back over its left shoulder.

He was an outsized male with a beautiful dark glossy coat, the rosettes on his skin standing out like clear-cut designs on a rich velvet ground. I had an unhurried shot with an accurate rifle at his right shoulder, at the short range of fifteen yards. By how little I missed his heart makes no matter, and while the bullet was kicking up the dust fifty yards away he was high in the air, and, turning a somersault, landed in the thick undergrowth he had a minute before left. For twenty, forty, fifty yards we heard him crashing through the cover, and then the sound ceased as abruptly as it had begun. This sudden cessation of sound could be accounted for in two ways: either the leopard had collapsed and died in his tracks, or fifty yards away he had reached open ground.

We had walked far that day; the sun was near setting and we were still four miles from home. This part of the jungle was not frequented by man, and there was not one chance in a million of anyone passing that way by night, and last, and the best reason of all for leaving the leopard, M. was unarmed and could neither be left alone nor taken along to follow up the wounded animal – so we turned to the north and made for home. There was no need for me to mark the spot, for I had walked through these jungles by day – and often by night – for near on half a century, and could have found my way blindfold to any part of them.

Night had only just given place to day the following morning when Robin – who had not been with us the previous evening – and I arrived at the spot I had fired from. Very warily Robin, who was leading, examined the ground where the leopard had stood, and then raising his head and snuffing the air he advanced to the edge of the undergrowth, where the leopard in falling had left great splashes of blood. There was no need for me to examine the blood to determine the position of the wound, for at the short range I had fired at I had seen the bullet strike, and the spurt of dust on the far side was proof that the bullet had gone right through the leopard's body.

It might be necessary later on to follow up the blood trail, but just at present a little rest after our four-mile walk in the dark would do no harm and might, on the other hand, prove of great value to us. The sun was near rising and at that early hour of the morning all the jungle folk were on the move, and it would be advisable to hear what they had to say on the subject of the wounded animal before going further.

Under a nearby tree I found a dry spot to which the saturating dew had not penetrated, and with Robin stretched out at my feet had finished my cigarette when a chital hind, and then a second and a third, started calling some sixty yards to our left front. Robin sat up and slowly turning his head looked at me, and, on catching my eye, as slowly turned back in the direction of the calling deer. He had travelled far along the road of experience since that day he had first heard the alarm-call of a langur, and he knew now – as did every bird and animal within hearing – that the chital were warning the jungle folk of the presence of a leopard.

From the manner in which the chital were calling it was evident that the leopard was in full view of them. A little more patience and they would tell us if he was alive. They had been calling for about five minutes when suddenly, and all together, they called once and, again, and then settled down to their regular call; the leopard was alive and had moved, and was now quiet again. All that we needed to know now was the position of the leopard, and this information we could get by stalking the chital.

Moving downwind for fifty yards we entered the thick undergrowth, and started to stalk the deer – not a difficult task, for Robin can move through any jungle as silently as a cat, and long practice has taught me where to place my feet. The chital were not visible until we were within a few feet of them. They were standing in the open and looking towards the north in the exact direction, as far as I was able to judge, in which the crashing sound of the evening before had ceased.

Up to this point the chital had been of great help to us; they had told us the leopard was lying out in the open and that it was alive, and they had now given us the direction. It had taken us the best part of an hour to acquire this information, and if the chital now caught sight of us and warned the jungle folk of our presence, they would in one second undo the good they had so far done. I was debating whether it would be better to retrace our steps and work down below the calling deer and try to get a shot from behind them, or move them from our vicinity by giving the call of a leopard, when one of the hinds turned her head and looked straight into my face. Next second, with a cry of 'Ware man', they dashed away at top speed. I had only about five yards to cover to reach the open ground, but quick as I was the leopard was quicker, and I was only in time to see his hindquarters and tail disappearing behind some bushes. The chital had very effectively spoilt my chance of a shot, and the leopard would now have to be located and marked down all over again – this time by Robin.

I stood on the open ground for some minutes, to give the leopard time to settle down and the scent he had left in his passage to blow past us, and then took Robin due west across the track of the wind, which was blowing from the north. We had gone about sixty or seventy yards when Robin, who was leading, stopped and turned to face into the wind. Robin is mute in the jungles, and has a wonderful control over his nerves. There is one nerve, however, running down the back of his hind legs, which he cannot control when he is looking at a leopard, or when the scent of a leopard is warm and strong. This nerve was now twitching, and agitating the long hair on the upper part of his hind legs.

A very violent cyclonic storm had struck this part of the forest the previous summer, uprooting a number of trees; it was towards one of these fallen trees, forty yards from where we were standing, that Robin was now looking. The branches were towards us, and on either side of the trunk there were light bushes and a few scattered tufts of short grass.

At any other time Robin and I would have made straight for our quarry; but on this occasion a little extra caution was advisable. Not only were we dealing with an animal who when wounded knows no fear but, in addition, we were dealing with a leopard who had had fifteen hours in which to nurse his grievance against man, and who could in consequence be counted on to have all his fighting instincts thoroughly aroused.

When leaving home that morning I had picked up the ·275 rifle I had used the previous evening. A good rifle to carry when miles have to be covered, but not the weapon one would select to deal with a wounded leopard; so instead of a direct approach, I picked a line that would take us fifteen yards from, and parallel to, the fallen tree. Step by step, Robin leading, we moved along this line, and had passed the branches and were opposite the trunk when Robin stopped. Taking the direction from him, I presently saw what had attracted his attention – the tip of the leopard's tail slowly raised, and slowly lowered – the warning a leopard invariably gives before charging. Pivoting to the right on my heels, I had just got the rifle to my shoulder when the leopard burst through the intervening bushes and sprang at us. My bullet, fired more with the object of deflecting him than with any hope of killing or even hitting him, passed under his belly and went through the fleshy part of his left thigh. The crack of the rifle, more than the wound, had the effect of deflecting the leopard sufficiently to make him pass my right shoulder without touching me, and before I could get in another shot he disappeared into the bushes beyond.

Robin had not moved from my feet, and together we now examined the ground the leopard had passed over. Blood we found in plenty, but whether it had come from the old wounds torn open by the leopard's violent exertions, or from my recent shot, it was impossible to say. Anyway, it made no difference to Robin, who without a moment's hesitation took up the trail. After going through some very heavy cover we came on knee-high undergrowth, and had proceeded about a couple of hundred yards when I saw the leopard get up in front of us, and before I could get the rifle to bear on him, he disappeared under a lantana bush. This bush with its branches resting on the ground was as big as a cottage tent, and in addition to affording the leopard ideal cover gave him all the advantages for launching his next attack.

Robin and I had come very well out of our morning's adventure and it would have been foolish now, armed as I was, to pursue the leopard further, so without more ado we turned about and made for home.

Next morning we were back on the ground. From a very early hour Robin had been agitating to make a start, and, ignoring all the interesting smells the jungle holds in the morning, would have made me do the four miles at a run had that been possible.

I had armed myself with a ·450/·400, and was in consequence feeling much happier than I had done the previous day. When we were several hundred yards from the lantana bush, I made Robin slow down and advance cautiously, for it is never safe to assume that a wounded animal will be found where it has been left hours previously, as the following regrettable incident shows.

A sportsman of my acquaintance wounded a tiger one afternoon, and followed the blood trail for several miles along a valley. Next morning, accompanied by a number of men, one of whom was carrying his empty rifle and leading the way, he set out intending to take up the tracking where he had left off. His way led over the previous day's blood trail, and while still a mile from the spot where the tiger had been left, the leading man, who incidentally was the local shikari, walked on to the wounded tiger and was killed. The rest of the party escaped, some by climbing trees and others by showing a clean pair of heels.

I had marked the exact position of the lantana bush, and now took Robin along a line that would pass a few yards on the lee side of it.

Robin knew all that was worth knowing about this method of locating
the position of an animal by cutting across the wind, and we had only
gone a short distance, and were still a hundred yards from the bush,
when he stopped, turned and faced into the wind, and communicated
to me that he could smell the leopard. As on the previous day, he was
facing a fallen tree which was lying along the edge of, and parallel to,
the thick undergrowth through which we had followed the leopard to
the lantana bush after he had charged us. On our side of the tree the
ground was open, but on the far side there was a dense growth of waist-
high basonta bushes. Having signalled to Robin to carry on along our
original line, we went past the lantana bush, in which he showed no
interest, to a channel washed out by rain-water. Here, removing my
coat, I filled it with as many stones as the stitches would hold, and with
this improvised sack slung over my shoulder returned to the open
ground near the tree.

Resuming my coat, and holding the rifle ready for instant use, I took
up a position fifteen yards from the tree and started throwing stones,
first on to the tree and then into bushes on the far side of it with the
object of making the leopard – assuming he was still alive – charge on
to the open ground where I could deal with him. When all my ammunition was exhausted I coughed, clapped my hands, and shouted, but
neither during the bombardment nor after it did the leopard move or
make any sound to indicate that he was alive.

I should now have been justified in walking straight up to the tree
and looking on the far side of it, but remembering an old jungle saying,
'It is never safe to assume that a leopard is dead until it has been
skinned', I set out to circle round the tree, intending to reduce the size
of the circles until I could see right under the branches and along the
whole length of the trunk. I made the radius of the first circle about
twenty-five yards, and had gone two-thirds of the way round when
Robin stopped. As I looked down to see what had attracted his attention, there was a succession of deep-throated, angry grunts, and the
leopard made straight for us. All I could see was the undergrowth
being violently agitated in a direct line towards us, and I only just had
time to swing half right and bring the rifle up, when the head and
shoulders of the leopard appeared out of the bushes a few yards away.

The leopard's spring and my shot were simultaneous, and side-
stepping to the left and leaning back as far as I could, I fired the second
barrel from my hip into his side as he passed me.

When a wounded animal, be he leopard or tiger, makes a headlong charge and fails to contact he invariably carries on and does not return to the attack until he is again disturbed.

I had side-stepped to the left to avoid crushing Robin, and when I looked down for him he was nowhere to be seen. For the first time in all the years we had hunted together we had parted company in a tight corner, and he was now probably trying to find his way home, with very little chance of being able to avoid the many dangers that lay before him in the intervening four miles of jungle. Added to the natural dangers he would have to face in a jungle with which, owing to its remoteness from home, he was not familiar, was the weak condition of his heart. It was therefore with very great misgivings that I turned about to go in search of him, and as I did so I caught sight of his head projecting from behind a tree trunk at the edge of a small clearing a hundred yards away. When I raised my hand and beckoned, he disappeared into the undergrowth, but a little later, with drooped eyes and drooping ears, he crept silently to my feet. Laying down the rifle I picked him up in my arms and, for the second time in his life, he licked my face – telling me as he did so, with little throaty sounds, how glad he was to find me unhurt, and how terribly ashamed he was of himself for having parted company from me.

Our reactions to the sudden and quite unexpected danger that had confronted us were typical of how a canine and a human being act in an emergency, when the danger that threatens is heard and not seen. In Robin's case it had impelled him to seek safety in silent and rapid retreat; whereas in my case it had the effect of gluing my feet to the ground and making retreat – rapid or otherwise – impossible.

When I had satisfied Robin that he was not to blame for our temporary separation, and his small body had stopped trembling, I put him down and together we walked up to where the leopard, who had put up such a game fight and had so nearly won the last round, was lying dead.

I have told you the story, and while I have been telling it Robin – the biggest-hearted and the most faithful friend man ever had – has gone to the Happy Hunting Grounds, where I know I shall find him waiting for me.

# 18

## Wild Life in the Village: an Appeal

It was a small village of some sixteen ploughs, differing in no respect from hundreds of similar villages scattered throughout the length of the bhabar. Originally the village had been surrounded by tree jungle interspersed with grass, and in this virgin jungle lived all the numerous denizens of the wild. To protect their crops the villagers erected thorn fences round their fields. As an additional safeguard a member of the depressed class was encouraged to settle in the village, and it was his duty to watch the crops at night and see they were not damaged by stray cattle or wild animals.

Owing to the abundance of game, tigers did not interfere with the village cattle and I cannot remember a single case of cow or bullock having been killed by a tiger. In the course of time a great change took place, not only in the villagers themselves but also in the jungle surrounding the village. Hindus, who formerly looked upon the taking of life as against their religious principles, were now clamouring for gun licences and were competing with each other in the indiscriminate slaughter of game. As profits from the sale of game increased, field work was neglected and land began to go out of cultivation. Simultaneously lantana, introduced into Haldwani as a pot plant, started to kill out the grass and basonta, until the village was surrounded with a dense growth of this noxious weed. Government now stepped in, and at great expense built a pukka wall all round the village. The building of this wall freed the villagers from the necessity of erecting fences and watching their crops and gave them more time to devote to the killing of the game. This heavy and unrestricted shooting of deer had the inevitable consequence of disturbing the balance in nature, with the result that tigers and leopards that had hitherto lived on game were now forced to live on the village cattle.

One morning in May of the present year [1932] I arrived in the village and pitched my tent in a little clearing just outside the cultivated land. News of my arrival soon spread through the village, and in a short time a dozen men were squatting in front of my tent. One and all had the same tale to tell. A tiger had taken up its quarters in the lantana and in the course of two years had killed 150 head of cattle, and unless it was destroyed the village would have to be abandoned.

While the men were pouring out their tale of woe I observed a pair of vultures circling low over a narrow stretch of lantana, running between the village wall and the public road. The two vultures were soon joined by others; so I picked up a rifle and set off to investigate. Progress through the lantana was difficult, but with the aid of a good hunting knife a way was eventually cut, and the remains of a horse, killed the previous day, found. There were plenty of pug marks round the kill, little of which remained, and it was easy to locate the tiger from his low, continuous growling, but impossible to see him in the dense cover. I returned to the road, which was only forty yards from the kill and little used at this time of year, and concealed myself behind a bush, in the hope that the tiger would follow me to see if I had left the locality, quite a natural thing for it to do. Half an hour later the tiger walked out on to the road and gave me an easy shot, as he stood facing me.

That evening after I had skinned the tiger – he was a very old animal and I took four old bullets and nine pellets of buckshot out of him – I called the villagers together and made an appeal to them on behalf of the few remaining deer in the jungle. On the side of the village opposite from my camp, irrigation water had been allowed to flow into the jungle. Over this water machans had been built in the trees, and in these machans men sat through the heat of the day, and all night long on moonlight nights, and shot down animals that came to drink. There was no other water within miles, and if a thirst-maddened animal avoided one machan it fell a victim to the next. I told the villagers that God had given water free for all, and that it was a shameful thing for man to sit over the water God had provided and shoot His creatures when they came to drink. To do this was to lower themselves below the level of a corpse-eating hyena, for even he, the lowest of all creation, did not lie in wait to kill defenceless animals while they were drinking. The men listened to me in silence, and when I had done, said they had not looked at the matter in this light. They promised that they would take down the machans, and in future would not molest the animals that came to the vicinity of the village to drink.

I stayed in the locality several weeks, taking bird and animal pictures, and am glad to say the men kept their promise. I believe that much of the slaughter of deer that is daily taking place throughout the length and breadth of the bhabar and terai would cease if an appeal was made to the better feelings of men.

I do not exaggerate the damage that is being done to our fauna by shooting over water. Let me give you but one instance. An acquaintance of mine living in a village in the bhabar adjoining mine, in one hot season, over one small pool of water, shot with a single-barrel muzzle-loading gun 60 head of chital and sambur, which he sold in a nearby bazaar at the rate of Rs 5 per chital and Rs 10 per sambur. It is no exaggeration to say that the banks of every little stream and every pool of water in the vicinity of bhabar villages are soaked with the blood of animals that never took toll of a single blade of the villagers' crops. I assert without fear of contradiction that for every shot fired on cultivated land, from guns provided for crop protection, a hundred shots are fired in the jungle over water. Pigs and nilgai are the only wild animals that damage the crops in the bhabar to any extent, and to keep them out of cultivated land Government has expended lakhs of rupees in building pukka walls.

It is asserted that in recent years tigers have increased. With this assertion I do not agree. It is a fact that more cattle are being killed every year, but this is not due to the tigers having increased. It is due to the balance in nature having been disturbed by the unrestricted slaughter of game, and also to some extent it is due to tigers having been driven out of their natural haunts, where they were seldom or never seen by man, by the activities of the Forest Department.

A country's fauna is a sacred trust, and I appeal to you not to betray this trust. Shooting over water, shooting over salt-licks, natural and artificial, shooting birds in the close season and when roosting at night, encouraging permit-holders to shoot hinds, fencing off of large areas of forest, and the extermination by the Forest Department of all game within these areas, making of unnecessary motor tracks through the forest and shooting from motor-cars, absence of sanctuaries, and the burning of forests by the Forest Department and by villagers at a time when the forests are full of young life, are all combining to one end – the extermination of our fauna. If we do not bestir ourselves now it will be to our discredit that the fauna of our province was exterminated in our generation, and under our very eyes, while we looked on and never raised a finger to prevent it.

## 19

## The Mohan Man-eater

I

Eighteen miles from our summer home in the Himalayas there is a long ridge running east and west, some 9,000 feet in height. On the upper slopes of the eastern end of this ridge there is a luxuriant growth of oat grass; below this grass the hill falls steeply away in a series of rock cliffs to the Kosi river below.

One day a party of women and girls from the village on the north face of the ridge were cutting the oat grass, when a tiger suddenly appeared in their midst. In the stampede that followed an elderly woman lost her footing, rolled down the steep slope, and disappeared over the cliff. The tiger, evidently alarmed by the screams of the women, vanished as mysteriously as it had appeared, and when the women had reassembled and recovered from their fright, they went down the grassy slope and, looking over the cliff, saw their companion lying on a narrow ledge some distance below them.

The woman said she was badly injured – it was found later that she had broken a leg and fractured several ribs – and that she could not move. Ways and means of a rescue were discussed, and it was finally decided that it was a job for men; and as no one appeared to be willing to remain at the spot, they informed the injured woman that they were going back to the village for help. The woman begged not to be left alone, however, and at her entreaty a girl, sixteen years of age, volunteered to stay with her. So, while the rest of the party set off for the village, the girl made her way down to the right, where a rift in the cliff enabled her to get a foothold on the ledge.

This ledge only extended half-way across the face of the cliff and ended, a few yards from where the woman was lying, in a shallow depression. Fearing that she might fall off the ledge and be killed on the rocks hundreds of feet below, the woman asked the girl to move her to this depression, and this difficult and dangerous feat the girl successfully accomplished. There was only room for one in the depression, so the girl squatted on the ledge facing the woman.

The village was four miles away, and once, and once again, the two on the ledge speculated as to the length of time it would take their companions to get back to the village; what men they were likely to find in the village at that time of day; how long it would take to explain what had happened; and finally, how long it would take the rescue party to arrive.

Conversation had been carried on in whispers for fear the tiger might be lurking in the vicinity and hear them and then, suddenly, the woman gave a gasp and the girl, seeing the look of horror on her face and the direction in which she was looking, turned her head and over her shoulder saw the tiger, stepping out of the rift on to the ledge.

Few of us, I imagine, have escaped that worst of all nightmares in which, while our limbs and vocal chords are paralysed with fear, some terrible beast in monstrous form approaches to destroy us; the nightmare from which, sweating fear in every pore, we waken with a cry of thankfulness to Heaven that it was only a dream. There was no such happy awakening from the nightmare of that unfortunate girl, and little imagination is needed to picture the scene. A rock cliff with a narrow ledge running partly across it and ending in a little depression in which an injured woman is lying; a young girl frozen with terror squatting on the ledge, and a tiger slowly creeping towards her; retreat in every direction cut off, and no help at hand.

Mothi Singh, an old friend of mine, was in the village visiting a sick daughter when the women arrived, and he headed the rescue party. When this party went down the grassy slope and looked over the cliff, they saw the woman lying in a swoon, and on the ledge they saw splashes of blood.

The injured woman was carried back to the village, and when she had been revived and had told her story, Mothi Singh set out on his eighteen-mile walk to me. He was an old man well over sixty, but he scouted the suggestion that he was tired and needed a rest, so we set off together to make investigations. But there was nothing that I could do, for twenty-four hours had elapsed and all the tiger had left of the brave young girl, who had volunteered to stay with her injured companion, were a few bits of bone and her torn and blood-stained clothes.

This was the first human being killed by the tiger which later was designated 'The Mohan Man-eater' in Government records.

After killing the girl, the tiger went down the Kosi valley for the winter, killing on its way – among other people – two men of the Public Works Department, and the daughter-in-law of our Member of the Legislative Council. As summer approached it returned to the scene of its first kill, and for several years thereafter its beat extended up and down the Kosi valley from Kakrighat to Gargia – a distance of roughly forty miles – until it finally took up its quarters on the hill above Mohan, in the vicinity of a village called Kartkanoula.

At the District Conference, to which reference has been made in a previous story, the three man-eating tigers operating at that time in the Kumaon District were classed as follows, in their order of importance:

1st — Chowgarh, Naini Tal District.
2nd—Mohan, Almora District.
3rd—Kanda, Garhwal District.

After the Chowgarh tiger had been accounted for I was reminded by Baines, Deputy Commissioner, Almora, that only a part of my promise made at the conference had been fulfilled, and that the Mohan tiger was next on the list. The tiger, he stated, was becoming more active and a greater menace every day, and had during the previous week killed three human beings, residents of Kartkanoula village. It was to this village Baines now suggested I should go.

While I had been engaged with the Chowgarh tiger, Baines had persuaded some sportsmen to go to Kartkanoula, but though they had sat up over human and animal kills they had failed to make contact with the man-eater and had returned to their depot at Ranikhet. Baines informed me I should now have the ground to myself – a very necessary precaution, for nerves wear thin when hunting man-eaters, and accidents are apt to result when two or more parties are hunting the same animal.

2

It was on a blistering hot day in May that I, my two servants, and the six Garhwalis I had brought with me from Naini Tal, alighted from the 1 p.m. train at Ramnagar and set off on our twenty-five-mile foot journey to Kartkanoula. Our first stage was only seven miles, but it was evening before we arrived at Gargia. I had left home in a hurry on receiving Baines's letter, and had not had time to ask for permission to occupy the Gargia Forest Bungalow, so I slept out in the open.

On the far side of the Kosi river at Gargia there is a cliff several hundred feet high, and while I was trying to get to sleep I heard what I thought were stones falling off the cliff on the rocks below. The sound was exactly the same as would be made by bringing two stones violently together. After some time this sound worried me, as sounds will on a hot night, and as the moon was up and the light good enough to avoid stepping on snakes, I left my camp bed and set out to make investigations. I found that the sound was being made by a colony of frogs in a marsh by the side of the road. I have heard land-, water-, and tree-frogs making strange sounds in different parts of the world, but I have never heard anything so strange as the sound made by the frogs at Gargia in the month of May.

After a very early start next morning we did the twelve miles to Mohan before the sun got hot, and while my men were cooking their food and my servants were preparing my breakfast, the chowkidar of the bungalow, two forest guards, and several men from the Mohan bazaar, entertained me with stories of the man-eater, the most recent of which concerned the exploits of a fisherman who had been fishing the Kosi river. One of the forest guards claimed to be the proud hero of this exploit, and he described very graphically how he had been out one day with the fisherman and, on turning a bend in the river, they had come face to face with the man-eater; and how the fisherman had thrown away his rod and had grabbed the rifle off his – the forest guard's – shoulder; and how they had run for their lives with the tiger close on their heels. 'Did you look back?' I asked. 'No, sahib,' said he, pitying my ignorance. 'How could a man who was running for his life from a man-eater look back?'; and how the fisherman, who was leading by a head, in a thick patch of grass, had fallen over a sleeping bear, after which there had been great confusion and shouting and everyone, including the bear, had run in different directions and the fisherman had got lost; and how after a long time the fisherman had eventually found his way back to the bungalow and had said a lot to him – the forest guard – on the subject of having run away with his rifle and left him empty-handed to deal with a man-eating tiger and an angry bear. The forest guard ended up his recital by saying that the fisherman had left Mohan the following day saying that he had hurt his leg when he fell over the bear, and that anyway there were no fish to be caught in the Kosi river.

By midday we were ready to continue our journey, and, with many warnings from the small crowd that had collected to see us off to keep a sharp look-out for the man-eater while going through the dense forest that lay ahead of us, we set out on our 4,000-foot climb to Kartkanoula.

Our progress was slow, for my men were carrying heavy loads and the track was excessively steep, and the heat terrific. There had been some trouble in the upper villages a short time previously, necessitating the dispatch from Naini Tal of a small police force, and I had been advised to take everything I needed for myself and my men with me, as owing to the unsettled conditions it would not be possible to get any stores locally. This was the reason for the heavy loads my men were carrying.

After many halts we reached the edge of the cultivated land in the late afternoon, and as there was now no further danger to be apprehended for my men from the man-eater, I left them and set out alone for the Foresters' Hut which is visible from Mohan, and which had been pointed out to me by the forest guards as the best place for my stay while at Kartkanoula.

The hut is on the ridge of the high hill overlooking Mohan, and as I approached it along the level stretch of road running across the face of the hill, in turning a corner in a ravine where there is some dense undergrowth, I came on a woman filling an earthenware pitcher from a little trickle of water flowing down a wooden trough. Apprehending that my approach on rubber-soled shoes would frighten her, I coughed to attract her attention, noticed that she started violently as I did so, and, a few yards beyond her, stopped to light a cigarette. A minute or two later I asked, without turning my head, if it was safe for anyone to be in this lonely spot, and after a little hesitation the woman answered that it was not safe, but that water had to be fetched and as there was no one in the home to accompany her, she had come alone. Was there no man? Yes, there was a man, but he was in the fields ploughing, and in any case it was the duty of women to fetch water. How long would it take to fill the pitcher? Only a little longer. The woman had got over her fright and shyness, and I was now subjected to a close cross-examination. Was I a policeman? No. – Was I a Forest Officer? No. – Then who was I? Just a man. – Why had I come? To try and help the people of Kartkanoula. – In what way? By shooting the man-eater. – Where had I heard about the man-eater? – Why had I come alone? – Where were my men? – How many were there? – How long would I stay? And so on.

The pitcher was not declared full until the woman had satisfied her curiosity, and as she walked behind me she pointed to one of several ridges running down the south face of the hill, and pointing out a big tree on a grassy slope said that three days previously the man-eater had killed a woman under it; this tree, I noted with interest, was only two or three hundred yards from my objective – the Foresters' Hut. We had now come to a footpath running up the hill, and as she took it the woman said the village from which she had come was just round the shoulder of the hill, and added that she was now quite safe.

Those of you who know the women of India will realize that I had accomplished a lot, especially when it is remembered that there had recently been trouble in this area with the police. So far from alarming the woman and thereby earning the hostility of the entire countryside I had, by standing by while she filled her pitcher and answering a few questions, gained a friend who would in the shortest time possible acquaint the whole population of the village of my arrival; that I was not an officer of any kind, and that the sole purpose of my visit was to try to rid them of the man-eater.

### 3

The Foresters' Hut was on a little knoll some twenty yards to the left of the road, and as the door was only fastened with a chain I opened it and walked inside. The room was about ten feet square and quite clean, but had a mouldy disused smell; I learnt later that the hut had not been occupied since the advent of the man-eater in that area eighteen months previously. On either side of the main room there were two narrow slips of rooms, one used as a kitchen, and the other as a fuel store. The hut would make a nice safe shelter for my men, and having opened the back door to let a current of air blow through the room, I went outside and selected a spot between the hut and the road for my forty-pound tent. There was no furniture of any kind in the hut, so I sat down on a rock near the road to await the arrival of my men.

The ridge at this point was about fifty yards wide, and as the hut was on the south edge of the ridge, and the village on the north face of the hill, the latter was not visible from the former. I had been sitting on the rock for about ten minutes when a head appeared over the crest from the direction of the village, followed by a second and a third. My friend the water-carrier had not wasted any time.

When strangers meet in India and wish to glean information on any particular subject from each other, it is customary to refrain from broaching the subject that has brought them together – whether accidentally or of set purpose – until the very last moment, and to fill up the interval by finding out everything concerning each other's domestic and private affairs; as, for instance, whether married, and if so, the number and sex of children and their ages; if not married, why not; occupation and amount of pay, and so on. Questions that would in any other part of the world earn one a thick ear are in India – and especially in our hills – asked so artlessly and universally that no one who has lived among the people dreams of taking offence at them.

In my conversation with the woman I had answered many of the set questions, and those of a domestic nature which it is not permissible for a woman to ask of a man were being put to me when my men arrived. They had filled a kettle at the little spring, and in an incredibly short time dry sticks were collected, a fire lit, the kettle boiled, and tea and biscuits produced. As I opened a tin of condensed milk I heard the men asking my servants why condensed milk was being used instead of fresh milk and receiving the answer that there was no fresh milk; and further that, as it had been apprehended that owing to some previous trouble in this area no fresh milk would be available, a large supply of tinned milk had been brought. The men appeared to be very distressed on hearing this and after a whispered conversation one of them, who I learnt later was the Headman of Kartkanoula, addressed me and said it was an insult to them to have brought tinned milk when all the resources of the village were at my disposal. I admitted my mistake, which I said was due to my being a stranger to that locality, and told the Headman that if he had any milk to spare I would gladly purchase a small quantity for my daily requirements, but that beyond the milk, I wanted for nothing.

My loads had now been unstrapped, while more men had arrived from the village, and when I told my servants where I wanted them to pitch my tent there was a horrified exclamation from the assembled villagers. Live in a tent – indeed! Was I ignorant of the fact that there was a man-eating tiger in this area and that it used this road regularly every night? If I doubted their word, let me come and see the claw-marks on the doors of the houses where the road ran through the upper end of the village. Moreover, if the tiger did not eat me in the tent it would certainly eat my men in the hut, if I was not there to protect them. This last statement made my men prick up their ears and add their entreaties to the advice of the villagers, so eventually I agreed to stay in the main room, while my two servants occupied the kitchen, and the six Garhwalis the fuel store.

The subject of the man-eater having been introduced, it was now possible for me to pursue it without admitting that it was the one subject I had wished to introduce from the moment the first man had put his head over the ridge. The path leading down to the tree where the tiger had claimed its last victim was pointed out to me, and the time of day and the circumstances under which the woman had been killed explained. The road along which the tiger came every night, I was informed, ran eastward to Baital Ghat with a branch down to Mohan, and westward to Chaknakl on the Ramganga river. The road going west, after running through the upper part of the village and through cultivated land for half a mile, turned south along the face of the hill, and on rejoining the ridge on which the hut was, followed the ridge right down to Chaknakl. This portion of the road between Kartkanoula and Chaknakl, some six miles long, was considered to be very dangerous, and had not been used since the advent of the man-eater; I subsequently found that after leaving the cultivated land the road entered dense tree and scrub jungle, which extended right down to the river.

The main cultivation of Kartkanoula village is on the north face of the hill, and beyond this cultivated land there are several small ridges with deep ravines between. On the nearest of these ridges, and distant about a thousand yards from the Foresters' Hut, there is a big pine-tree. Near this tree, some ten days previously, the tiger had killed, partly eaten, and left, a woman, and as the three sportsmen who were staying in a Forest Bungalow four miles away were unable to climb the pine-tree the villagers had put up three machans in three separate trees, at distances varying from one hundred to one hundred and fifty yards from the kill, and the machans had been occupied by the sportsmen and their servants a little before sunset. There was a young moon at the time, and after it had set the villagers heard a number of shots being fired, and when they questioned the servants next morning the servants said they did not know what had been fired at, for they themselves had not seen anything. Two days later a cow had been killed over which the sportsmen had sat, and again, as on the previous occasion, shots had been fired after the moon had set. It is these admittedly sporting but unsuccessful attempts to bag man-eaters that make them so wary, and the more difficult to shoot the longer they live.

The villagers gave me one very interesting item of news in connexion with the tiger. They said they always knew when it had come into the village by the low moaning sound it made. On questioning them closely I learnt that at times the sound was continuous as the tiger passed between the houses, while at other times the sound stopped for sometimes short, and other times long, periods.

From this information I concluded (*a*) that the tiger was suffering from a wound, (*b*) that the wound was of such a nature that the tiger only felt it when it was in motion, and that therefore (*c*) the wound was in one of its legs. I was assured that the tiger had not been wounded by any local shikari, or by any of the sportsmen from Ranikhet who had sat up for it; however, this was of little importance, for the tiger had been a man-eater for years, and the wound that I believed it was suffering from might have been the original cause of its becoming a man-eater. A very interesting point and one that could only be cleared up by examining the tiger – after it was dead.

The men were curious to know why I was so interested in the sound made by the tiger, and when I told them that it indicated the animal had a wound in one of its legs and that the wound had been caused either by a bullet, or porcupine quills, they disagreed with my reasoning and said that on the occasions they had seen the tiger it appeared to be in sound condition, and further, the ease with which it killed and carried off its victims was proof that it was not crippled in any way. However, what I told them was remembered and later earned me the reputation of being gifted with second sight.

4

When passing through Ramnagar I had asked the Tahsildar to purchase two young male buffaloes for me and to send them to Mohan, where my men would take them over.

I told the villagers I intended tying up one of the buffaloes near the tree where three days previously the woman had been killed and the other on the road to Chaknakl, and they said they could think of no better sites, but that they would talk the matter over among themselves and let me know in the morning if they had any other suggestions to make. Night was now drawing in and, before leaving, the Headman promised to send word to all the adjoining villages in the morning to let them know of my arrival, the reason for my coming, and to impress on them the urgency of letting me know without loss of time of any kills or attacks by the tiger in their areas.

The musty smell in the room had much decreased though it was still noticeable. However, I paid no attention to it, and after a bath and dinner put two stones against the doors – there being no other way of keeping them shut – and being bone-tired after my day's exertions went to bed and to sleep. I am a light sleeper, and two or three hours later I awoke on hearing an animal moving about in the jungle. It came right up to the back door. Getting hold of a rifle and a torch, I moved the stone aside with my foot and heard an animal moving off as I opened the door – it might, from the sound it was making, have been the tiger, but it might also have been a leopard or a porcupine. However, the jungle was too thick for me to see what it was. Back in the room and with the stone once more in position, I noticed I had developed a sore throat, which I attributed to having sat in the wind after the hot walk up from Mohan; but when my servant pushed the door open and brought in my early morning cup of tea I found I was suffering from an attack of laryngitis, due possibly to my having slept in a long-disused hut, the roof of which was swarming with bats. My servant informed me that he and his companion had escaped infection, but that the six Garhwalis in the fuel store were all suffering from the same complaint as I was. My stock of medicine consisted of a two-ounce bottle of iodine and a few tabloids of quinine, and on rummaging in my gun-case I found a small paper packet of permanganate which my sister had provided for me on a previous occasion. The packet was soaked through with gun oil, but the crystals were still soluble, and I put a liberal quantity of the crystals into a tin of hot water, together with some iodine. The resulting gargle was very potent, and while it blackened our teeth it did much to relieve the soreness in our throats.

After an early breakfast I sent four men down to Mohan to bring up the two buffaloes, and myself set off to prospect the ground where the woman had been killed. From the directions I had received overnight I had no difficulty in finding the spot where the tiger had attacked and killed the woman, as she was tying the grass she had cut into a bundle. The grass, and the rope she was using, were lying just as they had been left, as were also two bundles of grass left by her companions when they had run off in fright to the village. The men had told me that the body of the woman had not been found, but from the fact that three perfectly good lengths of rope and the dead woman's sickle had been left in the jungle, I am inclined to think that no attempt had been made to find her.

The woman had been killed at the upper end of a small landslide, and the tiger had taken her down the slide and into a thick patch of undergrowth. Here the tiger had waited, possibly to give the two women time to get out of sight, and had then crossed the ridge visible from the hut, after which it had gone with its kill straight down the hill for a mile or more into dense tree and scrub jungle. The tracks were now four days old, and as there was nothing to be gained by following them further, I turned back to the hut.

The climb back to the ridge was a very steep one, and when I reached the hut at about midday I found an array of pots and pans of various shapes and sizes on the veranda, all containing milk. In contrast to the famine of the day before there was now abundance, sufficient milk, in fact, for me to have bathed in. My servants informed me they had protested to no effect and that each man had said, as he deposited his vessel on the veranda, that he would take good care that I used no more condensed milk while I remained in their midst.

I did not expect the men to return from Mohan with the buffaloes before nightfall, so after lunch I set out to have a look at the road to Chaknakl.

From the hut the hill sloped gradually upwards to a height of about five hundred feet, and was roughly triangular in shape. The road, after running through cultivated land for half a mile, turned sharply to the left, went across a steep rocky hill until it regained the ridge, and then turned to the right and followed the ridge down to Chaknakl. The road was level for a short distance after coming out on the ridge, and then went steeply down, the gradient in places eased by hairpin bends.

I had the whole afternoon before me, and examined about three miles of the road very carefully. When a tiger uses a road regularly it invariably leaves signs of its passage by making scratch marks on the side of the road. These scratch marks, made for the same purpose as similar marks made by domestic cats and all other members of the cat family, are of very great interest to sportsmen, for they provide the following very useful information, (1) whether the animal that has made the mark is a male or a female, (2) the direction in which it was travelling, (3) the length of time that has elapsed since it passed, (4) the direction and approximate distance of its headquarters, (5) the nature of its kills, and finally, (6) whether the animal has recently had a meal of human flesh. The value of this easily acquired information to one who is hunting a man-eater on strange ground will be easily understood. Tigers also leave their pug marks on the roads they use and these pug marks can provide one with quite a lot of useful information, as, for instance, the direction and speed at which the animal was travelling, its sex and age, whether all four limbs are sound and, if not sound, which particular limb is defective.

The road I was on had through long disuse got overgrown with short stiff grass and was therefore not, except in one or two damp places, a good medium on which to leave pug marks. One of these damp places was within a few yards of where the road came out on the ridge, and just below this spot there was a green and very stagnant pool of water; a regular drinking place for sambur.

I found several scratch marks just round the corner where the road turned to the left after leaving the cultivated ground, the most recent of which was three days old. Two hundred yards from these scratch marks the road, for a third of its width, ran under an overhanging rock. This rock was ten feet high and at the top of it there was a flat piece of ground two or three yards wide, which was only visible from the road when approaching the rock from the village side. On the ridge I found more scratch marks, but I did not find any pug marks until I got to the first hairpin bend. Here, in cutting across the bend, the tiger had left its tracks where it had jumped down on to some soft earth. The tracks, which were a day old, were a little distorted, but even so it was possible to see that they had been made by a big, old, male tiger.

When one is moving in an area in which a man-eating tiger is operating progress is of necessity very slow, for every obstruction in one's line of walk, be it a bush, a tree, a rock, or an inequality in the ground capable of concealing death, has to be cautiously approached, while at the same time, if a wind is not blowing – and there was no wind that evening – a careful and a constant look-out has to be maintained behind and on either side. Further, there was much of interest to be looked at, for it was the month of May, when orchids at this elevation – 4,000 to 5,000 feet – are at their best, and I have never seen a greater variety or a greater wealth of bloom than the forests on that hill had to show. The beautiful white butterfly orchid was in greatest profusion, and every second tree of any size appeared to have decked itself out with them.

It was here that I first saw a bird that Prater of the Bombay Natural History Society later very kindly identified for me as the Mountain Crag Martin, a bird of a uniform ash colour, with a slight tinge of pink on its breast, and in size a little smaller than a Rosy Pastor. These birds had their broods with them, and while the young ones – four to a brood – sat in a row on a dry twig at the top of a high tree, the parent birds kept darting away – often to a distance of two to three hundred yards – to catch insects. The speed at which they flew was amazing, and I am quite sure there is nothing in feathers in North India, not excluding our winter visitor, the great Tibetan Swallow, that these Martins could not make rings round. Another thing about these birds that was very interesting was their wonderful eyesight. On occasions they would fly in a dead straight line for several hundred yards before turning and coming back. It was not possible, at the speed they were going, that they were chasing insects on these long flights, and as after each flight the bird invariably thrust some minute object into one of the gaping mouths, I believe they were able to see insects at a range at which they would not have been visible to the human eye through the most powerful fieldglasses.

Safeguarding my neck, looking out for tracks, enjoying nature generally, and listening to all the jungle sounds – a sambur a mile away down the hillside in the direction of Mohan was warning the jungle folk of the presence of a tiger, and a karker and a langur on the road to Chaknakl were warning other jungle folk of the presence of a leopard – time passed quickly, and I found myself back at the overhanging rock as the sun was setting. As I approached this rock I marked it as being quite the most dangerous spot in all the ground I had so far gone over. A tiger lying on the grass-covered bit of ground above the rock would only have to wait until anyone going either up or down the road was under or had passed it to have them at his mercy – a very dangerous spot indeed, and one that needed remembering.

When I got back to the hut I found the two buffaloes had arrived, but it was too late to do anything with them that evening.

My servants had kept a fire going most of the day in the hut, the air of which was now sweet and clean, but even so I was not going to risk sleeping in a closed room again; so I made them cut two thorn-bushes and wedged them firmly into the doorways before going to bed. There was no movement in the jungle near the back door that night, and after a sound sleep I woke in the morning with my throat very much better.

I spent most of the morning talking to the village people and listening to the tales they had to tell of the man-eater and the attempts that had been made to shoot it, and after lunch I tied up one buffalo on the small ridge the tiger had crossed when carrying away the woman, and the other at the hairpin bend where I had seen the pug marks.

Next morning I found both buffaloes sleeping peacefully after having eaten most of the big feed of grass I had provided them with. I had tied bells round the necks of both animals, and the absence of any sound from these bells as I approached each buffalo gave me two disappointments for, as I have said, I found both of them asleep. That evening I changed the position of the second buffalo from the hairpin bend to where the road came out on the ridge, close to the pool of stagnant water.

The methods most generally employed in tiger-shooting can briefly be described as (a) sitting up, and (b) beating, and young male buffaloes are used as bait in both cases. The procedure followed is to select the area most convenient for a sit-up, or for a beat, and to tie the bait out in the late evening using a rope which the bait cannot, but which the tiger can, break; and, when the bait is taken, either to sit up over the kill on a machan in a tree or beat the cover into which the kill has been taken.

In the present case neither of these methods was feasible. My throat, though very much better, was still sore and it would not have been possible for me to have sat up for any length of time without coughing, and a beat over that vast area of heavily wooded and broken ground would have been hopeless even if I had been able to muster a thousand men, so I decided to stalk the tiger, and to this end carefully sited my two buffaloes and tied them to stout saplings with four one-inch-thick hemp ropes, and left them out in the jungle for the whole twenty-four hours.

I now stalked the buffaloes in turn each morning, as soon as there was sufficient light to shoot by, and again in the evening, for tigers, be they man-eaters or not, kill as readily in the day as they do at night in areas in which they are not disturbed, and during the day, while I waited for news from outlying villages, nursed my throat, and rested, my six Garhwalis fed and watered the buffaloes.

On the fourth evening when I was returning at sunset after visiting the buffalo on the ridge, as I came round a bend in the road thirty yards from the overhanging rock, I suddenly, and for the first time since my arrival at Kartkanoula, felt I was in danger, and that the danger that threatened me was on the rock in front of me. For five minutes I stood perfectly still with my eyes fixed on the upper edge of the rock, watching for movement. At that short range the flicker of an eyelid would have caught my eyes, but there was not even this small movement; and after going forward ten paces, I again stood watching for several minutes. The fact that I had seen no movement did not in any way reassure me – the man-eater was on the rock, of that I was sure; and the question was, what was I going to do about it? The hill, as I have already told you, was very steep, had great rocks jutting out of it, and was overgrown with long grass and tree and scrub jungle. Bad as the going was, had it been earlier in the day I would have gone back and worked round and above the tiger to try to get a shot at him, but with only half an hour of daylight left, and the best part of a mile still to go, it would have been madness to have left the road. So, slipping up the safety-catch and putting the rifle to my shoulder, I started to pass the rock.

The road here was about eight feet wide, and going to the extreme outer edge I started walking crab-fashion, feeling each step with my feet before putting my weight down to keep from stepping off into space. Progress was slow and difficult, but as I drew level with the overhanging rock and then began to pass it, hope rose high that the tiger would remain where he was until I reached the part of the road from which the flat bit of ground above the rock, on which he was lying, was visible. The tiger, however, having failed to catch me off my guard, was taking no chances, and I had just got clear of the rock when I heard a low muttered growl above me, and a little later a karker went off barking to the right, and then two hind sambur started belling near the crest of the triangular hill.

The tiger had got away with a sound skin, but, for the matter of that, so had I, so there was no occasion for regrets, and from the place on the hill where the sambur said he was, I felt sure he would hear the bell I had hung round the neck of the buffalo that was tied to the ridge near the stagnant pool.

When I reached the cultivated land I found a group of men waiting for me. They had heard the karker and sambur and were very disappointed that I had not seen the tiger, but cheered up when I told them I had great hopes for the morrow.

## 5

During the night a dust-storm came on, followed by heavy rain, and I found to my discomfort that the roof of the hut was very porous.

However, I eventually found a spot where it was leaking less than in others, dragged my camp bed to it and continued my sleep. It was a brilliantly clear morning when I awoke; the rain had washed the heat haze and dust out of the atmosphere, and every leaf and blade of grass was glistening in the newly risen sun.

Hitherto I had visited the nearer buffalo first, but this morning I had an urge to reverse the daily procedure, and after instructing my men to wait until the sun was well up and then go to feed and water the nearer buffalo, I set off with high hopes down the Chaknakl road; having first cleaned and oiled my ·450/·400 rifle – a very efficient weapon, and a good and faithful friend of many years' standing.

The overhanging rock that I had passed with such trouble the previous evening did not give me a moment's uneasiness now, and after passing it I started looking for tracks, for the rain had softened the surface of the road. I saw nothing, however, until I came to the damp place on the road, which, as I have said, was on the near side of the ridge and close to the pool where the buffalo was tied. Here in the soft earth I found the pug marks of the tiger, made before the storm had come on, and going in the direction of the ridge. Close to this spot there is a rock about three feet high, on the khud [precipice] side of the road. On the previous occasions that I had stalked down the road I had found that by standing on this rock I could look over a hump in the road and see the buffalo where it was tied forty yards away. When I now climbed on to the rock and slowly raised my head I found that the buffalo had gone. This discovery was as disconcerting as it was inexplicable. To prevent the tiger from carrying the buffalo away to some distant part of the jungle, where the only method of getting a shot would have been by sitting up on the ground or in a tree – a hopeless proceeding with my throat in the condition it was – I had used four thicknesses of strong one-inch-thick hemp rope, and even so the tiger had got away with the kill.

I was wearing the thinnest of rubber-soled shoes, and very silently I approached the sapling to which the buffalo had been tied and examined the ground. The buffalo had been killed before the storm, but had been carried away after the rain had stopped, without any portion of it having been eaten. Three of the ropes I had twisted together had been gnawed through, and the fourth had been broken. Tigers do not usually gnaw through ropes; however, this one had done so, and had carried off the kill down the hill facing Mohan. My plans had been badly upset, but very fortunately the rain had come to my assistance. The thick carpet of dead leaves which the day before had been as dry as tinder were now wet and pliable and, provided I made no mistakes, the pains the tiger had been to in getting away with the kill might yet prove his undoing.

When entering a jungle in which rapid shooting might at any moment become necessary, I never feel happy until I have reassured myself that my rifle is loaded. To pull a trigger in an emergency and wake up in the Happy Hunting Grounds – or elsewhere – because one had omitted to load a weapon, would be one of those acts of carelessness for which no excuse could be found; so though I knew I had loaded my rifle before I came to the overhanging rock, I now opened it and extracted the cartridges. I changed one that was discoloured and dented, and after moving the safety-catch up and down several times to make sure it was working smoothly – I have never carried a cocked weapon – I set off to follow the drag.

This word 'drag', when it is used to describe the mark left on the ground by a tiger when it is moving its kill from one place to another, is misleading, for a tiger when taking its kill any distance (I have seen a tiger carry a full-grown cow for four miles) does not drag it, it carries it; and if the kill is too heavy to be carried, it is left. The drag is distinct or faint according to the size of the animal that is being carried, and the manner in which it is being held. For instance, assuming the kill is a sambur and the tiger is holding it by the neck, the hindquarters will trail on the ground, leaving a distinct drag-mark. On the other hand, if the sambur is being held by the middle of the back, there may be a faint drag-mark or there may be none at all.

In the present case the tiger was carrying the buffalo by the neck, and the hindquarters trailing on the ground were leaving a drag-mark it was easy to follow. For a hundred yards the tiger went diagonally across the face of the hill until he came to a steep clay bank. In attempting to cross this bank he had slipped and relinquished his hold of the kill, which had rolled down the hill for thirty or forty yards until it had fetched up against a tree. On recovering the kill the tiger picked it up by the back, and from now on only one leg occasionally touched, leaving a faint drag-mark which, nevertheless, owing to the hillside being carpeted with bracken, was not very difficult to follow. In his fall the tiger had lost direction, and he now appeared to be undecided where to take the kill. First he went a couple of hundred yards to the right, then a hundred yards straight down the hill through a dense patch of ringals (stunted bamboo). After forcing his way with considerable difficulty through the ringals he turned to the left and went diagonally across the hill for a few hundred yards until he came to a great rock, to the right of which he skirted. This rock was flush with the ground on the approach side, and, rising gently for twenty feet, appeared to project out over a hollow or dell of considerable extent. If there was a cave or recess under the projection it would be a very likely place for the tiger to have taken his kill to, so, leaving the drag, I stepped on to the rock and moved forward very slowly, examining every yard of ground below and on either side of me as it came into view. On reaching the end of the projection and looking over I was disappointed to find that the hill came up steeply to meet the rock, and that there was no cave or recess under it as I had expected there would be.

As the point of the rock offered a good view of the dell and of the surrounding jungle – and was comparatively safe from an attack from the man-eater – I sat down; and as I did so I caught sight of a red-and-white object in a dense patch of short undergrowth, forty or fifty yards directly below me. When one is looking for a tiger in heavy jungle everything red that catches the eye is immediately taken for the tiger, but I could also see his stripes. For a long minute I watched the object intently, and then, as the face you are told to look for in a freak picture suddenly resolves itself, I saw that the object I was looking at was the kill, and not the tiger; the red was blood where he had recently been eating, and the stripes were the ribs from which he had torn away the skin. I was thankful for having held my fire for that long minute, for in a somewhat similar case a friend of mine ruined his chance of bagging a very fine tiger by putting two bullets into a kill over which he had intended sitting; fortunately he was a good shot, and the two men whom he had sent out in advance to find the kill and put up a machan over it, and who were, at the time he fired, standing near the kill screened by a bush, escaped injury.

When a tiger that has not been disturbed leaves his kill out in the open, it can be assumed that he is lying up close at hand to guard the kill from vultures and other scavengers, and the fact that I could not see the tiger did not mean that he was not lying somewhere close by in the dense undergrowth.

Tigers are troubled by flies and do not lie long in one position, so I decided to remain where I was and watch for movement; but hardly had I come to this decision when I felt an irritation in my throat. I had not quite recovered from my attack of laryngitis, and the irritation grew rapidly worse until it became imperative for me to cough. The usual methods one employs on these occasions, whether in church or the jungle, such as holding the breath and swallowing hard, gave no relief until it became a case of cough or burst; and in desperation I tried to relieve my throat by giving the alarm-call of the langur. Sounds are difficult to translate into words, and for those of you who are not acquainted with our jungles I would try to describe this alarm-call, which can be heard for half a mile, as *khok, khok, khok,* repeated again and again at short intervals, and ending up with *khokorror.* Not all langurs call at tigers, but the ones in our hills certainly do, and as this tiger had probably heard the call every day of his life it was the one sound I could make to which he would not pay the slightest attention. My rendering of the call in this emergency did not sound very convincing, but it had the desired effect of removing the irritation from my throat.

For half an hour thereafter I continued to sit on the rock, watching for movement and listening for news from the jungle folk, and when I had satisfied myself that the tiger was not anywhere within my range of vision, I got off the rock and, moving with the utmost caution, went down to the kill.

## 6

I regret I am not able to tell you what weight of flesh a full-grown tiger can consume at a meal, but you will have some idea of his capacity when I tell you he can eat a sambur in two days, and a buffalo in three, leaving possibly a small snack for the fourth day.

The buffalo I had tied up was not full grown, but he was by no means a small animal, and the tiger had eaten approximately half of him. With a meal of that dimension inside of him I felt sure he had not gone far and, as the ground was still wet and would remain so for another hour or two, I decided to find out in what direction he had gone and, if possible, stalk him.

There was a confusion of tracks near the kill, but by going round in widening circles I found the track the tiger had made when leaving. Soft-footed animals are a little more difficult to track than hard-footed ones, yet after long years of experience tracking needs as little effort as a gun dog exerts when following a scent. As silently and as slowly as a shadow I took up the track, knowing that the tiger would be close at hand. When I had gone a hundred yards I came on a flat bit of ground, twenty feet square, and carpeted with that variety of short soft grass that has highly scented roots; on this grass the tiger had lain, the imprint of his body being clearly visible.

As I was looking at the imprint and guessing at the size of the animal that had made it, I saw some of the blades of grass that had been crushed down spring erect. This indicated that the tiger had been gone only a minute or so.

You will have some idea of the layout when I tell you that the tiger had brought the kill down from the north, and on leaving it had gone west, and that the rock on which I had sat, the kill, and the spot where I was now standing, formed the points of a triangle, one side of which was forty yards, and the other two sides a hundred yards long.

My first thought on seeing the grass spring erect was that the tiger had seen me and moved off, but this I soon found was not likely, for neither the rock nor the kill was visible from the grass plot, and that he had not seen me and moved after I had taken up his track I was quite certain. Why then had he left his comfortable bed and gone away? The sun shining on the back of my neck provided the answer. It was now nine o'clock of an unpleasantly hot May morning, and a glance at the sun and the tree-tops over which it had come showed that it had been shining on the grass for ten minutes. The tiger had evidently found it too hot and gone away a few minutes before my arrival to look for a shady spot.

I have told you that the grass plot was twenty feet square. On the far side to that from which I had approached there was a fallen tree, lying north and south. This tree was about four feet in diameter, and, as it was lying along the edge of the grass plot in the middle of which I was standing, it was ten feet away from me. The root end of the tree was resting on the hillside, which here went up steeply and was overgrown with brushwood, and the branch end (which had been snapped off when the tree had fallen) was projecting out over the hillside. Beyond the tree the hill appeared to be more or less perpendicular, and running across the face of it was a narrow ledge of rock which disappeared into dense jungle thirty yards further on.

If my surmise, that the sun had been the cause of the tiger changing his position, was correct, there was no more suitable place than the lee of the tree for him to have taken shelter in, and the only way of satisfying myself on this point was, to walk up to the tree – and look over. Here a picture seen long years ago in *Punch* flashed into memory. The picture was of a lone sportsman who had gone out to hunt lions and who, on glancing up on to the rock he was passing, looked straight into the grinning face of the most enormous lion in Africa. Underneath the picture was written, 'When you go out looking for a lion, be quite sure that you want to see him'. True, there would be this small difference, that whereas my friend in Africa looked up – into the lion's face, I would look down – into the tiger's; otherwise the two cases – assuming that the tiger *was* on the far side of the tree – would be very similar.

Slipping my feet forward an inch at a time on the soft grass, I now started to approach the tree, and had covered about half the distance that separated me from it when I caught sight of a black-and-yellow object about three inches long on the rocky ledge, which I now saw was a well-used game-path. For a long minute I stared at this motionless object, until I was convinced that it was the tip of the tiger's tail. If the tail was pointing away from me the head must obviously be towards me, and as the ledge was only some two feet wide, the tiger could only be crouching down and waiting to spring the moment my head appeared over the bole of the tree. The tip of the tail was twenty feet from me, and allowing eight feet for the tiger's length while crouching, his head would be twelve feet away. But I should have to approach much nearer before I should be able to see enough of his body to get in a crippling shot, and a crippling shot it would have to be if I wanted to leave on my feet. And now, for the first time in my life, I regretted my habit of carrying an uncocked rifle. The safety-catch of my ·450/·400 makes a very distinct click when thrown off, and to make any sound now would either bring the tiger right on top of me or send him straight down the steep hillside without any possibility of my getting in a shot.

Inch by inch I again started to creep forward, until the whole of the tail, and after it the hindquarters, came into view. When I saw the hindquarters I could have shouted with delight, for they showed that the tiger was not crouching and ready to spring, but was lying down. As there was only room for his body on the two-foot ledge, he had stretched his hind legs out and was resting them on the upper branches of an oak sapling growing up the face of the almost perpendicular hillside. Another foot forward and his belly came into view, and from the regular way in which it was heaving up and down I knew that he was asleep. Less slowly now I moved forward, until his shoulder, and then his whole length, was exposed to my view. The back of his head was resting on the edge of the grass plot, which extended for three or four feet beyond the fallen tree; his eyes were fast shut, and his nose was pointing to heaven.

Aligning the sights of the rifle on his forehead I pressed the trigger and, while maintaining a steady pressure on it, pushed up the safety-catch. I had no idea how this reversal of the usual method of discharging a rifle would work, but it did work; and when the heavy bullet at that short range crashed into his forehead not so much as a quiver went through his body. His tail remained stretched straight out; his hind legs continued to rest on the upper branches of the sapling; and his nose still pointed to heaven. Nor did his position change in the slightest when I sent a second, and quite unnecessary, bullet to follow the first. The only change noticeable was that his stomach had stopped heaving up and down and that blood was trickling down his forehead from two surprisingly small holes.

I do not know how the close proximity of a tiger reacts on others, but me it always leaves with a breathless feeling – due possibly as much to fear as to excitement – and a desire for a little rest. I sat down on the fallen tree and lit the cigarette I had denied myself from the day my throat had got bad, and allowed my thoughts to wander. Any task well accomplished gives satisfaction, and the one just completed was no exception. The reason for my presence at that spot was the destruction of the man-eater, and from the time I had left the road two hours previously right up to the moment I pushed up the safety-catch everything – including the langur call – had worked smoothly and without a single fault. In this there was great satisfaction, the kind of satisfaction I imagine an author must feel when he writes 'finis' to the plot that, stage by stage, had unfolded itself just as he desired it to. In my case, however, the finish had not been satisfactory, for I had killed the animal, that was lying five feet from me, in his sleep.

My personal feelings in the matter are, I know, of little interest to others, but it occurs to me that possibly you also might think it was not cricket, and in that case I should like to put the arguments before you that I used on myself, in the hope that you will find them more satisfactory than I did. These arguments were (a) the tiger was a man-eater that was better dead than alive, (b) therefore it made no difference whether he was awake or asleep when killed, and (c) that had I walked away when I saw his belly heaving up and down I should have been morally responsible for the deaths of all the human beings he killed thereafter. All good and sound arguments, you will admit, for my having acted as I did; but the regret remains that through fear of the consequences to myself, or fear of losing the only chance I might ever get, or possibly a combination of the two, I did not awaken the sleeping animal and give him a sporting chance.

The tiger was dead, and if my trophy was to be saved from falling into the valley below and being ruined, it was advisable to get him off the ledge with as little delay as possible. Leaning the rifle, for which I had no further use, against the fallen tree, I climbed up to the road and, once round the corner near the cultivated land, I cupped my hands and sent a cooee echoing over the hills and valleys. I had no occasion to repeat the call, for my men had heard my two shots when returning from attending to the first buffalo and had run back to the hut to collect as many villagers as were within calling distance. Now, on hearing my cooee, the whole crowd came helter-skelter down the road to meet me.

When stout ropes and an axe had been procured I took the crowd back with me, and after I had secured the ropes round the tiger, willing hands half carried and half dragged him off the ledge and over the fallen tree on to the plot of grass. Here I would have skinned him, but the villagers begged me not to do so, saying that the women and children of Kartkanoula and the adjoining villages would be very disappointed if they were not given an opportunity of seeing the tiger with their own eyes and satisfying themselves that the man-eater, in fear of whom they had lived for so many years, and who had established a reign of terror over the whole district, was really and truly dead.

While a couple of saplings, to assist in carrying the tiger back to the hut, were being felled, I saw some of the men passing their hands over the tiger's limbs, and knew they were satisfying themselves that their assertion that the tiger had not been suffering from any old, or crippling, wounds was correct. At the hut the tiger was placed in the shade of a wide-spreading tree and the villagers informed that it was at their disposal up to 2 o'clock – longer I could not give them, for it was a very hot day and there was fear of the hair slipping and the skin being ruined.

I myself had not looked closely at the tiger, but at 2 p.m., when I had laid him on his back to start the skinning, I noticed that most of the hair from the inner side of his left foreleg was missing, and that there were a number of small punctures in the skin, from which yellow fluid was exuding. I did not draw attention to these punctures and left the skinning of the leg, which was considerably thinner than the right leg, to the last. When the skin had been removed from the rest of the animal, I made a long cut from the chest to the pad of the festering left leg, and as I removed the skin drew out of the flesh, one after another, porcupine quills which the men standing round eagerly seized as souvenirs; the longest of these quills was about five inches, and their total number was between twenty-five and thirty. The flesh under the skin, from the tiger's chest to the pad of his foot, was soapy, and of a dark yellow colour; cause enough to have made the poor beast moan when he walked and quite sufficient reason for his having become – and having remained – a man-eater, for porcupine quills do not dissolve, no matter low long they are embedded in flesh.

I have extracted, possibly, a couple of hundred porcupine quills from the man-eating tigers I have shot. Many of these quills have been over nine inches in length and as thick as pencils. The majority were embedded in hard muscles, a few were wedged firmly between bones, and all were broken off short under the skin.

Unquestionably the tigers acquired the quills when killing porcupines for food, but the question arises – to which I regret I am unable to give any satisfactory answer – why animals with the intelligence, and the agility, of tigers, should have been so careless as to drive the quills deep into themselves, or be so slow in their movements as to permit porcupines – whose only method of defending themselves is by walking backwards – to do so; and further, why the quills should have broken off short, for porcupine quills are not brittle.

Leopards are just as partial to porcupines as our hill tigers are, but they do not get quills stuck in them, for they kill porcupines – as I have seen – by catching them by the head; and why tigers do not employ the same safe and obvious method of killing as leopards employ, and so avoid injury to themselves, is a mystery to me.

And now I have done telling you the story of the second of the three man-eating tigers mentioned at that District Conference of long ago and, when opportunity offers, I will tell you how the third tiger, the Kanda man-eater, died.

## 20

## Just Tigers

I think that all sportsmen who have had the opportunity of indulging in the twin sports of shooting tigers with a camera and shooting them with a rifle will agree with me that the difference between these two forms of sport is as great, if not greater, than the taking of a trout on a light tackle in a snow-fed mountain stream, and the killing of a fish on a fixed rod on the sun-baked bank of a tank.

Apart from the difference in cost between shooting with a camera and shooting with a rifle, and the beneficial effect it has on our rapidly decreasing stock of tigers, the taking of a good photograph gives far more pleasure to the sportsman than the acquisition of a trophy; and further, while the photograph is of interest to all lovers of wild life, the trophy is only of interest to the individual who acquired it. As an illustration I would instance Fred Champion. Had Champion shot his tigers with a rifle instead of with a camera his trophies would long since have lost their hair and been consigned to the dustbin, whereas the records made by his camera are a constant source of pleasure to him, and are of interest to sportsmen in all parts of the world.

It was looking at the photographs in Champion's book, *With a Camera in Tiger-Land*, that first gave me the idea of taking photographs of tigers. Champion's photographs were taken with a still camera by flashlight and I decided to go one better and try to take tiger pictures with a ciné camera by daylight. The gift by a very generous friend of a Bell & Howell 16-mm camera put just the weapon I needed into my hands, and the 'Freedom of the Forests' which I enjoy enabled me to roam at large over a very wide field. For ten years I stalked through many hundreds of miles of tiger country, at times being seen off by tigers that resented my approaching their kills, and at other times being shooed out of the jungle by tigresses that objected to my going near their cubs. During this period I learnt a little about the habits and ways of tigers, and though I saw tigers on, possibly, two hundred occasions I did not succeed in getting one satisfactory picture. I exposed films on many occasions, but the results were disappointing owing either to over-exposure, under-exposure, obstruction of grass or leaves, or cobwebs on the lens; and in one case owing to the emulsion on the film having melted while being processed.

Finally, in 1938, I decided to devote the whole winter to making one last effort to get a good picture. Having learnt by experience that it was not possible to get a haphazard picture of a tiger, my first consideration was to find a suitable site, and I eventually selected an open ravine fifty yards wide, with a tiny stream flowing down the centre of it, and flanked on either side by dense tree and scrub jungle. To deaden the sound of my camera when taking pictures at close range I blocked the stream in several places, making miniature waterfalls a few inches high. I then cast round for my tigers, and having located seven, in three widely separated areas, started to draw them a few yards at a time to my jungle studio. This was a long and difficult job, with many setbacks and disappointments, for the area in which I was operating is heavily shot over, and it was only by keeping my tigers out of sight that I eventually got them to the exact spot where I wanted them. One of the tigers for some reason unknown to me left the day after her arrival, but not before I had taken a picture of her; the other six I kept together and I exposed a thousand feet of film on them. Unfortunately it was one of the wettest winters we have ever had and several hundred feet of the film were ruined through moisture on the lens, under-exposure, and packing of the film inside the camera due to hurried and careless threading. But, even so, I have got approximately six hundred feet of film[1] of which I am inordinately proud, for they are a living record of six full-grown tigers – four males, two of which are over ten feet, and two females, one of which is a white tigress – filmed in daylight, at ranges varying from ten to sixty feet.

The whole proceeding from start to finish took four and a half months, and during the countless hours I lay near the tiny stream and my miniature waterfalls, not one of the tigers ever saw me.

The stalking to within a few feet of six tigers in daylight would have been an impossible feat, so they were stalked in the very early hours of the morning, before night had gone and daylight come – the heavy winter dew making this possible – and were filmed as light, and opportunity, offered.

[1] This film is preserved in the British Film Archive.

## 21

# On Man-eating

As many of the stories in this book are about man-eating tigers, it is perhaps desirable to explain why these animals develop man-eating tendencies.

A man-eating tiger is a tiger that has been compelled, through stress of circumstances beyond its control, to adopt a diet alien to it. The stress of circumstances is, in nine cases out of ten, wounds, and in the tenth case old age. The wound that has caused a particular tiger to take to man-eating might be the result of a carelessly fired shot and failure to follow up and recover the wounded animal, or be the result of the tiger having lost his temper when killing a porcupine. Human beings are not the natural prey of tigers, and it is only when tigers have been incapacitated through wounds or old age that, in order to live, they are compelled to take to a diet of human flesh.

A tiger when killing its natural prey, which it does either by stalking or lying in wait for it, depends for the success of its attack on its speed and, to a lesser extent, on the condition of its teeth and claws. When, therefore, a tiger is suffering from one or more painful wounds, or when its teeth are missing or defective and its claws worn down, and it is unable to catch the animals it has been accustomed to eating, it is driven by necessity to killing human beings. The change-over from animal to human flesh is, I believe, in most cases accidental. As an illustration of what I mean by 'accidental' I quote the case of the Muktesar man-eating tigress. This tigress, a comparatively young animal, in an encounter with a porcupine, lost an eye and got some fifty quills, varying in length from one to nine inches, embedded in the arm and under the pad of her right foreleg. Several of these quills after striking a bone had doubled back in the form of a U, the point and the broken-off end being quite close together. Suppurating sores formed where she endeavoured to extract the quills with her teeth, and while she was lying up in a thick patch of grass, starving and licking her wounds, a woman selected this particular patch of grass to cut as fodder for her cattle. At first the tigress took no notice, but when the woman had cut the grass right up to where she was lying the tigress struck once, the blow crushing in the woman's skull. Death was instantaneous, for, when found the following day, she was grasping her sickle with one hand and holding a tuft of grass, which she was about to cut when struck, with the other. Leaving the woman lying where she had fallen, the tigress limped off for a distance of over a mile and took refuge in a little hollow under a fallen tree. Two days later a man came to chip firewood off this fallen tree, and the tigress who was lying on the far side killed him. The man fell across the tree, and as he had removed his coat and shirt, and the tigress had clawed his back when killing him, it is possible that the smell of the blood trickling down his body as he hung across the bole of the tree first gave her the idea that he was something that she could satisfy her hunger with. However that may be, before leaving him she ate a small portion from his back. A day later she killed her third victim deliberately, and without having received any provocation. Thereafter she became an established man-eater and had killed twenty-four people before she was finally accounted for.

A tiger on a fresh kill, or a wounded tiger, or a tigress with small cubs, will occasionally kill human beings who disturb them; but these tigers cannot by any stretch of imagination be termed man-eaters, though they are often so called. Personally, I would give a tiger the benefit of the doubt once, and once again, before classing it as a man-eater, and whenever possible I would subject the alleged victim to a post-mortem before letting the kill go down on the records as the kill of a tiger or a leopard, as the case might be. This subject of post-mortems of human beings alleged to have been killed by either tigers or leopards or, in the plains, by wolves or hyenas, is of great importance, for, though I refrain from giving instances, I know of cases where deaths have wrongly been ascribed to carnivora.

It is a popular fallacy that *all* man-eaters are old and mangy, the mange being attributed to the excess of salt in human flesh. I am not competent to give any opinion on the relative quantity of salt in human or animal flesh; but I can, and do, assert that a diet of human flesh, so far from having an injurious effect on the coat of man-eaters, has quite the opposite effect, for all the man-eaters I have seen have had remarkably fine coats.

Another popular belief in connexion with man-eaters is that the cubs of these animals automatically become man-eaters. This is quite a reasonable supposition; but it is not borne out by actual facts, and the reason why the cubs of a man-eater do not themselves become man-eaters, is that human beings are not the natural prey of tigers, or of leopards.

A cub will eat whatever its mother provides, and I have even known of tiger cubs assisting their mothers to kill human beings; but I do not know of a single instance of a cub, after it had left the protection of its parent, or after that parent had been killed, taking to killing human beings.

In the case of human beings killed by carnivora, the doubt is often expressed as to whether the animal responsible for the kill is a tiger or leopard. As a general rule – to which I have seen no exceptions – tigers are responsible for all kills that take place in daylight, and leopards are responsible for all kills that take place in the dark. Both animals are semi-nocturnal forest-dwellers, have much the same habits, employ similar methods of killing, and both are capable of carrying their human victims for long distances. It would be natural, therefore, to expect them to hunt at the same hours; and that they do not do so is due to the difference in courage of the two animals. When a tiger becomes a man-eater it loses all fear of human beings and, as human beings move about more freely in the day than they do at night, it is able to secure its victims during daylight hours and there is no necessity for it to visit their habitations at night. A leopard, on the other hand, even after it has killed scores of human beings, never loses its fear of man; and, as it is unwilling to face up to human beings in daylight, it secures its victims when they are moving about at night, or by breaking into their houses at night. Owing to these characteristics of the two animals, namely, that one loses its fear of human beings and kills in the daylight, while the other retains its fear and kills in the dark, man-eating tigers are easier to shoot than man-eating leopards.

The frequency with which a man-eating tiger kills depends on (*a*) the supply of natural food in the area in which it is operating; (*b*) the nature of the disability which has caused it to become a man-eater; and (*c*) whether it is a male or a female with cubs.

Those of us who lack the opportunity of forming our own opinion on any particular subject are apt to accept the opinions of others, and in no case is this more apparent than in the case of tigers – here I do not refer to man-eaters in particular, but to tigers in general. The author who first used the words 'as cruel as a tiger' and 'as bloodthirsty as a tiger', when attempting to emphasize the evil character of the villain of his piece, not only showed a lamentable ignorance of the animal he defamed, but coined phrases which have come into universal circulation, and which are mainly responsible for the wrong opinion of tigers held by all except that very small proportion of the public who have the opportunity of forming their own opinions.

When I see the expression 'as cruel as a tiger' and 'as bloodthirsty as a tiger' in print, I think of a small boy armed with an old muzzle-loading gun – the right barrel of which was split for six inches of its length, and the stock and barrels of which were kept from falling apart by lashings of brass wire – wandering through the jungles of the terai and bhabar in the days when there were ten tigers to every one that now survives; sleeping anywhere he happened to be when night came on, with a small fire to give him company and warmth; wakened at intervals by the calling of tigers, sometimes in the distance, at other times near at hand; throwing another stick on the fire and turning over and continuing his interrupted sleep without one thought of unease; knowing from his own short experience and from what others, who like himself had spent their days in the jungles, had told him, that a tiger, unless molested, would do him no harm; or during daylight hours avoiding any tiger he saw, and when that was not possible, standing perfectly still until it had passed and gone, before continuing on his way. And I think of him on one occasion stalking half a dozen jungle-fowl that were feeding in the open, and on creeping up to a plum bush and standing up to peer over, the bush heaving and a tiger walking out on the far side and, on clearing the bush, turning round and looking at the boy with an expression on its face which said as clearly as any words, 'Hello, kid, what the hell are you doing here?' and, receiving no answer, turning round and walking away very slowly without once looking back. And then again I think of the tens of thousands of men, women, and children who, while working in the forests or cutting grass or collecting dry sticks, pass day after day close to where tigers are lying up and who, when they return safely to their homes, do not even know that they have been under the observation of this so-called 'cruel' and 'bloodthirsty' animal.

Half a century has rolled by since the day the tiger walked out of the plum bush, the latter thirty-two years of which have been spent in the more or less regular pursuit of man-eaters; and though sights have been seen which would have caused a stone to weep, I have not seen a case where a tiger has been deliberately cruel or where it has been bloodthirsty to the extent that it has killed, without provocation, more than it has needed to satisfy its hunger or the hunger of its cubs.

A tiger's function in the scheme of things is to help maintain the balance in nature and if, on rare occasions, when driven by dire necessity, he kills a human being or when his natural food has been ruthlessly exterminated by man he kills two per cent of the cattle he is alleged to have killed, it is not fair that for these acts a whole species should be branded as being cruel and bloodthirsty.

Sportsmen are admittedly conservative, the reason being that it has taken them years to form their opinions, and as each individual has a different point of view, it is only natural that opinions should differ on minor, or even in some cases on major, points, and for this reason I do not flatter myself that all the opinions I have expressed will meet with universal agreement.

There is, however, one point on which I am convinced that all sportsmen – no matter whether their viewpoint has been a platform on a tree, the back of an elephant, or their own feet – will agree with me, and that is, that a tiger is a large-hearted gentleman with boundless courage and that when he is exterminated – as exterminated he will be unless public opinion rallies to his support – India will be the poorer by having lost the finest of her fauna.

Leopards, unlike tigers, are to a certain extent scavengers and become man-eaters by acquiring a taste for human flesh when unrestricted slaughter of game has deprived them of their natural food.

The dwellers in our hills are predominantly Hindu, and as such cremate their dead. The cremation invariably takes place on the bank of a stream or river in order that the ashes may be washed down into the Ganges and eventually into the sea. As most of the villages are situated high up on the hills, while the streams or rivers are in many cases miles away down in the valleys, it will be realized that a funeral entails a considerable tax on the manpower of a small community when, in addition to the carrying party, labour has to be provided to collect and carry the fuel needed for the cremation. In normal times these rites are carried out very effectively; but when disease in epidemic form sweeps through the hills and the inhabitants die faster than they can be disposed of, a very simple rite, which consists of placing a live coal in the mouth of the deceased, is performed in the village and the body is then carried to the edge of the hill and cast into the valley below.

A leopard, in an area in which his natural food is scarce, finding these bodies, very soon acquires a taste for human flesh, and when the disease dies down and normal conditions are established, he very naturally, on finding his food supply cut off, takes to killing human beings.

Of the two man-eating leopards of Kumaon, which between them killed five hundred and twenty-five human beings, one followed on the heels of a very severe outbreak of cholera, while the other followed the mysterious disease which swept through India in 1918 and was called 'war fever'.

## *Looking Back*

Between the catapult and the muzzle-loader periods there was a bow-and-arrow interlude which I look back on with very great pleasure, for though I never succeeded in impaling bird or beast with an arrow I opened my credit account – with my small savings – with the Bank of Nature during that period, and the jungle lore I absorbed during the interlude, and later, has been a never-ending source of pleasure to me.

I have used the word 'absorbed', in preference to 'learnt', for jungle lore is not a science that can be learnt from textbooks; it can, however, be absorbed, a little at a time, and the absorption process can go on indefinitely, for the book of nature has no beginning, as it has no end. Open the book where you will, and at any period of your life, and if you have the desire to acquire knowledge you will find it of intense interest, and no matter how long or how intently you study the pages your interest will not flag, for in nature there is no finality.

Today it is spring, and the tree before you is bedecked with gay bloom. Attracted by this bloom a multitude of birds of many colours are flitting from branch to branch, some drinking the nectar from the flowers, others eating the petals, and others again feeding on the bees that are busily collecting honey. Tomorrow the bloom will have given place to fruit and a different multitude of birds will be in possession of the tree. And each member of the different multitudes has its allotted place in the scheme of nature. One to beautify nature's garden, another to fill it with melody, and yet another to regenerate the garden.

Season after season, year after year, the scene changes. A new generation of birds in varying numbers and species adorn the tree. The tree loses a limb – torn off in a storm – gets stackheaded and dies, and another tree takes its place; and so the cycle goes on.

On the path at your feet is the track of a snake that passed that way an hour before sunrise. The snake was going from the right-hand side of the path to the left, was three inches in girth, and you can be reasonably certain that it was of a poisonous variety. Tomorrow the track on the same path, or on another, may show that the snake that crossed it five minutes earlier was travelling from left to right, that it was five inches in girth, and that it was non-poisonous.

And so the knowledge you absorb today will be added to the knowledge you will absorb tomorrow, and on your capacity for absorption, not on any fixed standard, will depend the amount of knowledge you ultimately accumulate. And at the end of the accumulating period – be that period one year or fifty – you will find that you are only at the beginning, and that the whole field of nature lies before you waiting to be explored and to be absorbed. But be assured that if you are not interested, or if you have no desire to acquire knowledge, you will learn nothing from nature.

I walked with a companion for twelve miles through a beautiful forest from one camp to another. It was the month of April and nature was at her best. Trees, shrubs, and creepers were in full bloom. Gaily coloured butterflies flitted from flower to flower, and the air, filled with the scent of flowers, throbbed with the song of birds. At the end of the day my companion was asked if he had enjoyed the walk, and he answered, 'No. The road was very rough.'

I was travelling, shortly after World War I, from Bombay to Mombasa in the British India liner *Karagola*. There were five of us on the upper deck. I was going to Tanganyika to build a house, the other four were going to Kenya – three to shoot and one to look at a farm he had purchased. The sea was rough and I am a bad sailor, so I spent most of my time dozing in a corner of the smoke room. The others sat at a table nearby playing bridge, smoking, and talking, mostly about sport. One day, on being awakened by a cramp in my leg, I heard the youngest member of the party say, 'Oh, I know all about tigers. I spent a fortnight with a Forest Officer in the Central Provinces last year.'

Admittedly two extreme cases, but they will serve to emphasize my contention that if you are not interested you will see nothing but the road you walk on, and if you have no desire to acquire knowledge and assume you can learn in a fortnight what cannot be learnt in a lifetime, you will remain ignorant to the end.

# MORE OXFORD PAPERBACKS

Details of a selection of other books follow. A complete list of Oxford Paperbacks, including The World's Classics, Twentieth-Century Classics, OPUS, Past Masters, Oxford Authors, Oxford Shakespeare, and Oxford Paperback Reference, is available in the UK from the General Publicity Department, Oxford University Press (JH), Walton Street, Oxford OX2 6DP.

In the USA, complete lists are available from the Paperbacks Marketing Manager, Oxford University Press, 200 Madison Avenue, New York, NY 10016.

Oxford Paperbacks are available from all good bookshops. In case of difficulty, customers in the UK can order direct from Oxford University Press Bookshop, 116 High Street, Oxford, Freepost, OX1 4BR, enclosing full payment. Please add 10 per cent of published price for postage and packing.

# HINDUISM

## R. C. Zaehner

Hinduism is both a way of life and a highly organized social and religious system, but in the modern world its essentials, perhaps more than those of any other major religion, are undergoing a process of redefinition. What then are the key concepts of Hinduism?

Professor Zaehner's book traces these through the four-thousand-year development of Hinduism, and is concerned to elucidate, as the author puts it, 'the changeless ground from which the proliferating jungle that seems to be Hinduism grows'.

'the best short introduction to Hinduism in existence . . . a really first-class guide to its ancient roots and to its subtle blend of the mythological and the metaphysical' *Guardian*

An OPUS Book

# ISLAM

## *H. A. R. Gibb*

A knowledge of the tenets of Islam is crucial to our understanding of nations that have assumed an immense importance in the modern world. This book has become a standard work on a religion which is, after Christianity, the most widely diffused in the world. Beginning with Islam's origins as a practical religion in the Koran and the preaching of Muhammad, the author traces the growth of Islamic theology and the expansion of the Muslim social order, and the rise of the mystical Sufi movement. The concluding chapter analyses the problems that have confronted Islam in the twentieth century and its reactions to them.

An OPUS book

# MUHAMMAD

## Prophet and Statesman

### W. Montgomery Watt

A short account of the life and achievements of one of the great figures of history, this volume also serves as an excellent introduction to one of the world's major religions.

Dr Watt tells of Muhammad's call to prophethood as a result of visions. He recounts the writing down of the Prophet's revelations in the Qur'ān (with an explanation of its passages); Muhammad's betrayal, expulsion from Mecca, and migration to Medina, and his rise to political power in Arabia. Throughout, Dr Watt makes clear the social and political background out of which Islam was born, especially the influence of Judaism and Christianity.

'This book . . . admirably fulfills its purpose. It is written in a clear and interesting style, and the reader can be assured that it is not only an interesting book to read, but is also based on sound scholarship.' *Journal of Semitic Studies*

# SOE IN THE FAR EAST

*Charles Cruickshank*

The whole course of the Second World War in the Far East might have changed if the activities of Special Operations Executive had been given a free rein by the military and politicians. This is the startling conclusion of Dr Cruickshank's official history, based on secret files and the accounts of surviving agents.

'admirably vivid . . . a pleasure to read' *Listener*

'full of Cruickshank's dry wit and tales of startling bravery' M. R. D. Foot, *Times Literary Supplement*

'The author is as diverting as Le Carré.' *Glasgow Herald*

# BUKHARIN AND THE BOLSHEVIK REVOLUTION

## Stephen F. Cohen

For more than two decades Bukharin's career was central to the turbulent history of Soviet Russia and the communist movement: he made important contributions to Lenin's original leadership, and after 1917 was a Politburo member, editor of *Pravda,* head of the Comintern, chief theoretician, and, for three years, co-leader with Stalin of the Communist Party. He was tried as 'an enemy of the people' and executed by Stalin in 1938.

'Professor Cohen, in this brilliantly written, meticulously documented monograph, has not only reconstructed the tragedy of a fascinating man . . . he has also produced a classic study of the intellectual development of the foremost Bolshevik theoretician . . . He has, in a word, achieved a break-through in Soviet studies.' *Observer*

# THE ROOT AND THE FLOWER

## L. H. Myers

### Introduced by Penelope Fitzgerald

Myers's great trilogy, is set in exotic sixteenth-century India and records a succession of dynastic struggles during the ruinous reign of Akbar the Great Mogul. It is an absorbing story of war, betrayal, intrigue, and political power, but Myers's ultimate interests lie with the spiritual strengths and weaknesses of his major characters. The book explores a multitude of discrepancies—for example between the vastness of the Indian plains and the intricacy of an ants' nest—and yet attempts subtly to balance them. Throughout the trilogy Myers persists in his aim to reconcile the near and the far. *The Root and the Flower* demonstrates both his determination and his elegance in doing so, and, it has been said, 'brought back the aspect of eternity to the English novel'.

# A LESSON FROM ALOES

## *Athol Fugard*

*A Lesson from Aloes* centres on the farewell party given by an Afrikaner couple, Piet and Gladys, for Piet's Coloured friend Steve, a small-time political activist emigrating to England. Piet grows aloes in his backyard, and this plant, which can thrust its sharp leaves through the most barren soil, recurs throughout the play as a metaphor of survival for a group of people trying to find security and hope in a country where there is only betrayal.

'A parable of survival from South Africa's most uncompromising dramatist.' *Sunday Times*

# 'MASTER HAROLD' AND THE BOYS

## *Athol Fugard*

This is a powerful play by the South African playwright Athol Fugard that exposes, with unsparing simplicity, the roots of racism. If was first performed in the United States during 1982.

Master Harold is Hally, a white South African teenager, and the boys are Willie and Sam, two black men who work for his family; the setting is Port Elizabeth, South Africa, in 1950. The news that Hally's invalid and alcoholic father is to be allowed home from hospital violently upsets Hally who, in guilt and fear, suddenly turns on his lifelong friends, Willie and Sam, who have been to him a surrogate family. The shock of his outburst shows how the political and social realities of the time and place in which we live may dominate and distort our closest relationships.

# STATEMENTS

## Three Plays

### *Athol Fugard*

The three plays in this book, *Sizwe Bansi is Dead, The Island* and *Statements after an Arrest under the Immorality Act* are an effective indictment of the inhumanity of authoritarian regimes through a compassionate, humorous examination of the everyday lives of totally credible people.

'There is no mention of the theory of apartheid . . . but you experience with unique vividness what it is like to have a black skin and live in South Africa; you taste the flavour of life. This is possibly the greatest service that the theatre can render.' *Sunday Times*

'a dialogue between African innocence and experience; between country and the town; and between the masks the African is obliged to wear and the man within' *The Times*

# COLLECTED PLAYS 1

*Wole Soyinka*

The five plays in this collection are linked by their concern with the spiritual and the social, with belief and ritual as integrating forces for social cohesion. The plays are: *A Dance of the Forest, The Swamp Dwellers, The Strong Breed, The Road,* and *The Bacchae of Euripides*, an adaptation of the original Greek tregedy. In all these plays—whether concerned with the corruption of urban life or the power of superstition—Soyinka's language and imagination transcend the plays' immediate social contexts.

# COLLECTED PLAYS 2

*Wole Soyinka*

This volume contains five plays: *The Lion and the Jewel*, *Kongi's Harvest*, *The Trials of Brother Jero*, *Jero's Metamorphosis*, and *Madmen and Specialists*.

'*The Lion and the Jewel* alone is enough to establish Nigeria as the most fertile new source of English-speaking drama since Synge's discovery of the Western Isles.' *The Times*

# ON A CHINESE SCREEN

*W. Somerset Maugham*

## Introduction by H. J. Lethbridge

This remarkable book resulted from Maugham's travels in China between 1919 and 1920 and was first published in 1922. It presents in a sequence of vignettes and brief sketches an extraordinary range of the European types then resident there: missionaries and their wives, Catholic priests and nuns, consular and diplomatic officials, taipans and business men, soldiers and seafarers, and all the flotsam and jetsam of European communities in the East. There are Chinese among the portraits as well, including an official who was supremely sensitive to beauty in all its forms and yet grossly venal in his public life and a Chinese professor of comparative literature who made wonderfully bizarre evaluations of foreign writers.

Since Maugham visited China the treaty ports have gone, the privileged expatriate communites have vanished, and the visitor is no longer free to wander at will. *On a Chinese Screen* is now an important historical document.

# TURBOTT WOLFE

*William Plomer*

### *Introduced by Laurens van der Post*

When this novel first appeared in 1925 the wide critical appreciation it attracted in England was matched by the political controversy it caused in South Africa. It remains acutely relevant, and if, as Turbott Wolfe declares, 'Character is the determination to get one's own way', then history bears the marks of this book and testifies to the depth of its perception.

Plomer records the struggle of a few against the forces of prejudice and fear. The book is full of images of exploitation and atrocity. Yet it is also the love story of a man who finds beauty where others have seen only ugliness. The narrative, which never shrinks from witnessing the unforgivable, is also characterized by sensitivity and self-control, and in the end manages perhaps the most we are capable of: continuing bravery, the voice of individual affirmation.